One Week In April:
THE
MASTERS

ONE WEEK IN APRIL:
THE
MASTERS

Stories and Insights from Arnold Palmer,
Phil Mickelson, Rick Reilly, Ken Venturi, Jack Nicklaus, Lee Trevino,
and Many More About the Quest for the Famed Green Jacket

INTRODUCTION BY
Brad Faxon, eight-time winner on the PGA TOUR

FOREWORD BY
Don Wade, former senior editor at *Golf Digest*®

STERLING INNOVATION
An imprint of Sterling Publishing Co., Inc.

New York / London
www.sterlingpublishing.com

Library of Congress Cataloging-in-Publication Data Available

10 9 8 7 6 5 4 3 2 1

Published by Sterling Publishing Co., Inc.
387 Park Avenue South, New York, NY 10016
© 2008 by Sterling Publishing Co., Inc.
First published in hardcover in 2008 as *First Sunday in April: The Masters* by
Sterling Publishing Co., Inc.
Distributed in Canada by Sterling Publishing
c/o Canadian Manda Group, 165 Dufferin Street
Toronto, Ontario, Canada M6K 3H6
Distributed in the United Kingdom by GMC Distribution Services
Castle Place, 166 High Street, Lewes, East Sussex, England BN7 1XU
Distributed in Australia by Capricorn Link (Australia) Pty. Ltd.
P.O. Box 704, Windsor, NSW 2756, Australia

Sterling ISBN 978-1-4027-6537-7

For information about custom editions, special sales,
premium and corporate purchases, please contact Sterling Special Sales
Department at 800-805-5489 or specialsales@sterlingpublishing.com.

TABLE OF CONTENTS

FOREWORD

There is a truism which holds that "the smaller the ball, the better the writing." That is made abundantly clear in this wonderful and engaging collection of pieces about one of the world's premier sporting events, the Masters Golf Tournament.

What is also apparent is that the tournament and the press have enjoyed an affair of the heart that began in 1934 and continues to this day. There are any number of reasons for this.

First and foremost was Bobby Jones himself, the supreme champion of his time who, in the constellation of athletes that made the Golden Age of Sports possible in the 1920s and 30s, shone the brightest of them all. Jones's record is well known. He won four U.S. Opens, five U.S. Amateurs, three British Opens, and the 1930 British Amateur. It was in that same year, 1930, that he won all four of these major championships of his era in one season—the historic Grand Slam. That done, he essentially retired from competitive golf at age 28.

The reasons for Jones's popularity transcended his playing record. He was the embodiment of the amateur ideal at a time when that truly mattered. He was instinctively gracious and had a keen mind. He had an engineering degree from the Atlanta School of Technology (now Georgia Tech), a degree in literature from Harvard, and was a practicing attorney.

And, for the purposes of this book, he respected sportswriters and counted among his closest friends the columnist Grantland Rice (one of the early members at Augusta National and the honorary chairman of the first Augusta National Invitation tournament, as it was known in its first five years) and O.B. Keeler, his close friend who chronicled Jones's career for the *Atlanta Journal*. Keeler, in effect, played Boswell to Jones's Dr. Johnson, a relationship that proved profitable and advantageous for both men. In the cases of both Rice and Keeler, the close relationship between the two and the club—let alone Jones himself—would be frowned upon, if not scandalous, today. Be that as it may, among the easiest shots in journalism is to measure people against the standards of our day and not their day.

It's worth noting here that from the earliest years of the club and the tournament, journalists were accorded uncommonly gracious treatment. This was at a time not far removed from the era when golf professionals and newspapermen were treated as second-class citizens, generally banned from entering clubhouses. This was particularly true in the British Isles, where the "Upstairs, Downstairs" mentality reigned supreme. For example, in the 1923 British Open at Royal Troon, professionals were banned from the clubhouse, so the irrepressible Walter Hagen ordered his limousine to park in front of the clubhouse, where a table set with the finest china and silver was prepared and Hagen was served a lavish lunch. Naturally, the members were outraged. Everyone else was thrilled.

It was at about this time when writers covering one British Open were assigned to an old potting shed. This proved to be too much and a protest was filed by the newspapermen. Soon a committee of members and officials from the Royal & Ancient Golf Club of St. Andrews were assigned to investigate. As they approached the shed, one member of the committee pointed to the lone writer laboring over his story.

"Look," he said. "There's one of them in there now."

There would be none of that at Augusta National.

Aside from the affection and admiration the writers had for Jones, there were two other factors working in the tournament's favor in the early years.

First, Jones played in the first few Masters and this alone was reason enough for editors to assign coverage to the events. His absence from competitive play was evidenced by his score in the inaugural tournament. He opened with a 76, shot a 74 in the second round, and had a pair of even-par 72s in the final two rounds to finish a respectable tie for thirteenth with Hagen and Denny Shute, who had won the British Open the previous year.

Second, the tournament's spring dates coincided with the end of baseball's spring training, which meant that the writers would be heading north, making it convenient for them to spend a few days in Augusta, luxuriating amidst the magnolias, azaleas, and dogwoods.

One reason journalists particularly enjoy the Masters is that it offers so many storylines, as readers will appreciate when they read the pieces in this book.

For one thing, as an invitational event, the Masters has always featured the finest players at any given time, including international players—something Jones insisted upon since he realized that golf is the most international of all sports.

Jones also insisted that the finest amateurs be invited. To that end, amateurs have always played a special role in the Masters, where it is often the first time they appear, and on the game's grandest stage no less. Take the case of Curtis Strange, who was the low amateur at the 1976 Masters.

"I was brought into the pressroom for an interview by an older member who had white hair, a moustache, and an unbelievable southern accent," said Strange, who would go on to earn a place in the World Golf Hall of Fame. "The reporters asked me a few questions, but they were really more interested in what was going on out on the course. There was a long pause and I thought we were done when the member said, 'Curtis, I have a question. You went to Wake Forest on an Arnold Palmer scholarship. How did it *feeeel* to play your first round in the Masters Tournament with the great Arnold Palmer?'

"'Sir, I didn't play with Arnold in the first round,' I told him.

"'Oh,' he said. 'Well then you must have played with Jack Nicklaus. How did it *feeel* to play in the first round of the Masters Tournament with the great Jack Nicklaus?'

"'Well sir, I didn't play with Jack in the first round,' I explained.

"'Well then, who did you play with in the first round of the Masters Tournament?' he asked.

"'Gay Brewer,' I said.

"There was a pause and one of the writers, mimicking the member's accent, said 'Tell us, Curtis, how'd it *feeel* to play in the first round of the Masters Tournament with the great Gay Brewer?'"

But the true masterstroke was the decision to extend invitations to all Masters champions. This meant that many of the game's legendary players would return year after year, not so much to compete as to refresh their memories and to reunite with old friends. In a sense, it is this atmosphere of reunion that helps make the Masters special. It is a place where the golf world—players, press, its officialdom, and fans who make an annual pilgrimage to Augusta National—gathers to reminisce and welcome the beginning of another golf season.

And since the Masters featured the game's best players, it also was a gathering of the best writers covering the game. That some of them happened to be fascinating characters in their own right simply added to the pageantry of it all.

One cannot think of the Masters without remembering Herbert Warren Wind, who covered golf so elegantly for *Sports Illustrated* in that publication's early years, and later for *The New Yorker*. Wind, who died at age 88 in 2005, was a classicist. He was a fine player who competed in the 1950 British Amateur. He received degrees from both Yale and Cambridge University and it was at the latter where he developed a love for the classic Scottish courses and became a confirmed Anglophile. At Augusta and other major golf events, no matter how hot and humid it might be, Herb Wind was always in full tweed (including, of course, a tweed cap) with his tie knotted tightly at the collar of his white shirt.

Wind, who christened the 11th, 12th, and 13th holes "Amen Corner" after an old jazz standard, "Shouting at the Amen Corner," was a dear friend of Bobby Jones and had a deep love and reverence for Augusta National and the Masters, which was reflected in his beautifully crafted writings.

Herb Wind and I both grew up near Boston, and since he was a friend of 1913 U.S. Open champion Francis Ouimet and I was a Ouimet Scholar in college, he took an interest in my writing and career. One year I ran into him just as he arrived at Augusta National.

"Tell me," he asked. "How are the greens?"

After I assured him that the greens were just fine, we visited for a few minutes and then, just as we were to part, he said, "Your writing is coming along nicely."

Winning a Pulitzer couldn't have meant more.

In 2001, when he was 85 and hadn't been to the Masters in ten years, he sat down with Jim McCabe, the respected golf writer from *The Boston Globe*.

"Towards the end of the interview, he asked, 'Tell me, is Augusta still beautiful?' I told him that it was and he said, 'Good, that pleases me. Bob would be pleased, too.'"

The other equally influential golf writer of years from the 1960s on is Dan Jenkins. Jenkins was from Ft. Worth and enjoyed a deep friendship with Ben Hogan. He made his national reputation first at *Sports Illustrated* and then moved on to *Golf Digest*.

If Herb Wind was a sentimentalist, even a romantic, about the game, Jenkins looks at everything in golf—and probably life for that matter—with the gimlet eye of a humorist (but not as a cynic, a crucial distinction). This definitely includes the Masters and Augusta National. Jenkins is a brilliant observer and writer but it is his humor—the hardest trick to pull off in writing—that sets him apart.

While Wind and Jenkins were polar opposites in nature and in their writing, I've long thought that they should be measured, in part, by their profound influence on generations of writers who followed them and who, in many respects, emulated their styles. It would be interesting, I think, for people reading this book to read the Wind and Jenkins pieces first and then move on to other writers, trying to determine who was influenced by Wind's and who was more taken by Jenkins's style. For example, going through this anthology, I would put John Feinstein and Tom Callahan in the Wind school while the writings of Rick Reilly and Gary Van Sickle remind me more of Jenkins. See what you think.

No discussion of writers and the Masters would be complete without mentioning Bob Drum, who began covering golf when he was at the

Pittsburgh Press just as a kid named Arnold Palmer was starting to attract attention as a top junior golfer. "The Drummer" covered Palmer's remarkable career but particularly enjoyed coming to Augusta National in the spring, where he was a fixture on the clubhouse verandah with his friend, Dan Jenkins. His devotion to Palmer and the Masters was absolute, as you will see.

"In March 1961, I was diagnosed with cancer," said the Drummer. "The doctor told me this was serious stuff and then he wanted to operate right away. I told him to forget it. I had to get down to Augusta because Arnold was the defending champion. I told him he could operate right after the Masters. That way I'd be fixed up in time for the Open at Oakmont in June, where Arnold was also the defending champion.

"You'd think that after all I went through, Arnold could have won at least one of them," said Drummer.

Herb Wind is gone now and so is the Drummer and Dick Taylor, the former editor of *Golf World*, and Charlie Price, who wrote *A Golf Story: Bobby Jones, Augusta National, and the Masters Tournament*. Gone, too, are Sam Snead, Byron Nelson, Gene Sarazen, and so many others whom I came to look forward to seeing at Augusta in the spring and who made the Masters, in the words of the incomparable Jim Nantz of CBS Sports, "a tradition unlike any other."

Their spirit is captured here.

I hope you enjoy this literary stroll down Magnolia Lane.

—Don Wade

INTRODUCTION

Augusta National Golf Club is one of the most famous golf courses in the world and home to my favorite tournament—the Masters. The club was founded in 1933 by the legendary amateur champion Bobby Jones. He collaborated with one of history's most famous architects, Alister MacKenzie. MacKenzie designed Cypress Point in California and Royal Melbourne in Australia, among others, but there is little doubt Augusta National is his crown jewel. The Masters Tournament is equally rich in history with long standing traditions, including the Wednesday par-3 tournament, the ceremonial opening tee-shot by the likes of Sam Snead, Byron Nelson, and Arnold Palmer, the Butler cabin interviews and, of course, the presentation of the green jacket by the defending champion on the 18th green.

Growing up as a golfer in Rhode Island, to me the Masters signaled the advent of spring. With the final round played the second Sunday of every April, the tournament, which has been televised majestically by CBS over the last fifty years, provided viewers with the most meticulously manicured golf course in the world. It's as if Augusta National has a magical switch somewhere that causes the azaleas, the dogwoods, and every other flower to bloom perfectly, right as that first tee shot is struck! Likewise, the greens must be sprinkled with a secret dust that speeds them up dramatically between the final practice round on Wednesday and the opening round on Thursday. The Masters is the only major tournament played on the same course every year so that viewers are intimately familiar with the course. So much so, I knew how to play the course long before ever setting foot on the hallowed grounds of Augusta National.

Any Masters fan knows the famous adage that the tournament doesn't begin until the back nine on Sunday! If you can navigate your way through holes 10, 11, and 12 without a disaster and keep your scores around par then you are bound to pick up a few shots on the field. There are few scarier shots in golf than the second into the 11th, fronted by a menacing pond that catches any shot hit even slightly to the left. The trouble doesn't end there as you play the 12th, the most famous par 3 in tournament golf. The confounding winds and the narrowest green on the course put you at the mercy of the golfing gods. Who could forget when Freddie Couples's ball held up on the bank and didn't trickle into the creek in 1992? With that unexpected break, he went on to win the tournament and no one has seen a ball stay up since!

The back nine also provides the most exciting stretch of golf from the 13th tee to the 16th green. With attackable pin placements on Sunday, players can make birdies and eagles in bunches. When this happens, the fans let loose with the loudest roars on the course, just as they did when Phil Mickelson made three birdies during this stretch before draining the winning putt on the 18th hole in 2004. And the same golfing gods who rewarded Freddie Couples tempted Curtis Strange to go for the green in two shots on both par-5s in 1985, only to see both balls end up in what Ben Wright called a "watery grave." Likewise, Seve Ballesteros suffered a similar fate when he made a double bogey 7 on the 15th hole and saw his chances of winning the tournament slip away after his ball landed in the water. Yet Zach Johnson proved in 2007 that there's no shame in hitting a wedge into holes 13 and 15 for your third shot. He did it every round and went on to win the tournament.

The 16th hole is a highlight reel of memorable golf moments. The par 3 is the site of Jack Nicklaus's knife-in-the-back birdie putt in 1975 with Johnny Miller and Tom Weiskopf watching from the tee-box and the tournament in the balance. His reaction is still vivid: Nicklaus with his right arm extended, putter raised high and jumping for joy. And this hole is also where, in 2005, Tiger Woods made the most suspenseful chip in golf history when his ball hung on the lip for what seemed like an eternity before dropping in the hole for birdie. He celebrated with a fist pump that would have knocked Muhammad Ali out cold.

The 17th and 18th holes were often criticized for being easy finishing holes, so in recent years the tournament committee went about making them more difficult by lengthening them tremendously—and, in the case of the 17th, adding new pine trees along the right side of the fairway. But even before these changes were made, the 18th produced great drama and heartache such as Arnold Palmer's double bogey in his 1961 playoff loss to Gary Player, and Ed Sneed's missed short par putt in 1979, which led to him losing to Fuzzy Zoeller in the first ever sudden death play-off. The hole has also seen its share of triumph, such as Sandy Lyle's miraculous fairway bunker shot to hold off Mark Calcavecchia in 1988 and become the first Scottish golfer to win the tournament, or Mark O'Meara's birdie putt in 1998 to pull ahead of David Duval and Freddie Couples on the final hole of the tournament.

Just as the television coverage brought the course alive, it also brought the players to life. Jack Nicklaus began to supplant Arnold Palmer as the greatest player in the game largely because of his five Masters victories in the 1960s and 1970s. My most indelible Nicklaus memory, like many of you no doubt, is his Sunday back-nine charge in 1986 when he went on to win his sixth green jacket by out-dueling Seve Ballesteros, Greg Norman, and Tom Kite. Augusta is where players like Miller, Weiskopf, Trevino, and Watson would challenge Nicklaus on golf's greatest theater. The television coverage was also my first exposure to international golfers like Gary Player, the aforementioned Ballesteros and Norman, and multiple-time champions Nick Faldo and Bernhard Langer. By studying the names on the Masters leaderboard, it was evident golf was indeed a global game. You noticed how the course design challenged all types of players in many different ways. Length was an asset, but a great short game was mandatory for success. Scramblers could do well at Augusta, just as short and accurate plodders could. I dreamed of playing there and practiced many of the shots the course demanded, like a high draw off the 13th tee or a delicate pitch from the back of the 3rd green. As a junior golfer, I often played practice rounds with three balls: one was Nicklaus, one was Watson, and one was Faxon. This was fun!

I promised myself I would never play Augusta National until I qualified to play in the Masters. In 1991, after qualifying by winning the Buick Open,

Brad Boss, my long-time friend and a member at Augusta, called and said, "Let's go next February!" Needless to say, television did not do the course justice. That first tee shot of the first round had me as excited as any tournament I had ever played. After reaching the green on the opening hole, I witnessed the magnificence, and the treachery of MacKenzie's design. The undulations on the greens were beyond comparison—the ultimate measuring stick, even today, for any other club's greens. It was a truly memorable few days, made even more memorable when Brad made a hole-in-one on the 16th during the first round we played. The entire experience far and away exceeded my greatest expectations and made the day well worth the wait.

Augusta National is a magical place. I have played in twelve Masters Tournaments, and the thrill never wanes. Each and every round is special and the experience one to cherish. Your mind is challenged on every shot and every hole. You are more tired mentally than physically when you finish a tournament round. I have no doubt the Masters is the most compelling major every year and I can't wait to get back and play in the tournament one more time. I hope thirteen will be a lucky number for me.

—Brad Faxon
October 2007

THE TRADITIONS

The Men of the Masters

from *A Good Walk Spoiled: Days and Nights on the PGA Tour*
by John Feinstein

Tradition is one of the most important words in the lexicon of golf. There is no doubt that tradition is a key element in explaining what draws people to the game. If you walk the Old Course at St. Andrews and are not moved by the tradition that is spread out before you every step of the way, then the sport has not connected with you or you with it. If you don't hear, at least faintly, the footsteps of Old Tom Morris and Young Tom Morris, then you are wasting your time from the moment you arrive in Scotland.

The same can be said—and is often said—of the Augusta National Golf Club. But while there are hundreds of years of tradition and memories at St. Andrews, there are only sixty at Augusta. While it was the Scots who invented golf, it is the men who wear the green jackets of Augusta National who believe they are the ones who got it right.

The Masters is the greatest golf tournament in the world. Ask the men in the green jackets. If you do not treat the Masters with a reverence that goes beyond all other golf tournaments, it is quite possible you will be asked not to return. Jack Whitaker learned that in 1966 when he referred to a crowd around the hallowed 18th green as "a mob." The Men of the Masters told CBS he would not be welcome the following year and CBS meekly complied with that request. Twenty-eight years later, Gary McCord commented that the greens were so slick they looked like they had been bikini-waxed. The MOTM again made their displeasure known to CBS and, again, the network did as it was told. McCord was not invited to return in 1995.

The Masters *is* all about tradition. The only green jacket that ever leaves the premises is the one worn by the current champion. The members and past champions wear theirs only at the club. Every year, Masters week at Augusta is the same, from the champions dinner on Tuesday to the par-three tournament on Wednesday, to the ceremonial tee-off on Thursday, to the four minutes per hour of commercials on Saturday and Sunday, to the members dinner with the new champion on Sunday night.

Every April it is the same, and every April the Masters is seen as a signal of rebirth. The gorgeous azaleas and Georgia dogwood are in bloom, the huge pine and oak trees are as stunning and sturdy as ever, and golf is at its most poetic, especially during those final nine holes on Sunday when, as the TV voices are required to say at least 4,567 times each year, "The golf tournament really begins."

There is no doubting the greatness or the beauty of the golf course that Bobby Jones created as his legacy to the game. The back nine, with two reachable par-fives and water in play at five of the first seven holes, is a perfect setting for the final holes of a major championship.

But there is also no doubting that Augusta National is not a comfortable place for most people. It is a place golf people go every April because (of course) it is a tradition. Players know that a Masters victory ensures them a hallowed place in the pantheon of the sport. It also means you can come back and play in the tournament for the rest of your life and that you will be treated with an extra measure of respect wherever you go in the golf world.

To some extent, this is true of any major. Not like the Masters.

Andy North won the U.S. Open twice and some people still point to those victories as proof that the Open isn't as great a championship as it is cracked up to be. A British Open champion is a hero in Europe but often unnoticed in the United States. And to this day there are players who claim that the PGA shouldn't be considered a major because it allowed forty club pros into the field each year (until dropping the number to twenty in 1995) and is almost always played in brutal August heat.

Jeff Sluman, who won the PGA in 1988, has heard the arguments that his victory shouldn't count as a major. "Fine," he says, "I'll accept the fact that I can't count mine as a major when you go and tell Nicklaus that his *five* don't count."

No one questions a Masters champion whether he is Nicklaus or Palmer, Tommy Aaron or Charles Coody. You have worn the green jacket, you have selected the menu for the champions dinner and dined with the members. You have driven up Magnolia Lane to the clubhouse instead of coming in the main gate off Washington Street the way mere mortals do.

Tradition means rules, and Augusta has more rules than anyone.

There is no running allowed anywhere on the grounds, and while you may ask for autographs on the parking lot side of the clubhouse, you may not do so on the golf course side. On the practice days, a sign posted on the first tee instructs players to play "only one ball please." If you want to play two or three balls from a certain spot, you are more than welcome to do so—next week at Hilton Head.

The chairman of the club, currently Jackson Stephens, meets with the media every Masters Wednesday at precisely 11 A.M. That is the only time he speaks to the media and he speaks briefly. The same two club members—Charlie Yates and Dan Yates—have moderated the press conferences for as long as anyone can remember. Both men were excellent golfers in their day, especially Charlie, who won the British Amateur in 1938; Dan's son, Dan Jr., was once the runner-up in the U.S. Amateur and a member of the U.S. Walker Cup team and has played in sixteen Masters.

The Yates brothers are both well into their seventies now. They still address female reporters as "pretty little ladies" and, on occasion, will babble on for a while at the start of an interview while a player and reporters sit fidgeting uncomfortably waiting for them to finish. It was Blackie Sherrod of the *Dallas Morning News* who hung the nicknames "Big Silly" and "Little Silly" on them years ago.

Race and gender are still uncomfortable topics at Augusta—as they are at almost all golf clubs worldwide. Augusta has no female members and admitted its first black member four years ago, after the Shoal Creek debacle forced everyone in golf to make some attempt to open doors previously closed to blacks. During the 1994 tournament there was talk that Augusta might be getting ready to admit a *second* black member.

There is no shortage of black faces around Augusta National however. Blacks work as waiters, caddies, and members of the grounds crew. Most of them come in through gate seven, on the far corner of the grounds, report to their work stations, and leave through gate seven in the evening. Once a year, the club invites them all to a barbecue and picnic.

There are even rules for television at Augusta. Unlike any other sports event in the world, the Masters is paid far less than market value for its television rights. On an open market, during a time when NBC is paying the U.S. Open $13 million a year for the next three years, the Masters would be worth at least that much—perhaps more. Instead, CBS, which has televised the tournament for the last thirty-nine years, pays in the neighborhood of $4 million a year.

Why? So that the Masters can remain in complete control of the telecast. That means not only having the right to fire announcers like Whitaker and McCord, but the right to approve any announcer before he (no women announcers here either) is handed a microphone. It also means that someone from the club (the chairman until 1994, when vice chairman Joe Ford did the honors) asks the champion the first question on the air when he arrives at Butler Cabin to receive the green jacket.

And it also means that there are only four minutes of commercials per hour—two minutes for Cadillac and two minutes for Travelers Insurance—because the Men of the Masters don't want their telecasts glutted by commercials. Naturally, they have final approval of all commercial copy. You aren't likely to see any Miller Lite commercials on the Masters anytime soon. Since CBS pays a lower rights fee, the lack of commercial time doesn't create a problem.

The members' approach is simple: This is *our* tournament. If you do not like the way we do business, you are free not to do business with us. If you find our past policies on race or our current policies on gender offensive, you need not attend the tournament, televise the tournament, write about the tournament, or, for that matter, play in the tournament.

If you doubt the power of the Men of the Masters, consider the column that appeared in *Golf World* magazine a couple of weeks after the announcement that McCord had been banned from Augusta. "I applaud their decision," it read. "In the contract with CBS, they have the right to evaluate the announcers and decide who personifies the muted rituals of restraint. I am a loud wail."

The author of the column was Gary McCord.

No one is above the laws of Augusta. Several years ago, Pat Summerall, who did his twenty-sixth and last Masters for CBS in 1994 and was given what amounted to a royal sendoff by the MOTM (a gold badge, which grants him lifetime access to the tournament), was about to climb the steps to the tower behind the 18th green, when a Pinkerton guard stopped him.

"You need a pass to get up there," the guard said.

Summerall had left his pass in the CBS trailer. He explained that to the guard, noted that he had taken these same steps every day all week and for many years. The guard didn't care. No pass, no passage. The argument got heated, and Summerall was dragged off to the proper authorities. There, he had to be freed by a great deal of apologetic pleading by his boss, Frank Chirkinian.

Chirkinian has produced the Masters telecasts for thirty-six years.

For twenty of those years he lived at Augusta. He has been friends with all the club chairmen, plays the course every year, and produces the pictures and sounds that make America wax poetic about the Masters each year.

In 1994, Chirkinian arrived for the tournament and was told that CBS's ticket allotment had been cut by twenty-five, a disaster since the network flies in all sorts of clients as a major perk. When Chirkinian asked why, he was told "because."

"Arbitrary decision," he grumbled later in the week. Then he caught himself. "Of course, it's their ballpark."

It sure is. That's why when Summerall's partner, Ken Venturi, parked his car in a space where he wasn't supposed to park, Chirkinian got another call. Venturi could move his car—within the next fifteen minutes—or it would be moved—towed—for him.

"If I can just get into the truck and do my job, I can enjoy the week," Chirkinian said. "Until then... "

Until then, he was like everyone else, a guest of the Men of the Masters— as long as he behaved.

The best moments of every Masters are the first ones. They come early on Thursday morning when Gene Sarazen, Byron Nelson, and Sam Snead make their way to the first tee. This is one of the traditions that makes the Masters unique. All three are past champions, each a living, breathing legend. Snead, the kid in the group at eighty-one, played in forty-four Masters, winning three times. Nelson is eighty-two, also a three-time Masters champion. More than anyone, though, it is Sarazen, now ninety-two, who helped make the Masters what it is.

It was his historic double eagle at the 15th hole in 1935—the second year the tournament was played—that not only won the title, but put the Masters on the map. To this day, when you talk about "the shot heard 'round the world" to golfers, they think not of Bobby Thompson at the Polo Grounds in 1951, but Gene Sarazen at the Masters in 1935.

It is quite possible that these are the only three men in the world that Jackson Stephens ever waits for. Shortly after 8 A.M. Stephens stood on the first tee, wearing a floppy white golf hat that looked incongruous with his green jacket, and waited for the threesome that was scheduled to begin the tournament at 8:15.

To his left, on the board where the players' names are posted before they tee off, the three slots read: Sarazen-92; Nelson-82; Snead-81. The number usually tells the fan what number a player's caddy is wearing on his white overalls. The defending champion is always assigned number 1 and Jack Nicklaus is given 86 in honor of the year he won the last·and most extraordinary of his six titles. The first threesome's numbers need no explanation.

Sarazen played his last nine holes at Augusta in 1991. For several weeks, prior to the '94 tournament, he had been concerned that shoulder miseries would make it impossible to take his one swing. A year earlier, Nelson, bothered by hip and knee problems, couldn't take his turn, and Sarazen was concerned he would be the spectator in the group this time.

At 8:12, he walked resolutely onto the tee, dressed in his trademark knickers and floppy hat, carrying a walking stick. The spectators, most of whom had ignored the Pinkertons' "no running" pleas when the gates opened at 8 o'clock, in order to jockey for position around the tee, burst into loud applause when Sarazen appeared.

Sarazen rubbed his left shoulder and, noting the breezy 51 degree temperature, said, "Cold out here for these old guys."

He took a driver out of the bag he had borrowed from Rick Fehr and began swinging easily to get loose. Nelson appeared a few moments later, followed by CBS's Ken Venturi, who once led the Masters after three rounds as an amateur. "I don't know if I can hit the ball," Nelson said, "but I found me a good boy here to tee it up for me."

Snead was the last to arrive, bursting onto the tee right at 8:15.

"Jack, how is everything," he said, shaking hands with Stephens as if the chairman were his caddy.

They posed for pictures, then Stephens grabbed a hand microphone and introduced the three men. The other eighty-six players in the field would each receive exactly the same introduction on the first tee:

"Fore, please, [fill in a name] now driving."

Period. Sarazen, Nelson, and Snead did considerably better. Stephens, whose voice always quavers a bit, went through their accomplishments in detail. "... In 1945, when Byron won eleven straight tournaments, his scoring average for the year was, I believe, 68.33."

"That's correct," Nelson confirmed, smiling.

"... And Gene Sarazen won the U.S. Open in 1922 and 1932, the British Open in 1932 ..." He paused. "Don't forget the PGA," Sarazen said.

Sarazen, whose ball had been placed on the tee for him before he arrived, hit first. He lofted a shot about 120 yards down the left side. As the applause washed over him, he smiled, relieved that he had been able to get his shoulders turned.

Nelson, after his "boy," the 1964 U.S. Open champion, had teed the ball for him, hit a short, low line drive down the middle. He was clearly thrilled at being able to swing the club again.

Snead needed no help. He teed the ball himself, took that picture-perfect swing that produced eighty-one tournament victories, and hit the ball well down the fairway. He grinned and looked around as if to say, "Anybody looking for a game?"

"The fifty-eighth Masters is now officially under way," Stephens said.

Everyone headed for the warmth of the clubhouse, although it was hard to believe it would feel any warmer in there than it had felt on the windswept tee for those brief, sweet moments.

"How come," Sarazen said to his partners as they walked off, "I'm the only one who gets older every year?"

The cool morning gave way to a picture-postcard afternoon. By the end of the day it was apparent that no one was going to challenge the tournament record of 271 co-held by Nicklaus and Raymond Floyd. The breezes and the greens were turning everyone into grinders.

Larry Mize had the lead at 68 when everyone was finished, with Tom Kite and Fulton Allem one shot back. Tom Watson shot 70 in spite of chipping into the water at the 15th and making a triple-bogey 8 there. Greg Norman also went into the water at 15, but saved par and also shot 70.

The 15th was the talk of the locker room. The embankment in front of the green just over the water had been cut so short that any ball that landed in front of the green was going to roll back and get wet. In fact, some balls that landed *on* the front of the green and spun also ended up wet.

If Norman was the favorite going in, favorites 1-A and 1-B were the two Nicks: Faldo and Price. Both struggled, Price to a 74, Faldo to a 76. Faldo came off the course mumbling about his putting and, after a brief chat with the media, went directly to the putting green.

There are two places at the Masters where players talk to the media. One is the interview room, where the leaders are brought in each day and put through their paces by the Yates brothers. The other is underneath the giant oak tree that stands just outside the entrance to the clubhouse.

Exactly how this particular tradition has grown up, no one is quite sure, but almost every player knows it and follows it. When you finish a round and you know you aren't going to be asked to the interview room, you march up the hill from the 18th green, step inside the ropes that stop the public from going farther, walk about five more paces, and find a spot under the oak tree. The tree is so huge that there is room for at least half a dozen players to spread out in different places and talk.

Occasionally, a reporter or two will follow a player into the locker room once he is finished under the oak tree, but most players do their talking there. The exception to this rule and tradition was John Daly, who walked past the oak tree each of the first three days (76-73-77) pursued by a bevy of reporters and never stopped to talk to anyone.

Only on Sunday, after finishing with a triple-bogey 7 at the 18th to shoot 76, did he pause to talk. He had been paired, by luck of the draw, for four straight rounds with Ian Woosnam, the Welshman who had won the tournament in 1991.

"Me and Woosie are talking about getting married," joked Daly, who was in the middle of an ugly divorce. "He told me this was the longest relation-ship I've ever had."

Standing at the bar inside the clubhouse, he sipped a Diet Coke.

Someone asked if he could feel the support of the fans. "Sure could," he said. "Can't understand it."

He was asked if he had perhaps rushed a little bit on the back nine, gotten careless. He shrugged. "I'm damn sure not going to play slow when nothing's going right. At twelve, I hit me a seven-iron I thought was in the hole and it went in the water. That'll make you impatient. Tell the truth, all I was trying to do today was get me some crystal."

The Masters gives out crystal to any player who makes an eagle during the tournament. Jeff Maggert had made a double eagle that day at the 13th, the third in tournament history. "Knowing this place," Daly said, "they'll probably tell him a double eagle doesn't count."

He put down the Diet Coke and headed for the door. He had been funny and charming and antsy all at once. Being near him gave one a sense of discomfort, as if a wrong question or comment might set him off. He had played the last round as if getting some crystal and getting out of Dodge were the only two things on his mind. The enigma grew.

By Friday evening at most majors, the list of contenders and pretenders has shrunk. The Masters is the only major tournament that repairs after the first round, meaning that the Thursday leaders go out last the way the leaders normally do at other tournaments only on Saturday and Sunday. By the time Larry Mize got to the clubhouse in the late-afternoon gloaming on Friday, he had shot 71 for 139 and he still had the lead. The list of those chasing him had changed considerably.

Norman was still there, one shot back after shooting 70 again. Tom Lehman, who had finished third in his first Masters a year earlier, had also shot a second straight 70. The two biggest moves of the day had been made by two men who knew what it felt like to contend on Sunday and come up short: Dan Forsman, who had led the tournament in 1993 until he knocked his ball into Rae's Creek at the 12th hole and made an eight, had produced a 66, the low round of the tournament, to tie Norman and Lehman. And Jose Maria Olazabal, who had stood on the 18th tee tied for the lead in 1991 only to bogey the hole and lose by one shot to Ian Woosnam, had come back from an opening 74—identical to Forsman—to shoot 67. He was two shots back of Mize along with the rising young South African star Ernie Els and a trio of forty-something Americans: Hale Irwin, Kite, and Watson.

Olazabal's presence on the leader board was intriguing since he had become golf's version of the invisible man in 1993. He had been labeled the "next Seve" when he first began making a name for himself by winning two tournaments on the European Tour in 1986 at the age of twenty. A year later, he had started his famous Ryder Cup partnership with Ballesteros. He wasn't as classically handsome or charismatic as his older countryman, but he did have the same sort of magic touch around the green and a similar ability to extricate himself from seemingly impossible spots. When he won the World Series of Golf in 1990 at the age of twenty-four by a stunning twelve shots, it seemed to be only a matter of time before he began winning major championships.

Then he lost the 1991 Masters to Woosnam and his ascendancy stopped. He was still a good player, but he was not the same. In 1993, he failed to win on the European Tour for the first time in six years and dropped out of the top ten on the Order of Merit. In fact, he didn't even qualify for the Ryder Cup team and made the team only as a captain's pick.

He went from shy but charming to angry and aloof. He was constantly telling reporters to leave him alone and, during the Ryder Cup, Ballesteros did virtually all his talking for him. People wondered if all of the "next Seve" pressure had gotten to him the way all the "next Nicklaus" rhetoric had gotten to many young American players.

Olazabal said no, he just needed to tinker with his swing a little. He worked over the winter on his consistency and switched to a metal driver. Right from the start, he had played better in 1994 and had finished second in New Orleans the week before the Masters. When his name popped onto the leader board Friday, eyebrows went up all over the grounds.

The same was true of Els, the tall twenty-four-year-old South African with the long, dreamy-looking swing and easygoing manner. Els had already won seven times around the world, but more important than that, he had shown a knack for playing his best golf in the majors. This was his eighth major and he came in with four top-ten finishes. He had length comparable to Daly's, only he made it look much easier. And he had the good fortune not to be called the "next Gary Player," if only because, at a shade under 6-foot-4, he was almost nine inches taller than Player and played a game so different that the only thing they had in common was South African birth.

The real surprise, though, was who *wasn't* on the leader board: the two Nicks. Price and Faldo both struggled in with 73s on Friday, meaning both would play on the weekend—Price at 147 and Faldo right on the number at 149—but neither was likely to contend, barring a miraculous round on Saturday.

Price, who had never won the Masters and knew that the lightning-fast greens probably would make it the most difficult major for him to win, was disappointed but sanguine. He knew, the way the course was set up, with the pins practically sitting on cliffs, that he would have to be at his very best with the putter and he just wasn't. "It's not as if I'm hitting the ball badly," he said. "I just can't make any putts on these greens."

Faldo wasn't quite as philosophical. He had won the Masters twice, in 1989 and 1990, and knew he was perfectly capable of making putts on Augusta's greens. Only he wasn't. Each day he walked up the hill from 18 to the oak tree, stood with his arms folded, and in a voice that couldn't be heard by anyone standing more than five feet away, kept saying, "It's horrible, terrible. Can't make a thing." The inquisition finished, he would find his caddy, Fanny Sunneson—one of a handful of female tour caddies—and head for the putting green.

For most top players, the goal during the first two days of any golf tournament is simple: don't lose the tournament. That is especially true at a major, where the pressure on every shot beginning on Thursday seems to quadruple.

"You can always tell the first day of a major the minute you walk into the locker room," Jeff Sluman says. "The line for the bathroom is always a *lot* longer."

The great players rarely lead majors on Saturday morning. No one really *wants* to go wire-to-wire at a major because the pressure of sleeping with the lead for three straight nights can be unbearable.

It does happen. During the course of winning eighteen times, Nicklaus had to lead start to finish a few times. At Baltusrol in 1980, he shot 63 in the first round and led all the way, and he ran away with the Masters in 1965. Raymond Floyd led the Masters all four rounds when he tied Nicklaus's record in 1976 and also was in command for all four rounds when he won his second PGA title at Southern Hills in 1982.

More often than not, though, the real leader board—the one that will produce the winner—doesn't take shape until Saturday afternoon. Tom Watson never once led wire-to-wire on his way to eight major wins. In fact, even in 1977 at the British Open, when he and Nicklaus eventually lapped the field by 10 shots, they were not the leaders after two rounds. Roger Maltbie was one shot ahead of both of them.

"You want to play well on Thursday and Friday at a major," Nicklaus said. "But you want to save your best golf for Saturday and Sunday."

Most of the time, if you bet against the thirty-six-hole leader, you will win. In 1993 the only thirty-six-hole leader at a major who went on to win was Lee Janzen at the U.S. Open. That doesn't mean that no one took Larry Mize seriously after thirty-six holes at the Masters. After all, he had won the tournament before and had played the best golf of his career in 1993, winning two tour events and an IMG-run megabucks made-for-TV tournament in December. There, he had beaten an elite field by 10 shots to win $550,000. No question, Mize could win.

But not many people expected him to. The name that had been mentioned most often before the tournament began was Greg Norman. On Saturday morning, very few people had changed their opinion. Norman had done nothing to lose on Thursday and Friday and sat very comfortably one shot behind Mize.

"It's a little bit like going down the road with a ten-foot alligator running right behind you," Mize said.

Norman was trying to go the low-key route, refusing to get caught up in the hype that surrounded him. He had always liked little sayings; his first boss as a young assistant pro had always told him that the key to success in life came down to DIN and DIP—Do-It-Now and Do-It-Properly. He still believed in that. At Augusta, he said, the keys were the two Ps—Patience and Putting. Norman hadn't yet gotten on a roll with his putting, but he was patiently waiting for that to happen.

To most Masters veterans, there was something missing on this Augusta Saturday. For the first time in forty years, no one named Palmer or Nicklaus was around for the weekend. In one sense, this was no shock. Palmer hadn't made a Masters cut since 1983 and, at sixty-four, wasn't likely to make one again. Ironically, Nicklaus hadn't missed the last two rounds since that year. He didn't actually miss the cut in '83 either, but had been forced to withdraw Friday morning when his back began to spasm on the practice tee.

That was the first time that the media began speculating that his days as a serious contender were behind him. After all, he was forty-three. At forty-six, he won the tournament again. As recently as 1993 he had been tied for the first-round lead before finishing tied for twenty-seventh on Sunday.

But he had struggled with his game since January, when he started the year by winning the senior division of the Mercedes (don't call it Tournament of Champions) Championships. He hadn't made a cut on the regular tour in five tries, so missing at the Masters wasn't that surprising except for the fact that the cut at Augusta is probably easier to make than at any other tournament on tour.

Since the field is almost never more than ninety players (eighty-six in 1994) and everyone within 10 shots of the leader plays on the weekend, the cut is usually around 150. That was true this year—51 players made the cut at 149 or better—but Nicklaus at 152 and Palmer at 155 were not among them.

Saturday is always called "moving day" on tour because it is the day when those who are way behind must make a move if they want to have any chance to win on Sunday. About once a year, someone will win a tournament after making the cut on the number, proving that it is worth grinding on Friday to make the cut because you never know when you are going to discover something on the range or get hot with your putter.

If you don't move on Saturday, your chances of winning on Sunday are nil. Not only are you going to be too many shots back, but you are going to be behind too many people. There is a big difference between being four shots behind the leader in third place starting Sunday and being four shots behind tied for fourteenth. If you have only two people ahead of you, the chances that both will falter are halfway decent. But if you have thirteen people ahead of you, there is no way that every one of them is going to collapse. You might shoot 67 and move up to third or fourth, but the odds are that at least one or two people will play well enough to stay ahead of you.

Norman was in the second-to-last group of the day Saturday, paired with Tom Lehman. Jose Maria Olazabal and Ernie Els were right in front of them and Mize and Dan Forsman behind. The day was warm and cloudy with enough breeze to toughen the course even more than on the first two days.

The Norman-Lehman pairing was intriguing, if only because they both were playing with the same irons—one for big money, the other for no money. Lehman had switched at the beginning of the year to the irons Cobra made for Norman even though it meant giving up some endorsement money from Cleveland Classics. He liked the Cobra irons better than Cleveland's new VAS irons and decided to play them even though the company wasn't going to pay him to do so. Norman appeared in commercials for Cobra all the time, pitching its King Cobra woods. He carried one King Cobra club—the driver—in his bag.

Norman was thirty-nine, a multi-multi-millionaire. Lehman was thirty-five, a veteran of every mini-tour there was, someone who had been off the tour between 1985 and 1992. He had gotten so discouraged at one point that he almost took the job as golf coach at the University of Minnesota for $29,000 a year. "I probably would have done it," he said, "but they wanted me to rent cross-country skis out of the pro shop in the winter."

Golf courses don't check resumes. And so it was Lehman who shot 34 on the front nine and Norman who shot 38. That tied Lehman for the tournament lead with Olazabal and Mize at six under. Norman had gone from one shot back to four back.

Still, there was no reason to panic. The back nine at Augusta is the place where players make their move. Once you get by 10 and 11, both long, difficult par-fours, the next six holes can be attacked. That is what makes Augusta the perfect setting for a major. Most years, the leader cannot play safe on the back nine because if he does someone will catch him.

When Bobby Jones built the course, he created the back-nine par-fives, 13 and 15, as par-four-and-a-halfs where a player in contention almost has to go for the green in two, but faces real peril—water and shallow, treacherous greens—in doing so. The kind of golf the back nine at Augusta can produce was never more evident than in 1991 when Tom Watson made a double-bogey five at the tiny 12th, then made eagle three at both 13 and 15 to tie for the lead.

Norman arrived at 13 on Saturday knowing that moving day was rapidly drawing to a close and the only move he had made was backward. He was now three over par for the day and trailed the leaders, Olazabal and Mize, by five. Lehman, having just bogeyed 12, was one shot behind them.

The 13th is the last hole of "Amen Comer," the three famous holes where water can turn the tournament around in one quick splash. The 12th, the par-three with the tiny green that almost never calls for more than a nine-iron but often decides the tournament because of Rae's Creek meandering along in front of the green and the bunkers behind it, is a hole where everyone just tries to make his par and escape.

The 13th isn't as simple. It is a dogleg left, with azaleas, dogwood, and the creek running along the left side of the fairway and trees most of the way down the right. The narrow slice of water in front of the green is almost invisible from where you play your second shot, except inside the mind.

Norman hit a perfect drive and, as is the case when you hit the ball straight off the tee at 13, had only an iron—a four—left to the green. He hit perhaps his best shot of the day and the ball checked up 18 feet beyond the flag. The huge crowd surrounding the green was going crazy. It was time for the Shark to stop this silliness and climb back into contention. An eagle would do just that. He would be three shots back with five to play, including the equally reachable 15th.

Norman was thinking the same thing. His goal on the tee had been to make a birdie—he hadn't had one all day—but now, as he surveyed the putt, he knew it was makable and he knew what it would mean to him—and to those he was chasing—if he made it. "I went for it too hard," he said later. "I wasn't thinking about anything except making that one, which was a mistake."

The putt was left of the cup all the way, the kind of pull that often comes off the putter when someone is trying too hard. Worse than that, it rolled a good six feet past. Now Norman had a tricky putt coming back just to make birdie. Still, if he could make this and get an eagle at 15...

He couldn't. The putt slid just past the right edge. A three-putt par. In the meantime, Lehman made *his* birdie and moved into a three-way tie for the lead. Norman was deflated. He wasn't hitting the ball poorly, but nothing was happening with the putter.

Now he had to birdie 15. He parred 14 and hit a good drive at 15. But this time he missed the green, hitting his second safely over the water, but to a tough place to chip from. He got to within 10 feet, but again, the putter wouldn't work. He had gone 5-5 at two holes where 4-4 was an absolute must and 3-3 should not have been out of the question. Lehman, over the green in two, chipped to within two feet and made another birdie. He was now seven under. At 16, he had a 50-foot, curling birdie putt and somehow rolled that one in too. He was eight under and leading the Masters by two shots. The cheers echoing off the pines and oaks were for him, not for his far more famous and wealthy playing partner, who had started the day even with him and was now seven shots behind.

"When I heard the cheers walking off sixteen, my eyes got a little bit wet," Lehman said. "I mean, who would have thought a kid from Minnesota could lead the Masters?"

The kid turned human on 18, making a bogey from the middle of the fairway. That left him one shot ahead of Olazabal, two ahead of Mize, and three ahead of Tom Kite. Norman parred the last three holes, finishing with a birdie-less 75. Only once did he show his frustration. When he walked on the green at 18, knowing that most of the cheers were for Lehman, he marked his ball, then threw it to his caddy, Tony Navarro, who was still 100 yards down the fairway because he had just finished raking the fairway trap where Norman had put his drive.

It wasn't a heave, and Navarro scooped the ball up on a hop like a shortstop and cleaned it just as he would have done if Norman had calmly handed him the ball on the green. But the toss was telling. Norman wanted to get the round done and be gone. He had gone from a tie for second, one shot back in perfect position, to a three-way tie for eighth, six shots back.

While Lehman was being taken to the interview room to tell the gathered media his life story—a day earlier he had been asked four questions, now he was asked closer to forty—Norman stood under the oak tree and calmly told everyone he still didn't think he was out of the golf tournament, that he had hit the ball well and had every reason to believe he could go low on Sunday and catch the leaders.

As he started to walk away, with all the cameras and tape recorders still rolling, he spotted Tim Rosaforte of *Sports Illustrated,* who had just been elected president of the Golf Writers Association of America. Norman grinned and shook Rosaforte's hand. "Hey, Mr. President," he said cheerfully, "congratulations!"

He walked into the locker room and was about to make his escape when a freelance writer from Boston, who had been standing under the oak tree and had witnessed Norman's cheery analysis of the day, approached.

"Greg, I know this may be a bad time ..." he began.

"You're certainly right about that," Norman said and kept on walking.

That was how Norman really felt about the day.

The four longest days of the golfing year are the Sundays at the major championships. The leaders have to wait until mid afternoon to tee off on a day when they probably haven't slept very much and aren't likely to sleep very late even knowing they will have several hours to kill once they get out of bed.

Tom Lehman was up early on Masters Sunday to go to church. He had promised Ann Davis, the woman who ran the child-care center for the players at the tournament, that he would speak at her church that morning, and leading the Masters was not, in his opinion, any reason to back out.

Lehman spoke briefly to the congregation at Marks United Methodist Church. His message was simple and direct: He felt no pressure playing the last round of the Masters because he knew that because of his faith in God he was loved and eternally accepted whether he shot 70 or 80 or 90. Lehman is a devout Christian, but, like Paul Azinger, he doesn't talk about his faith publicly unless he is asked.

Lehman and Jose Maria Olazabal, who would make up the last pairing of the day, both arrived at the golf course shortly before noon. When Olazabal opened his locker, he found a piece of white notebook paper lying on the top shelf. It was a note from Seve Ballesteros.

Written in Spanish it said: "Be patient today. Remember, you are the best player. Wait for the others to make their mistakes and you will win ... Seve."

Ballesteros had left the note just before he teed off at 12:06—two and a half hours before Olazabal would tee off. He had arrived at the golf course that morning and remembered a note Gary Player had left in his locker before he played his final round in 1980. It had said approximately the same thing. Ballesteros won that day (and again in 1983) and never forgot the gesture. He thought he owed Olazabal, his longtime protégé and Ryder Cup partner, similar words of encouragement.

Olazabal picked up the note, walked outside the locker room, and sat in a rocking chair on the porch overlooking the first fairway. He read the note, smiled, read it again, then put it in his pocket. He sat in the rocking chair for several long minutes by himself, staring out toward the first tee.

Golf is the most solitary sport there is, never more so than on the last day of a major. There is no time for lessons or pep talks. You will be watched by thousands (millions on TV), but you and your game will be all alone on the golf course. Now, though, Olazabal wouldn't be completely alone. He would take Seve's note with him.

Most Sundays at Augusta are roller-coaster rides. Players race up the leader board, then fall back. Someone almost inevitably comes out of the pack to challenge, perhaps win. Player had shot 64 on the last day in 1978 to win, and Nicklaus had shot 65 on that amazing afternoon in 1986 when he shocked the world—not to mention Greg Norman—by stealing the green jacket. That is what makes the back nine of the Masters so special: the chance to go low is always there, especially when you get to 13 and 15.

But the Men of the Masters had outsmarted themselves this time. By setting up the golf course to keep players from going low, they had robbed the tournament of a good deal of its usual Sunday drama. On a golf course famous for yielding low Sunday scores, no one shot lower than 69 on this final day and only three players produced that score.

That meant the tournament would be decided by the players in the last three groups. Realistically, no one more than four shots out of the lead was going to win. By the time those final six players began to make their way to the back nine (where, as we all know, the tournament really starts on Sunday) the list of possible winners was down to three: Lehman, Olazabal, and Mize.

Norman's hopes for a Sunday charge had faded early. He three-putted the par-five second hole for a bogey, then hit his tee shot way left at number four and made another bogey. "It was over after number two," he said. "I walked on that green thinking I could make four and walked off it with a six. The thought crossed my mind right there that it wasn't going to be my day."

He slogged home with a 77. Standing under the tree again, he admitted that Saturday's round had hurt. "I lost all my spark," he said. "I tried to get it back going to the first tee today, but it wasn't there. The number I had in mind was sixty-six." He forced a laugh. "I guess I was a little off."

He started toward the locker room, pursued this time by Bob Drum, a veteran reporter and onetime CBS pundit who still did some work for the network. Norman's friend Frank Chirkinian had sent Drum to tell him that Chirkinian wanted him to sit in Butler Cabin with host Jim Nantz and analyze the last few holes of the tournament on TV. CBS often asks players—especially Norman—to do this when they finish early and, almost without exception, they comply especially Norman.

When Norman heard Drum calling his name, he stopped and turned around. He listened as Drum repeated Chirkinian's request. For several seconds, he said nothing. Then, slowly, he shook his head. "No, Drummer, I can't," he said. "Tell Frank, I'm sorry. Next week, anything he wants, but not today. I just can't."

Drum didn't answer, he just stood there waiting for Norman to reconsider. "You sure, Greg?" he said, finally.

Norman sighed. "I'm sure."

"Any other tournament, I could have handled it," he said later. "But I just couldn't bear the thought of sitting there describing how someone *else* had won the Masters. It would have hurt too much. I just had to get out of there."

Several other players made brief moves on Sunday. Tom Watson, starting at two under (five behind Lehman) birdied number two, but promptly bogeyed three of the next four. Ernie Els, six shots back at the start, eagled the eighth to get to four under and birdied 12 to get to five. But he went for too much on his drive at 13, put it into the azaleas on the left, and made a bogey. Tom Kite got to five under with a birdie at the second, but bogeyed the fifth and never got closer than five under again.

And so it was left to the onetime champion (Mize), the onetime wunderkind (Olazabal), and the onetime mini-tour lifer (Lehman) to decide the tournament on the back nine. They were tied at eight under through 11. Then the 12th stepped in again. All three players—Mize was playing in the group right in front of Lehman and Olazabal—knocked their tee shots over the green trying to be sure not to get wet. Only Olazabal was able to chip close enough to make par.

He led by one. Mize was the only one to birdie 13, and that tied him with Olazabal again until he missed a five-footer at 14 to drop back. He never made another birdie and finished third. Olazabal and Lehman both parred 14, so they went to 15 with Olazabal still leading by one.

Lehman's drive was 25 yards past Olazabal's. Knowing Lehman would almost surely reach the green, Olazabal had to go for it, even though he had

215 yards to the hole and had to hit a three-iron as hard as he could to have a chance to clear the water. The ball hung in the air for what seemed like days, bounced on the upslope in front of the green, and seemed to hang there. Dozens of similar shots during the week had rolled back into the creek. But just as Fred Couples's ball had somehow not rolled into Rae's Creek at number 12 in 1992, this ball held on the front fringe 35 feet short of the pin.

"A foot shorter and he's in the creek," Lehman said. Undeterred, he hit a four-iron to within 15 feet.

If Lehman knocked in his eagle putt and Olazabal made a two-putt birdie, they would be even with three holes to play. Olazabal, off the green, left the pin in. His putt swooped left to right and headed straight for the cup. Five feet away, everyone knew it was in. Olazabal punched a fist in the air and, for the first time all day, smiled. He was ten under.

Now Lehman had to make his three to stay within one. His putt also looked perfect. But at the last possible second, it slid just over the right edge and stopped an inch away. Lehman stared in disbelief for a moment, then leaped into the air in agony, went to his knees and pounded the green in frustration.

"Sometimes," he said, "you put so much into a putt and when it doesn't go in, it just hurts."

Olazabal led Lehman by two, Mize by three. It was his tournament to lose now. On the 16th tee, Lehman said softly, "Great putt."

Deep down, he knew that Olazabal had just won the Masters. Not that Lehman stopped trying. He had birdie chances at 16 and 17, but couldn't convert. Olazabal bogeyed 17 (his second bogey in three days) to make the 18th suspenseful, but when Lehman made bogey there, all Olazabal had to do was two-putt from six feet to win. He didn't need the second putt. He shook his fist again, but didn't jump up and down or dance on the green. A number of people who remembered him dancing on the green after Europe had won the Ryder Cup in 1987 asked him why he had been so sedate.

"This is Augusta," he said, smiling. "You have to behave properly." Here was a champion the Men of the Masters would happily dine with that evening. He was the sixth foreigner invited to Sunday dinner at Augusta in seven years. First, though, he needed a green jacket. After surviving the always-awkward TV ceremony, Olazabal walked onto the putting green shortly after 7 o'clock to join the assembled officials and fans. Jack Stephens introduced him as "Josay Marie OlaZabal," pronouncing the *Z* instead of the proper *TH*. The new champion didn't care. He gave Stephens a thumbs-up for trying.

The sun was beginning to set behind the oaks and pines when 1993 champion Bernhard Langer slipped the green jacket (a 41-long) onto Olazabal's shoulders. The son of a greenskeeper had a huge smile on his face as Langer led the applause for him.

It was a warm moment in a wonderful setting, a scene worthy of the Masters. Which, as the Men of the Masters would hasten to tell you, is saying quite a lot.

My First Time at Augusta

from *A Golfer's Life* by Arnold Palmer with
James Dodson

I remember like it was yesterday the feeling as I drove up Magnolia Lane
into Augusta National Golf Club for the first time. I'd never seen a place
that looked so beautiful, so well manicured, and so purely devoted to golf, as
beautiful as an antebellum estate, as quiet as a church. I remember turning
to Winnie, who was as excited as I was by the sight of the place, and saying
quietly, probably as much in awe as I've ever been: "This has got to be it,
Babe ..." I felt a powerful thrill and unexpected kinship with the place.
Perhaps that's partially because Augusta was built by Bob Jones, who was
one of my childhood heroes, but also because the Masters, though still a rel-
atively modest event in terms of money, was like a family gathering of the
game's greatest players, ruled with a firm, unbending hand by Clifford
Roberts. They were all there—Jones, Sarazen, Snead, Nelson, Hogan.
Though I'd met them all before, just seeing their names together on pairing
sheets or chatting with each other on those perfect putting surfaces was an
almost religious experience for me. Privately, I admitted to Winnie that it

was like dying and going to heaven. I was there, of course, courtesy of my National Amateur title, and though I was rendered a bit agog by the lush surroundings and famous players, I was also surging with confidence. After weeks of playing courses on tour that were rock hard and in some cases in pretty woeful shape, coming to Augusta's exquisitely manicured fairways and pristine greens was a royal treat I was anxious to experience. As it was not an official Tour event, I also stood to pocket some much-needed moola.

I played pretty well, all things considered, in that first Masters outing. I opened with a pair of discouraging 76s, but then settled down a bit and shot 72 in the third round, followed by a final round of 69. Ironically, standing on the tenth tee on Sunday, I calculated that if I got home in 32 on Augusta's famous back nine I might be a serious factor in the tournament's outcome. That realization got me so worked up, I regret to say, I made a double-bogey six on ten and wound up finishing in tenth place. I made a paycheck for $696 that week—money that came just when we needed it most—but more importantly, I had made the acquaintance of a special place and numerous people who would soon mean more to Winnie and me than I could ever have imagined.

At first glance, the course, designed by Alister MacKenzie with helpful insights from Bob Jones, didn't particularly suit my style of game. There were numerous places where a high, soft fade worked best, and the undulating and fast putting surfaces favored approach shots that stuck like darts rather than ricocheted like bullets, as mine sometimes did. I quickly saw there were things I would need to learn to do if I intended to conquer the golf course and win the Masters—notably, hit the ball a bit higher and know when to back off intelligently at a hole where finesse and not power would bear more fruit.

As Pap would have pointed out, though, you're invariably stuck with the golf swing you're born with, and I wasn't going to alter that much of my game to try to tailor it to Augusta's swirling winds and daunting putting surfaces. I learned, instead, *where* to hit my drives in order to have approaches to greens I was comfortable with—in other words, put the ball where I could hit into the green on a straight, low line. In time I became pretty adept at knowing Augusta's "angles," as I thought of it, knowing where I could roll a ball through an opening or use a mound or hillside to pull off a shot and snug the ball close.

I remember meeting Clifford Roberts, the club's legendary chairman, then at the height of his power, and being almost instantly scared to death of him. Though a New York investment banker by profession, he reminded me of an old schoolteacher, reserved, tough, a headmaster brooking no opposition or even debate on any subject. He was clearly a one-man show, and the small membership of Augusta National obviously liked it that way. I was determined to stay out of his way, recalling that a few years before he'd tossed Frank Stranahan off the premises for allegedly hitting extra practice balls during a round—something that was against the club's policy. Being friends with Clifford Roberts, I would discover, was like learning Augusta National's proper angles—it took time, but the friendship, when it evolved, would be a lasting and genuine one.

I met Bob Jones there, too—by then far past his playing prime and only a year or so away from being stricken by the illness (syringomelia) that would rack his body and eventually force him to use a customized golf cart to get around the grounds to see players and meet people. Mr. Jones, as I called him from the outset, was as unfailingly polite and kind-spirited as anybody I ever met at Augusta. Perhaps because amateur golf had meant so much to him—he won the Grand Slam as an amateur in 1930 and then retired from the game, as he described it, before he "needed" to make money in order to play—Jones harbored a special affection for amateur champions who found their way to Augusta, treating each and every one like the special young men he thought they were, myself included.

I'd seen Ben Hogan at various tournaments and even played in a group close to him at Wilmington, but I met him for the first time in Augusta. To be honest, I was so in awe of the man, and so naturally shy, I felt he was utterly unapproachable. At the Masters someone introduced us, and we shook hands. He was polite enough, but I felt the cool distance others sensed while in his presence. Hogan was still limping from his 1950 car crash but remained the most dangerous player of his age, maybe the best ball-striker who ever lived.

I was at first surprised by—and later angered about—the fact that he never, in the years I knew him, called me by my first name. Ten million golf fans have felt completely comfortable calling me "Arnie," but Mr. Hogan never spoke my real name. He only called me "fella." To give him the benefit of the doubt, he called lots of young, ambitious players "fella." Perhaps he couldn't remember their names (after all, a lot of talent was streaming out of the college ranks into the professional ranks), or maybe he sensed the others and I were gunning for his records, which of course we were. But he was a living legend and inspiration. Golf is, at its core, life's most good-hearted and socially complex game—one of the "most humbling things on earth," as my good friend George Low once quipped—and I wouldn't have minded being called "Arnie" by a man I only admired from afar and played for on a Ryder Cup team. But it never happened. You draw your own conclusions from that.

I learned a valuable lesson at that first Masters—that *wanting* something so much I could almost taste it wasn't the best approach to winning golf tournaments, especially major ones. I learned that, at a place like Augusta National, where every shot is potentially so decisive, I couldn't afford to get ahead of myself as I did that Sunday afternoon on the final nine, blowing myself right out of contention. I had to play my own game, shot by shot, and not permit myself the luxury of thinking what it could mean—a lesson I was destined to learn and a mistake I was destined to repeat. But that's a tale to come.

Sam Snead and I had met before, but we got to be pretty good friends at that first Masters. I always enjoyed my time with Sam, the rounds we played together, the rustic pearls of wisdom he dropped about the game and life, even the colorful and sometimes downright raunchy jokes he told and tall tales he spun. Sam had a dark side that emerged when his game faltered, but he was at heart a big old country boy who loved golf and had a zest for life, swallowing it in gulps (especially if someone else was buying the beer—he was also one of the tightest guys with a buck I ever met), and surely one of the most natural talents who ever swung a golf club.

The Masters Its Ownself

from *Fairways and Greens*: *The Best Golf Writing of Dan Jenkins*
by Dan Jenkins

Something mystical happens to every writer who goes to the Masters for the first time, some sort of emotional experience that results in a search party having to be sent out to recover his typewriter from a clump of azaleas. The writer first becomes hypnotized by the "cathedral of pines," down around the tenth fairway normally; then he genuflects at the Sarazen Bridge on the fifteenth, and eventually takes up a position on the Augusta National veranda, there to wait for an aging wisteria vine to crawl up his sleeve and caress his priceless clubhouse badge. It is a peculiar state of mind, a sort of sporting heaven in which the writer feels that if Bobby Jones could only waggle a hickory shaft once more, it would instantly turn him into F. Scott Damon "Ring" Hemingway. My own problem is that I still feel this way after more than forty consecutive years of covering this unique event.

Where has the time gone? Yesterday it was 1951. I'm a college sophomore but a working journalist following Ben Hogan every step of the way to report on the color of Ben's slacks and the contents of Valerie's thermos to the readers of the now-deceased *Fort Worth Press*. Now it's all these years later but I'm still a fixture in my favorite area, the upstairs grill and balcony, wondering how much fun it would have been to have stood around there with Granny Rice and Bob Jones.

As it is, I make do with an assortment of rogues: golfers, ex-pro football players, TV folks, poets, and other privileged souls who turn up in the clubhouse every year. I'm accused of having done a record amount of time in the upstairs grill and on that balcony overlooking the veranda. It's true that I've spent a lot of hours up there, but I can tell you that eggs, country ham, biscuits, red-eye gravy, a pot of coffee, a morning paper, a table by the window, and the idle chitchat of competitors, authors, and philosophers hasn't exactly been a bad way to start off each day at the Masters all these years.

That room, the upstairs Men's Grill, was once the interview area, so designated by those writers who wished to include quotes in their stories. Strangely enough, not every writer wanted quotes in his story forty years ago. Many believed that their own observations were all their readers deserved. I was always a quote guy, trained by Blackie Sherrod, my mentor, a Texas sportswriting legend, to pick up the good quote, not just any old quote. So trained were a few other writers, such as my old friend Bob Drum, then with the *Pittsburgh Press*.

In those early 1950s, we would ordinarily have the daily leaders all to ourselves upstairs at the completion of their rounds. Then more quote guys began coming out of the dogwood as the press corps of the Masters started to double, triple, and upward. And suddenly one year, Hogan and Snead found themselves being smothered on separate sofas while journalists stood, knelt, and shouted, "What'd you hit to the sixth?" . . . "How long was the putt on twelve?" . . . "Where was the pin on fifteen?" They practically swung from chandeliers.

This was the first time I heard Ben use a line he would rely on again in the future. He said, "One of these days a deaf-mute is going to win a golf tournament, and you guys won't be able to write a story."

Cliff Roberts, the Masters chairman, observed this scene one day, saw things were getting out of hand, and ordered an interview room installed in the press building, which used to be a tent and then a Quonset hut before it became a structure to accommodate the largest number of journalists who attend any of the four majors. The problem these days with the interview area is that the interviews themselves have become so orchestrated by Masters edict that the interview area is quite possibly the worst place in Augusta, Georgia, to look for news. Locker rooms and grill rooms are still the best places to find out things you don't know—at the Masters or any other golf tournament.

Thinking back on all of the Masters Tournaments to which I've been assigned, I'm sure that my affection for the event has something to do with the fact that such folklore characters as Ben Hogan, Sam Snead, Arnold Palmer, Jack Nicklaus, Gary Player, Ray Flord, Tom Watson, Seve Ballesteros, Ben Crenshaw, and Nick Faldo had the wisdom and moral fiber to win most of them for me.

It's only human (some sportswriters are human) and even built into the craft that the words come easier, more quickly, and often more engagingly if the winner is already accepted by the world as a certified immortal or celebrity. Names make news, to be sure, and names have absolutely made the Masters. It wasn't Gene Kunes who holed out that shot for a double eagle, it was Gene Sarazen. And if there's anybody who likes a name more than a sportswriter, it's his boss. This is the guy back in the office who can be relied upon to create more space for your gifted prose and fatten the headline if the Masters winner is a familiar personality. I once worked for a managing editor at *Sports Illustrated* who was a great man in most ways, except that he tended to hold me personally responsible when Palmer or Nicklaus failed to win the Masters—or any other major, for that matter. I'm determined that the closest I ever came to being sentenced to a penal colony was back in 1971 at Augusta when I committed the heinous crime of Charles Coody, and again in 1973 when I was guilty of Tommy Aaron.

There is, of course, something else that helps shape the Masters into this very special event, a week to which many of us have become so devoted we can't even tolerate the thought of not being there. It's the set decoration, which is another way of saying it's the atmosphere.

The atmosphere surrounds you in two ways at the Augusta National. First of all, there's the ever-present awareness of the beauty of the course—its hills, valleys, forests, ponds, flower beds—even when you aren't especially looking at any of it. And then there are all of the old friends and associates with whom you congregate each spring over a five- or six-day period for no other purpose than to eat, drink, watch, and listen to golf.

Listening to golf becomes as important as anything if you're a writer. Much of it involves listening to the tales one hears in the locker rooms, bars, grillrooms, and dining rooms, although you generally can't print most of these tales without causing wholesale divorces. But there's also outdoor listening, to the roars from out on the course. You learn to interpret the roars.

Let's say, for example, that it's one o'clock in the afternoon, that you know Nicklaus teed off at 12:24, and you hear a roar from down in the valley. That qualifies the seasoned vet to turn immediately to someone on the veranda and calmly say, "Jack birdied two."

Most often, you'll be right. Minutes later the fact will be substantiated when a number goes up on the gigantic leader board that confronts the veranda from an age-old spot between the eighteenth and tenth fairways.

Learning to interpret roars over the years allows you to make other observations, such as:

"Watson eagled thirteen."

"How could Seve birdie ten after that drive?"

"Arnold must have hitched up his pants."

It seems to me that the old roars were more revealing, if not more fun. The loudest and most passionate roars were always those for Palmer, whereas the longest and most approving were always for Hogan. Sam Snead's roars, as I recall, never equaled Hogan's, just as the roars for

Nicklaus when he was at his best never quite matched Arnold's when he was at *his* best.

Today's roars have a boring kind of sameness to them, I think. This could be a statement about the current demographics of the Masters galleries. While the crowds are still mannerly—a guy doesn't want to lose his badge, after all—they may not be as knowledgeable as they once were. I don't miss the old roars as much as I simply distrust the roars of the '90s. I mean, it could be Craig Parry, Vijay Singh, Brett Ogle—almost anybody—who made that eagle these days.

I probably remember the 1954 Masters more vividly than any of the others. No doubt it has something to do with the fact that Hogan and Snead were involved, and it was only my fourth year there, and I was still as awed as a teenager standing around a country club swimming pool decorated with shapely adorables.

I'm not willing to argue that the '54 Masters was the most thrilling of them all. The competition is too stiff. There was 1960, for example, the tournament where Arnold Palmer roared out of nowhere to introduce Ken Venturi to serious heartbreak. Venturi was in the clubhouse, looking like a sure winner, when Arnold birdied the last two holes to beat him. This was the start of something—something called Arnold Palmer.

There was 1962 when Palmer birdied two of the last three holes to tie Gary Player and Dow Finsterwald, and then dusted them off in an 18-hole playoff during which the scoreboard operators showed no favoritism whatsoever when they posted "GO ARNIE" signs all over the golf course. And I couldn't overlook 1975, the year a trim, now-beloved Jack Nicklaus waged a Sunday birdie war—and won—over Tom Weiskopf and Johnny Miller.

But 1954 was special. It was important, too, because Hogan and Snead, the two great players of the era, were in it all the way and wound up in a tie that forced a playoff. And the tournament proper was all the more exciting because of Billy Joe Patton, an obscure amateur from North Carolina. He very nearly won, and would have if he'd known how to play safe at the thirteenth and fifteenth holes in the final round.

The last round began with Hogan in the lead by three strokes over Snead. Keep in mind that this was a Ben Hogan who had merely scored a Triple Crown the year before by capturing the Masters, the U.S. Open, and the British Open, and this was a Sam Snead who had merely won the Masters twice and the PGA twice in the four previous years. We're talking legends here.

Meanwhile, there was Billy Joe Patton, who had never won anything. Which I largely attributed to his fast backswing. Nevertheless, Billy Joe had stolen the hearts of the huge crowds, not to forget the press, by taking every conceivable risk on the course and babbling about it with everybody in the gallery. Billy Joe had surprisingly led through 18 and 36, but now he trailed by five—only not for long that Sunday.

My friend Bob Drum and I, being quote guys, went out early with Billy Joe. Ben and Sam—and the tournament—would come along later. At the sixth hole, a par 3 that then had an enormous hump in the green (a mound that was once known as "the hill where they buried the elephant"), it will be to my everlasting embarrassment that I left Drum in the crowd behind the green and went to a nearby concession stand only seconds before Billy Joe struck his tee shot. The roar was deafening, similar to the kind we would hear for Palmer in later years, only this one trailed off in irregular Rebel whoops. Billy Joe had made a hole in one.

"What did it look like?" I said, having rushed back to Drum.

"It looked like a hole in one, whaddaya think it looked like?"

Drum, a large man who was even larger then, has a guttural Irish voice that has often been compared with the percussion section of the Ohio State band.

"Did it go in on the fly, bounce in, roll in, or what?" I wondered.

"It looked like a one!" said Drum, a man not known for his patience, a writer who cared little for detail in those days. "Here's the cup and here's the ball. The ball did this. That's a one!"

He scribbled something on a pairing sheet.

"Here, this is what a two looks like," he said. "That's not as good as a one. Okay? Let's go before Mush Mouth's gallery tramples us."

Mush Mouth was every golfer or writer Drum ever knew who came from the Old South.

I suppose I should interject that Drum and I became friends in the first place when we had been accidentally seated next to each other in the press emporium at my first Masters. Who could resist striking up a friendship with a man who would lean back and laugh so raucously, so often, at his own copy? I confess that he would catch me doing the same thing on occasion. We were to joke in future years that if Arnold Palmer had ever actually said the things we made up for him, he could have had his own lounge act in Vegas.

But back to '54 and Billy Joe. The amateur reclaimed the Masters lead that Sunday after he birdied the eighth and ninth holes, and by the time he reached the par-5 thirteenth, the Masters was his to win or lose.

We were standing within a few feet of Billy Joe at the thirteenth after his drive had come to rest in an awkward lie in the upper right-hand rough. He pulled a spoon out of the bag, and Drum and I looked at each other. A wooden club from a bad lie in the rough to a green guarded by water? When you're leading the Masters? On Sunday? When maybe you can be the last amateur ever to win a major? When you've probably got Hogan and Snead beaten—and we've got Pulitzers riding on it?

Billy Joe only grinned at us and the crowd, and said, "I didn't get where I am by playin' safe!"

"Great!" Drum said to me. "Where does this guy want his body shipped?"

Billy Joe didn't hear my pal, not that it would have mattered. All week long, Billy Joe had heard nothing but his own muse. And he was too far away to hear his shot when it splashed in the creek. He made a seven. Minutes later, at the fifteenth he did it again—went for the green on his second. He found the water again, made a six. History books record that Billy Joe Patton played those two holes in three over par that Sunday, holes he could easily have parred by laying up, and he only missed tying Hogan and Snead by one stroke. With those pars, he would have won the Masters by two.

Even touring pros are sometimes aware of historic importance. Many in the field stayed over on Monday to watch the Hogan-Snead playoff. Bob Jones and Cliff Roberts rode along in a golf cart. From tee to green, it was a clinic, but neither player could make a putt on those old scratchy but lightning rye greens. They used to say you could actually hear the ball rolling across the barren rye. Snead won with a two-under 70 to Hogan's 71, and the difference was a 30-foot chip shot that Sam holed from just off the tenth green.

I lost a hundred dollars to Drum on the playoff, a hundred dollars that neither of us had. Knowing he admired Hogan's game as much as I did, I later asked him why he had wanted to bet on Snead.

"It ain't the Open," he had said, having outsmarted me again.

While it's true that I missed seeing Billy Joe's ace, I wasn't always in the wrong place at Augusta. On the night before Art Wall, Jr., birdied five of the last six holes to win the 1959 Masters, I ran into him in the lobby of the ancient Bon Air Hotel, once the only place to stay before it became a retirement home. The Bon Air was headquarters for everyone, just as the old Town Tavern in downtown Augusta used to be the only place to stand in line and try to bribe your way in for dinner.

Art and I were making small talk that evening when he was recognized by one of your typical Augusta fans, a red-faced, overbeveraged Southerner in an ill-fitting blazer.

"Hey!" the man said. "Ain't you Art Wall?"

Art smiled, nodded.

"Ain't you the fellow who's supposed to make all them hole in ones?"

"That's him," I said.

"Thirty or forty of them suckers? Something like that?"

"It's up to thirty-four now," said Art politely.

"*Thirty-four?*" the man frowned. "Boy, who you tryin' to kid? Bobby didn't make but *three!*"

At a more recent Masters, I was lolling around on the veranda with Mike Lupica, a columnist for the *New York Daily News*. He's considerably younger than I—this was maybe his second Masters—and I guess I momentarily forgot that Mike is noted for his mouth. He was thumbing through the Green Book, the press guide, looking for lore items, when he said, "Your first year was fifty-one?"

"Yeah."

He started to count something.

Then he said, "Do you realize your first year was only the fifteenth Masters they'd played?"

I'd never thought of it that way.

"I'll be damned," I muttered, feeling some strange sense of accomplishment at having seen so many of them, of having outlasted so many old friends.

"So what about it, old-timer?" he said with a glint. "Were the greens really *that* fast in those days?"

I almost made the mistake of answering him seriously. Happily, a wisteria vine grabbed me around the neck and prevented it.

The Wearing of the Green Masters Jacket

"Simple, Stylish, Sporty" and Oh-So Traditional

by Craig Dolch, *Palm Beach Post*, April 11, 2002

The most coveted garment in golf is made of wool and polyester, costs about $250 and is given its own gaudy shade of green.

It's uglier than your uncle's plaid sport coat, but Mr. Blackwell of Worst-Dressed list fame once called it "simple, stylish and sporty."

It's the Masters green jacket, or greencoat, as the locals say.

Tiger Woods, always thinking ahead, ordered a 42-long after his first victory five years ago so he could grow into it. Craig Stadler, uh, outgrew his. "It never fits because I'm so darn fat," the Walrus said.

Gary Player broke an early Augusta National rule by taking his jacket home to South Africa, prompting a call from tournament co-founder Clifford Roberts:

"I believe you've taken the jacket home. You're not supposed to."

"Come and fetch it," Player replied.

Jack Nicklaus, winner of six Masters titles? Well, he's lucky he even has a jacket.

More on jacket-less Jack in a moment. First, some history.

Green jackets at Augusta National Golf Club began not with the players, but with the members. In 1937, tournament co-founders Bobby Jones and Roberts wanted the members to be easily identifiable on the course so patrons could know where to go to get "reliable information."

The idea of a green jacket being awarded to the Masters winner started in 1949, with Sam Snead being the first to slip one on. Augusta National spokesman Glen Greenspan said, "Where and who that idea came from, we still don't know." The tradition was expanded where the year's previous champion would help the new winner put on his coat.

Every Masters champion receives his own green jacket, but Nicklaus apparently needed his own tailor.

He didn't get his jacket until 1998—35 years after he won his first Masters. How could the man who's been linked to this course like no other not have a green jacket?

Easy. He never asked for one.

"They never said anything to me," Nicklaus said, "and I wasn't going to say anything to them."

The slight started when Nicklaus first won in 1963. The Golden Bear was a little bigger back then, so before the presentation ceremony the club steward pulled a 46-large out of the closet where members' jackets are kept. The fit wasn't even close.

"It was like an overcoat," Nicklaus said. "It just hung on me."

The jacket was used for the ceremony, but Nicklaus was to have one tailored for him when he returned to Augusta the next year. One year later, no green jacket in his locker.

Not wanting to make a fuss, Nicklaus borrowed a jacket from club member Thomas Dewey—the former New York governor and "Dewey defeats

Truman" headline legend—and wore it to the champions' dinner. Nicklaus won again in 1965 and '66, but still no jacket.

By the time Nicklaus won his fourth Masters title in 1972, Dewey's jacket was about to give out.

Nicklaus had an endorsement contract with Hart, Schaffner and Marx, so he asked the Cincinnati-based clothing company to make him a green jacket.

It wasn't the same material or the right color, Nicklaus said. Yet nobody noticed. Soon, Nicklaus was back to borrowing jackets from members, even after his memorable victory in 1986.

It wasn't until 1997, when Nicklaus casually mentioned to then-Chairman Jack Stephens that he never had received a green jacket, that the oversight was corrected. When Nicklaus returned in 1998, there was a green jacket sitting in his locker.

Years earlier, Player didn't realize you couldn't take your jacket home, but Roberts agreed to let him keep it.

"He said that was fine, just don't wear it out," Player said. "I put it in a plastic case in my closet and I've never taken it out. It still sits in the plastic case."

The rule was changed, allowing the reigning champion to keep the jacket for a year, but it only could be worn at ceremonial gatherings, not for commercial purposes. Augusta pooh-bahs weren't happy when Nick Faldo was spotted wearing his on a talk show.

Fuzzy Zoeller never has made that mistake. "I'm not a show dog," he said. "I'm sure there are guys who wear it all the time. I just wear it every Tuesday night (at the champions dinner)."

So who presents the jacket when a player wins back-to-back titles? Jones persuaded Nicklaus to slip on his own coat when he repeated in 1966, but Faldo had tournament Chairman Hord Hardin assist him when he successfully defended in 1990. If Woods defends Sunday, Chairman Hootie Johnson said Wednesday he'll put it on Woods.

The jacket Woods received after his 1997 victory was so comfortable he went to sleep wearing it.

The jackets used to be tailored by Augusta haberdasher John Alfieri, but the Cincinnati-based Hamilton Tailoring Co. has taken over the job for the past 35 years. The single-breasted, single-vent jacket's color closely resembles Kelly green, but has been dubbed "Masters green." It was selected to match the rye grass that Augusta National uses on its fairways.

A Masters jacket takes four days to earn, but about a month to cut, assemble and sew. It's made of 2 1/2 yards of light tropical weight wool. The custom-crafted brass buttons inscribed with the club's insignia are from the Waterbury Co.

There used to be a steakhouse in town called The Green Jacket. The city's minor-league baseball team's nickname is the "GreenJackets."

But there is just one green jacket as far as golfers are concerned.

"It's the ultimate," 1976 champion Raymond Floyd said, and that's no fashion statement.

Masters Sets the Standard for Civility

by Ron Agostini, *The Modesto Bee*, April 14, 1993

A visitor walks the grounds of Augusta National on Masters week. He's surrounded by small acts of kindness, and he questions the world.

Why can't such decent behavior extend outside these prestigious gates?

We're talking about little things: an "excuse me" for an accidental bump, a picked-up-and-returned pen to a total stranger, a "thank you" and a smile that actually seemed sincere at a concession stand, a general atmosphere of human respect and civility.

Before we go further, a caveat: This is not meant to be a treatise on Augusta-as-utopia. Too many writers, blow-dried TV announcers and fans talk about The Masters Tournament as though it's a metaphysical experience.

It's not. Its warts are far too real.

The club membership includes one black man and no women. The black waiters at the bridal white clubhouse remain an ugly reminder of oppression and slavery. The imperfections are many on this otherwise pristine property.

But today's discussion centers on the setting of standards. And that's why we hope the Masters, apart from the above, never changes.

The reason the tournament is held above the rest is because of the people who run it. They insist that commercial logos are covered, TV advertisements are limited and the prize money—though large—is not announced until near the end of the tournament.

The point is that money, ever-present among the CEOs that grace Augusta's membership list, is downplayed on tournament week. The honor of victory is deemed to be more important than the financial reward.

In today's material-world society, a refreshing concept.

Such high-mindedness began with the tournament founder, Bobby Jones, a championship gentleman golfer of unquestioned integrity. Because of him, the Masters would be different from the rest.

How many televised events—outside PBS—use chamber music as their theme? The Masters fairly demands its own special mood.

Spectators, the so-called Masters "patrons," also must do their part. No one is admitted who doesn't respect golf's tradition. Good behavior and proper attire are mandatory. You don't see overweight men in tank-tops basking in the sun.

That's the easiest way to be quickly banished from the course. For life.

Look around you. Standards have been lowered on our priority list. We bring fame to rogue ballplayers, slob actors, lying politicians and everything's-fair businessmen.

The signs—growing drug abuse, soaring crime, greed—indicate the country is in decline. That's why we need events like the Masters to tell us it's still OK to reach for higher ground.

Golf, the splendid marriage of athleticism and mental presence, can't ask for a better soapbox than Augusta in early April each year.

It's here that good golf is revered, good manners are appreciated, and faith in the human condition is restored.

If the standards ever fall at the Masters, we all might be in trouble.

THE
PERSONALITIES

Charles de Clifford Roberts, Jr.

from the Introduction to *The Masters: Golf, Money, and Power in Augusta, Georgia* by Curt Sampson

Charles de Clifford Roberts, Jr., sat in his apartment on Park Avenue and East Sixty-first, a seventy-four-year-old man with a polished scalp, blue eyes, and a whiskey-reddened nose. Never an imposing man physically—five-nine in his prime—Roberts had shrunk with age, surrendering about an inch. He drank a glass of burgundy in the late afternoon, and as he surveyed his domain, he moved his head in a birdlike way, trying to choose the right view through his trifocals.

His apartment building didn't impress much, either, just a fourteen-story brown brick rectangle with a plain-Jane façade. New York City had hundreds just like it. But 535 Park Avenue was a prestigious address, and expensive. Two uniformed doormen attended the entrance, and Central Park loomed just two blocks to the west. Roberts could go to his window, incline his head to the left, and if he wished to, see huge elms and oaks, prematurely crimson and orange in the cold fall of 1968.

Roberts sat alone. Once he'd been a social dynamo in his adopted hometown. His days between the wars and after World War II had been filled with business lunches and golf games at either of his two clubs, Blind Brook and Deepdale near New York City, or at Maidstone or National Golf Links, a hundred miles away on Long Island. At night, he played—expertly—in the Two-Cent Bridge Club. From time to time he took in a fight at Madison Square Garden. Now, with so many of his cronies dead or retired to a warmer place, he didn't go out much.

He missed Bob Jones the most. Robert Tyre "Bobby" Jones, Jr., had been the second-brightest star in the glittering Golden Age of Sports—only Babe Ruth shone more brightly—and Clifford Roberts carried his spears. Other men's egos shrunk in the face of greatness, but Roberts's swelled. For years he counted on constant telephone and letter contact with Jones, his partner, his friend, his hero. Together they'd founded the Augusta National Golf Club and created the Masters. Later they'd gone into other business together. Now they rarely spoke. Disease had trapped Jones in his white-columned mansion on Tuxedo Road in Atlanta—a rare neurological disorder had made his spine as brittle and weak as an old stick, and it had curled his hands into unfeeling claws. Jones lived in a wheelchair or in his bed. Someone had to light his cigarettes for him, and the only way he could sign his name was by grasping a tennis ball skewered with a pen. Roberts had recently told Jones that he no longer looked well enough to perform the traditional chat with the new Masters champion on TV after the tournament. This was true enough—Jones looked ghastly—but his feelings had been deeply hurt at having it pointed out. Jones excused himself from the telecast.

For almost forty years, Jones proposed and Roberts disposed, but time and decay had flipped their relationship upside down. Now Roberts was telling Jones what to do.

Together they had started the golf course in 1932, then the tournament in 1934, and had made both grow beyond anyone's expectations, especially their own. Jones was president of the club, Roberts was chairman. Jones, cerebral, graceful, well educated, and above all enormously popular, provided the enterprise's guiding light. Roberts, whose formal education ended upon his graduation from a dinky high school in South Texas, was Jones's antipode; one Augusta National member referred to him as "our designated bastard." Yet everything this oddly complementary couple did together worked, including Joroberts, Inc., the company they formed to bottle Coca-Cola in South America. Pepsi couldn't keep up in Uruguay and Brazil, and the pesos and cruzeiros poured in. Thrilled to work with a man he idolized, Roberts gloried in their spectacularly successful early ventures, but even better ones beckoned.

In 1948, the year Jones was diagnosed with syringomyelia and began his long, slow decline, Roberts met General Dwight D. Eisenhower, who was to World War II what Jones had been to golf. One was born to command, the other to soldier, and they formed an immediate bond. Within months of their meeting, the general joined Augusta National, told Roberts to "call me Ike," and began to consider him one of his leading advisers and perhaps his closest friend. Within a few more months, Eisenhower received a staggering half-million-dollar advance for a book on the war in Europe; Roberts, the ultimate insider, helped arrange both the huge payment from Doubleday and the sales-boosting serialization of the book in the *New York Herald Tribune*. "He [Eisenhower] promptly handed the money over to me," Roberts later recalled proudly, "and asked me to put it in income securities for him." Roberts brokered stocks for Reynolds and Company, a New York investment banking firm (he owned one sixth of the company), and he was good at it; Eisenhower's portfolio quadrupled over the next fifteen years, with minimal risk. In one of his best gambits, Roberts got the general into Gulf Oil at sixty dollars in 1949. The stock raced up to ninety-five dollars a share within two years, then split two for one. Ike, along with several dozen other Augusta National members, also invested in Joroberts.

With Jones in decline, the pairing of Ike and Cliff solidified. Four years after they met, Roberts's wonderful new friend was elected president of the United States. Further glorious adventures unfolded: fund-raising, vacations, card games, conventions, campaigns, golf, and intimate counsel, all with or for the Most Powerful Man on Earth. Roberts hung a pair of pajamas and a toothbrush in the White House for eight years, and the staff at the presidential mansion came to refer to the Red Room as "Mr. Roberts's bedroom." Ike, in turn, visited Augusta so frequently that in 1953 Roberts arranged for the construction of a residence for his friend the president on the club grounds. The day after Ben Hogan won the Masters that April, Eisenhower flew in to Augusta and held his grandson David's hand as they watched a crew pour the foundation for his new house.

Because Eisenhower liked to fish, in the fall of 1949 Roberts built him a pond, not more than a skulled nine-iron from where the future First Hacker's house would stand. Store-bought bluegill and black bass soon swam in the shady little lagoon.

No subject was out of bounds between them. At least twice during the first presidential campaign, Roberts wrote to Eisenhower about religion. "[Several friends] urge me to advise you to join a church," Roberts wrote, although he believed Ike's "independence from formal affiliation with a particular denomination was an asset politically rather than a liability." Abraham Lincoln's parents were Baptists, Roberts informed Eisenhower, and Mary Todd Lincoln, his wife, had been Episcopalian, but Lincoln attended a Presbyterian church. Soon thereafter, Ike began gracing a pew. He never missed a Sunday at Reid Memorial Presbyterian over the scores of weekends he spent in Augusta.

Roberts, on the other hand, didn't attend. "Some think he was an atheist," recalls an Augustan who worked closely with the club chairman for many years. "At least, he never set foot in a church here."

"Dear Cliff," Eisenhower wrote in February 1951. "Anglo-Saxon men do not spend much time telling each other, face to face, anything of their mutual affection and regard," he began, then described at length his appreciation of his friend's thoughtfulness, devotion, and attention to the growth of the Eisenhower family fortune. The already profound friendship between Ike and Roberts grew even deeper during the presidential years.

When John F. Kennedy moved into the White House in 1961, Eisenhower departed for his farmhouse in Pennsylvania and for Palm Springs in the Southern California desert. From his most recent visit to Ike and Mamie, Roberts knew his dear friend had lost his vitality; by March 1969, in fact, Eisenhower would be dead. What with Vietnam, rioting students, and another Democrat, Lyndon Johnson, in the White House, the whole world was going to hell. Even the last Masters tournament had seemed a part of the larger chaos. There had been a rules dispute, and for twenty tortuous minutes after the conclusion of play, no one was sure who won.

Letitia Roberts provided no succor. Roberts and his second wife, the former Letitia Anderson Shearer, married since Christmas 1958, stood just three years away from a divorce court in Port-au-Prince. But the relationship ended long before 1964. Roberts knew one thing from his first divorce: a marriage isn't healthy one day and dead the next.

Roberts had also been denied the comfort that fatherhood and grandfatherhood might have provided. Or rather, he'd denied it to himself. Roberts didn't like children, and in fact believed that overpopulation would be the death of us all—believed it so profoundly that he left most of his fortune to Planned Parenthood. A man who'd sired five kids was once up for an invitation to join Augusta National. Everybody else at the club liked him, but Roberts looked over his dossier and vetoed the prospective member. "Anyone who is stupid enough to have five children isn't smart enough to belong to Augusta National," he said.

Roberts, golf's last autocrat, wielded power like the Old Testament God, with lots of rules—and no mercy.

Now, back in his New York apartment, Roberts waited for summer to end. The club didn't open until October, and Roberts wouldn't return to Augusta until then. The phone rang. John Mason, who ran the oral history department at Columbia University, would like to pay a visit. General Eisenhower's first postwar job had been as president of Columbia. As part of the Eisenhower Research Project, the amiable Mr. Mason explained, he would appreciate the opportunity to tape-record Mr. Roberts's memories of his time with Ike between 1948 and 1960. Mason seemed like a nice guy, and he was someone to talk to. Moreover, Roberts regarded himself as a historical figure, worthy of just this sort of recognition. So he agreed to the interview, but with one condition, which he announced on page one of the transcript: "I desire to place the following restriction on my memoir: that no use of any kind whatsoever is to be made [of it] until 20 years after my death."

The one interview Mason expected turned into fifteen, conducted over the next four years. The transcript of their talks fills 878 pages; if the interviewer hadn't run out of tape several times, it would have been more. By comparison, Clare Boothe Luce, Ike's ambassador to England, reminisced for 108 pages; Attorney General Herbert Brownell, Jr., 402; and Marion Bayard Folsom, Eisenhower's second secretary of Health, Education and Welfare, 163. Cliff Roberts, of course, had no official capacity at the Eisenhower White House. But the fact that he slept there overnight 120 times showed how close he was to the seat of power.

The obsessively organized Roberts brought notes to the tapings to refresh his memory. "Wasn't he a Republican?" Mason asked about some political figure. Roberts's reply required 1,200 words, four-plus double-spaced pages. Roberts spoke concisely, with no stumbles or repetitions—but with frequent pauses and *ah, ah*'s during which he searched for just the right word. He often interjected lawyerly turns of phrase: "I undertook to determine," for example, instead of "I tried to find out."

Professor Mason was struck by how lonely Roberts seemed and how anxious he was to talk—about almost anything.

The Eisenhower campaign needed money. "Well, I used to go over to Pete's office [Peter Jones, the preternaturally generous president of Cities Service, and a member at Augusta National] or he'd come over to my office and he'd give me $25,000 at a time in currency," Roberts recalled. "Pete and I were skirting around the fringes of the law [but] everybody violated those rules so regularly every year and nobody went to jail for violating them, so neither Pete nor I were worried too much."

Ike had woman trouble. Cliff met with the woman, Kay Summersby, who had written a book that hinted at a World War II romance with the general. "The Jewish writer that did the actual writing told a reasonably accurate story, as recited by Miss Summersby," Roberts said, "but there were a number of sentences in the book [*Eisenhower Was My Boss*, published in 1948] which, if lifted out of context and headlined separately, could be classified as double meanings, and the second meaning suggested a considerable degree of intimacy between the girl and Ike.

"I studied the woman rather closely during our two hour talk and came to the conclusion that she had never been General Ike's mistress.... I had sized him up as being one of those rather rare individuals like Bob Jones, for example, who was strictly a one-woman man. But I also felt that Summersby did not have sufficient physical appeal to tempt the average man, let alone a man such as General Ike."

Mason asked Roberts to comment on the 1957 civil rights disturbance in Little Rock, when, in perhaps the worst domestic crisis in his two terms, Ike sent federal troops to Arkansas to protect the black students who had enrolled at Little Rock's Central High. Roberts blamed the whole affair on the state's "worthless sort of a governor," Orval Faubus. "Southerners were very rational about most any other subject in the world, but when it came around to this thing, almost to a man they just said, 'Integration means one thing. It means mixed marriage.' . . . Those people were a lot more right about it than I thought they were at the time. . . . Where you had complete equality, since 1880 in Brazil, you go down there and look at the end result, I'll be damned if it's anything to look at being constructive.

"The mixed are the worst. But if [Brazilian businessmen] had their choice, they'd hire white people to work for them entirely, and secondly, their second choice would be 100 percent black people, and the third choice would be mixed, that they are the most worthless of all in every respect."

The Roberts tapes reveal a flawed and self-righteous man who harbored views on race that were and remain fairly common but are seldom so unashamedly revealed for the record. None of his views distinguished him from others of his class and age. His several compensating strengths also show through: loyalty, intelligence, a remarkable attention to detail, and brilliance at operating as a power behind the throne. In the behind-the-scenes string puller's traditional field, public relations, Roberts was somehow simultaneously a genius and an ignoramus.

The memoir disappoints in only two ways. Roberts didn't much discuss the Masters or Augusta National, where his peculiar talents helped create an institution golfers revere. And he didn't foreshadow his death.

Roberts killed himself five years after his final interview for the oral history. Researchers may open the five big, black binders expecting a confession, some preamble to Roberts's suicide note. But they won't find it.

The 1942 Masters

from *Byron Nelson: An Autobiography* by Byron Nelson

Starting out in '42, I tied for sixth in Los Angeles, which kept the L.A. Open on my list of important tournaments I still wanted to win. Then in Oakland I did win, by five shots. This is how I did it: The greens there were quite soft, and all eighteen had a definite slope from back to front. I noticed that we were all hitting at the flag, and our balls were spinning back, sometimes off the green. I changed tactics after the last practice round, and aimed for the top of the flag. Then, when my ball spun back, it ended up closer to the hole. That's the main reason I won. I remember the pro there was Dewey Longworth, brother to my good friend Ted Longworth from Texarkana. He was a good player and a nice man, just like Ted.

Our next stop, the San Francisco Open, was played at the California Golf Club where my friend Eddie Lowery was a member. I played well but putted very poorly and finished eighth. I've already said that most of us pros didn't spend much time on putting, because of the difference in the greens and so on, but I had another reason. I had originally learned to putt on stiff bermuda greens, where you had to hit the putt rather than roll it. I never really got over that, and I didn't work on it enough because we tend not to work on things we're not good at, and that certainly was true for me. I didn't three-putt much, but my bad distance was eight to fifteen feet. Those were the ones I didn't make as often as I should have.

Hogan won at San Francisco, though he was still hooking quite a bit then. On the 18th, which was a dogleg right, Hogan hooked a 4-wood high up over the trees and back into the fairway, because he just couldn't fade the ball or even count on hitting it straight then. Though he hooked it, he used the same swing and did the same thing every time, so he got to be pretty consistent.

At the Crosby and the Western I didn't do very well. I'd occasionally have several weeks when I wasn't chipping or putting well, either one. But I practiced some, and by the Texas Open, I was doing better, finished eighth, then sixth at New Orleans, and second at St. Petersburg. Still couldn't make much headway in the Miami Four-Ball, though—got knocked out in the second round again, this time with Henry Picard as my partner. But at least it was someone else beating us—Harper and Keiser instead of Runyan and Smith.

My game was getting better all along, but of course, so was everyone else's. Our on-the-job training was working for quite a few of the players, from those who had loads of natural talent to those who had some talent and a lot of persistence. There still were no real teachers to go to like the boys have today. Most of the older club pros were still making the transition to steel shafts, or even teaching the old way of pronating and all, so they really couldn't help anyone much. We had to figure things out on our own for the most part, and some fellows were better at it than others. But it was getting more and more important to have most of your rounds under 70, if you wanted to have a chance to win.

After Miami, I played in the Seminole Invitational again, enjoyed all their good food and being with the other players, and won $50. Well, at least the food was free, there was no entry fee, and my caddie only cost $8, so I had $42 more when I left than I did when I arrived.

I did better in the North and South, but had a bad last round of 73, tied for third, and won $500. At Greensboro, I had another poor last round of 74 and tied for fourth. Back then, they sometimes had prizes for low round of the day, and I tied in the third round with a 68, so I got another $25. Then I finished third at Asheville, and won $550. In my last five tournaments, I'd finished second once, third twice, and fourth once. I was definitely getting steadier, despite final rounds I wasn't very happy with.

During that Asheville tournament, I realized there hadn't been any pictures or publicity about me. It seemed the articles were all about the other players. I figured the press had gotten tired of writing about me, and I had gotten just enough used to all the attention that I kind of missed it. Anyway, about the third round, I was playing just so-so and was tied for the lead or leading. On the 16th hole, I put my ball in the left bunker, which was over six feet deep. I got in there and was trying to figure out how to get out and close enough to one-putt, and stuck my head up and looked over the bank to see the pin. Right above the bunker, on the green to my left, was a photographer, getting ready to photograph me as I played my shot. I said to him, "Where have you been all this week? Just get out of my way!" I did get up and down, but I felt bad about what I'd said, so I looked the fellow up afterwards and apologized, and he said, "That's no problem, I shouldn't have been where I was."

Along about this time, McSpaden and I were on a train together, talking about the money to be made on the tour. We figured then that with an interest rate of about 10%, if we could make $100,000 during our careers, we could retire and live quite comfortably on that annual interest of $10,000. That seemed quite reasonable at the time, but it's a ridiculous idea now.

Next was the Masters, but before the tournament started, I played a match there with Bob Jones against Henry Picard and Gene Sarazen. We were all playing well that day, including Bob, and on the back nine, Henry and Gene made seven straight birdies—but never won a hole from us. Jones shot 31 on the back nine that day. Amazing.

Then the tournament began, and fortunately, I played very well, ending the first round with 68. Paul Runyan led nearly the whole first round, and ended up tied with Horton Smith at 67. Sam Byrd was tied with me at 68, and Jimmy Demaret was behind us with 70. The second round, Horton led by himself for one hole, then I tied him with a birdie at the second hole. It was kind of huckledy-buck between Paul, Horton, and me for the next five holes, but I pulled ahead of them both with a birdie at the par-5 eighth. I was leading then for the rest of the second round, when I shot 67, and all through the third, but lost a little steam in the fourth when I bogeyed six, seven, and eight. Hogan had caught up with me when he birdied the eighth himself. He was several groups ahead of me, of course, so I couldn't see how he was doing. I birdied 9 to lead again, and led till the last hole despite bogeying 17.

When I stepped up to hit my drive on 18, I noticed the tee box was kind of soft and slick. As I started my downswing, my foot slipped a little and I made a bad swing, pushing my tee shot deep into the woods on the right. By now I knew Ben had shot 70, and I had to have a par just to tie. When I got to my ball, I was relieved to find I had a clear swing.

The ball was just sitting on the ground nicely, and there was an opening in front of me, about twenty feet wide, between two trees. I took my 5-iron and hooked that ball up and onto the green fifteen feet from the pin and almost birdied it—but I did make my par. So you can see why I felt very fortunate to tie.

Then came the playoff. This was one of the rare occasions when I was so keyed up my stomach was upset, even during the night. I lost my breakfast the next morning, which I thought might be a good sign, because I had always played well when I became that sick beforehand, and it always wore off after the first few holes. When I saw Hogan in the clubhouse, he said, "I heard you were sick last night," and I said, "Yes, Ben, I was." He offered to postpone the playoff, but I said, "No, we'll play." I did have half of a plain chicken sandwich and some hot tea, which helped a little, but you can see in the picture that was made of Ben and me when we were on the first tee that I was very nervous and tense.

This was probably one of the most unusual playoffs in golf, in that at least twenty-five of the pros who had played in the tournament stayed to watch us in the playoff. I don't recall that ever happening any other time. Ben and I were both very flattered by that.

Flattered or not, though, I started poorly. On the first hole, I hit a bad drive into the trees and my ball ended up right next to a pine cone, which I couldn't move because the ball would move with it. On my second shot, the ball hit more trees in front of me, so I ended up with a 6 while Ben made his par. We parred the second and the third. Then, on the fourth, a long par 3, I thought the pin was cut just over the bunker, but my long iron was short and went in the bunker, so I made 4 while Ben made 3. We'd played four holes and I was 3 down.

The 5th hole had a very tough pin placement at the back of the green, but we both parred it. The par-3 6th, I began to come alive a little and put my tee shot ten feet away, while Hogan missed his to the left and made 4. I put my ten-footer in for birdie, so I caught up two shots right there.

We both parred the 7th. Next, I eagled 8 and Ben birdied, so now we were even. I picked up three more shots on the next five holes, including a shot on 12 that rimmed the hole and stopped six inches away. But Ben didn't get rattled much. Though his tee shot stopped short on the bank, his chip almost went in for a 2.

When we arrived at the 18th tee. I was leading by 2, and Ben's approach shot ended up way at the back of the green, with the pin way at the front. I played short of the green on purpose, not wanting to take a chance on the bunker, because in those days, a ball landing in the bunker would bury, and then you really had your hands full. But I figured I might chip up and make par, or no worse than 5, while I was pretty sure Ben couldn't make his putt from up on the top ledge. I was right—he two-putted, I made 5 and won by one shot.

Louise and Valerie had stayed together up at the clubhouse during the playoff, and they were both very happy for me. Valerie was a very gracious lady, and Ben was always fine whether he won or lost. It was a great victory for me, and more so because I'd been able to beat Ben, who by then was getting to be a very fine player. The fact that he had come from well behind everyone else here showed that he had a lot of determination and persistence.

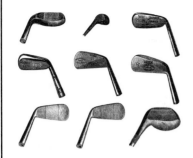

Call It Sam's Place, Augusta

by Tom Callahan, *Golf Digest*, April 2003

President Eisenhower has a pond, a cabin and a tree; Gene Sarazen, Byron Nelson and Ben Hogan have bridges; Arnold Palmer and Jack Nicklaus plaques. John Rae has a creek, Charlie Bartlett a lounge. But "Sam Snead" isn't etched on anything at Augusta National, and it belongs on everything. Snead's unbroken string of 44 Masters Tournaments began in 1937, the year the members broke out their green jackets. Twelve springs later, when coats started going to the winners, Sam got the first one.

"The Sam Snead Par-3 Contest" would work. Sam won the inaugural running in 1960 with a four-under-par 23. He won the 15th edition (at the age of 61) with a 23. Sam went on to lose two playoffs: the first after a 23, the last in 1991 (when he was a few weeks shy of 79), after a 24. He was getting older.

Any of the great loblolly pines might be named for Sam, maybe the tallest one blocking the turn at 13. Wasn't it there, during a practice round, that he told Bobby Cole, "You know, Bobby, when I was your age, I used to hit my drive straight over that tree"? As Cole's ball was pin-balling around in the upper branches, Sam went on, "Of course, when I was your age, that tree was only about this high."

The Champions Dinner could be Sam's as well. "We all looked forward to him telling stories," Tiger Woods says, "and to the next year's joke." Nick Faldo says, "Usually Byron was at one end of the table, with the serious players. I'd try to sit on the other end, with Sam."

It was Hogan's suggestion in 1952, the year Ike won the presidency, that all of the past champions be feted annually by their newest member. But Hogan eventually tired of everyone's company. The ice water in his veins ultimately froze his heart. "Don't ever get a blood transfusion from Ben," Sam said. "You'll die of pneumonia."

Almost any of the rolling greens call Snead to mind. Too competitive to let the yips shelve him, he was putting sidesaddle at the end only because Bobby Jones brought legislation throughout golf to outlaw Snead's between-the-legs technique. Like at all games—absolutely every game—Sam was just too damn good at croquet. (He was pretty good at sidesaddle.)

In my first Masters, 1972, a month before his 60th birthday, sidesaddler Snead shot 69 in the opening round to trail Nicklaus by one stroke. That Thursday, they were the only two in the field to break 70. Think of it. Rattling off his bogeys and birdies in the Bartlett Lounge, Sam kept saying, "I just hit a little Cutty Sark in there and—what do you know?—I made it."

Remembering his satin swing, wouldn't Sam's name look just right on the tee markers? Last year, when he was 89, Slammin' Sammy kicked off the tournament for the final time by slamming a customer right between the eyes. Lucky so-and-so. For a little while, that man could reel around drunkenly with "Wilson" written backward on his forehead. All across the wide property, he was the only printed monument to Snead.

Of course Sam's there, everywhere, in a breeze, in a smile, in a Panama hat.

Everyone knows how reluctant we are in this precinct to tell other people what to do. We're as famous for butting out as Augusta National is for accepting unsolicited advice. But I think the best place for Sam's name is on the gold plaque on the door of the Champions Locker Room upstairs. That was Sam Snead's chapel. He filled it with laughter. No one will ever go in there without thinking of him, anyway.

Thanks, Arnie

Through 50 Masters Tournaments, the Presence of Palmer Could Not Be Denied

by John Boyette, *The Augusta Chronicle*, April 4, 2004

The dream struck Arnold Palmer at an early age, when he was just a boy learning to play golf in Latrobe, Pa.

Go to Augusta and play in the Masters Tournament.

It consumed him as he became a successful amateur, making a name for himself on the East Coast and playing collegiately at Wake Forest.

Compete against the legends of the game at Augusta National Golf Club.

The dream came to fruition in 1954, when Palmer won the U.S. Amateur.

Drive down Magnolia Lane and meet Bobby Jones, your boyhood idol.

When Arnold Daniel Palmer struck his first Masters shot April 7, 1955, he could not have imagined the journey he was about to embark on.

He could only dream about it.

"From the first day I walked on Augusta, it was something special to me," Palmer said. "It was something I'd looked forward to for 25 years. To get there was a great thrill."

Four green jackets and one premature farewell later, the journey is coming to a close. This week, Palmer will hitch up his pants and play in his final Masters, a record 50th in a row, and dismiss Arnie's Army one last time.

Instead of pulling a trailer into Augusta, Palmer will fly his private jet from Orlando, Fla. His longtime assistant, Doc Giffin, probably will accompany him from the airport to Augusta National.

"Invariably, when he pulls in, he comes through that front gate and stops and chats with the guards," Giffin said. "He always enjoys it and chats with them before he goes on."

Then Palmer will make that trip down Magnolia Lane—the one he dreamed of taking so long ago—one last time as a competitor.

A MODEST DEBUT

Nothing about Palmer's opening round in his first Masters suggested anything special on the horizon.

The young professional struggled to 76, then followed it up with another 76 that left him 15 shots behind eventual winner Cary Middlecoff.

Fortunately for Palmer, the Masters did not institute a 36-hole cut until 1957. He was able to play on the weekend, and he made the most of his opportunity.

An even-par 72 on Saturday moved him up the leaderboard, then he shot 69 to finish in a tie for 10th. He received a crystal vase for Sunday's low round and, more importantly, earned $696.

For a first-year pro on probation and following the tour with his wife, Winnie, in a mobile trailer, the cash was important.

"I was very, very excited about it," Palmer said of his initial appearance. "It's difficult to describe something that you look forward to from your youth. To be there was the fulfillment of something that I thought was the beginning."

It didn't take Palmer long to live up to his reputation as a promising player. He won the 1955 Canadian Open, beginning a streak in which he won a PGA Tour event for 17 straight years. In 1956-57, he won eight more times.

Success at Augusta National was limited. He wound up 21st in 1956, soaring to 79 in a final round played in brutally tough conditions. A year later, he trailed 54-hole leader Sam Snead by just one stroke. But a final-round 76 dropped him into a tie for seventh.

> "Today, Cliff (Roberts) and I were watching Palmer at 13, and the same exhilaration came over me as did when I watched (Gene) Sarazen from that mound in 1935. I said to Cliff, 'He really hit that one.' It stopped 18 feet from the cup, and he holed it, and that was the deciding factor of the tournament."
> —Bobby Jones, on Palmer's play in 1958.

A LEGEND IS BORN

By 1958, when Palmer arrived in Augusta for his fourth Masters, he was one of the game's emerging stars. Now he needed a win in a major championship to elevate his status.

Ken Venturi, who had suffered a final-round collapse two years before as an amateur, was the pacesetter. He held the lead after 18 and 36 holes, but Palmer wasn't far behind after opening with rounds of 70 and 73.

Palmer shot 68 in the third round to forge a tie with Sam Snead. Venturi slipped to 74 and was three back, and he was paired with Palmer for the final round.

Ron Green Sr., a longtime *Charlotte Observer* columnist, recalled bumping into Palmer and Winnie that Saturday night. They had a drink at the old Richmond Hotel together.

Then, the next morning, Green and a friend saw the Palmers and joined them for breakfast.

"That afternoon he won his first Masters," Green said. "We did it the next year, and it didn't work. That's a fond memory for me."

Another writer, Herbert Warren Wind, first used the phrase "Amen Corner" to describe the action at the 11th, 12th and 13th holes that year. Wind took the expression from the jazz recording Shouting at Amen Corner, and, from Palmer's standpoint, it was appropriate.

Because of heavy rains the night before, a local rule offering relief from plugged lies was put into place.

Palmer was 1-over par for the day when he reached Amen Corner. He managed to make par at the 11th, but his tee shot on the par-3 12th flew long and plugged into a bank behind the green.

Confusion ensued because Palmer and the rules official were uncertain whether he was entitled to relief. Palmer played the muddy ball and carded a double-bogey five.

Then he played a second ball. After taking a drop, he pitched his ball close to the pin and made par.

The Masters rules committee, including Bobby Jones and Clifford Roberts, conferred on the matter. No immediate ruling was given, so Palmer had to continue playing.

On the next hole, the par-5 13th, Palmer played aggressively and reached the green in two. He made the 18-foot putt for eagle.

Two holes later, Palmer was told he had been entitled to a free drop on the 12th and his par with the second ball would stand.

Palmer, who would become famous in later years for his final-round charges, limped home with bogeys on two of his final three holes. But he still had the lead and could only watch as Doug Ford and Fred Hawkins came to the 18th hole with chances to tie him. Both missed birdie putts, and Palmer won his first Masters and the green coat that came with it.

"There was no doubt in my heart that it was a three," Palmer told reporters after the round about his free drop. "It was just a matter of the officials having to make a decision, and I thought I had a three. I wanted to protect myself, though, and that's the reason I played both balls, so there could be no question one way or the other."

Venturi, who never won the Masters and became a television analyst for CBS, isn't so sure that Palmer followed the rules correctly in 1958.

Venturi alleges in a new book, *Getting Up and Down: My 60 Years in Golf,* that Palmer did not declare he was going to play a second ball until after making a double bogey with the first one in 1958.

"Nobody, not even Palmer, is bigger than the game," Venturi said in the book. "I firmly believe that he did wrong and that he knows that I know he did wrong."

The two discussed the incident in the scorer's tent after the round, Venturi wrote. But Palmer remained adamant that the correct decision had been made.

"There was never any doubt that I was right. I had that confidence," Palmer told *The Augusta Chronicle* in February. "(The official) came out and announced that I was right, and I was very elated about that and pleased. It only confirmed what I felt about the club and the tournament and everything else."

The win also gave Palmer an additional boost.

"It put me in a position to feel a little more confidence in my game. To then go on and win it three more times was sort of icing on the cake," he said. "That was my first major objective—to win the Masters."

TV IDOL

The Masters was shown on television for the first time in 1956, and viewers were able to tune in and see coverage from Augusta National's final four holes.

Those early black-and-white broadcasts were crude by today's standards, but that would soon change thanks to two men.

Up-and-coming CBS producer Frank Chirkinian would supply the innovations that would make the telecasts more enjoyable, and Arnold Palmer would supply the electricity that made a live sporting event must-see TV.

Chirkinian, who worked on Masters telecasts for nearly 40 years, introduced relation-to-par scoring, multiple cameras, microphones on tees and aerial blimps during his award-winning career. He can still recall the first time he saw Palmer on television at the Masters. It was in 1959.

"Here comes Arnold, at the brow of the hill on 15, and this is my first experience with Arnold," Chirkinian said. "And you know, the camera either loves you or hates you. The camera fell in love with him, standing there next to his caddie, hitching his trousers, wrinkling his nose, flipping a cigarette to the ground. He hitched his trousers again and grabbed a club from his caddie. And he hits it on the green.

"I thought, 'Holy mackerel, who is this guy?' He absolutely fired up the screen. It was quite obvious this was the star. We followed him all the way."

Palmer finished third that year as Art Wall Jr. birdied five of the final six holes to win. But in Chirkinian's mind, a star was born.

"It was electrifying. He was just magic," he said. "It's been a long love affair."

> "I couldn't look. I didn't see it, but I heard it. It sounded like the best putt of the tournament."
> —Winnie Palmer, after Arnold's birdie on the 17th hole in the final round in 1960.

VISIONS OF A SLAM

Bobby Jones set the standard for golf's greatest year with his Grand Slam season of 1930.

Ben Hogan won all three of the majors he entered in 1953, and Tiger Woods won all four majors in a row over a two-year span.

In 1960, Palmer enjoyed his finest year as a professional and in the process rekindled talk of golf's Grand Slam.

The year started with a bang for Palmer. He won the Bob Hope Desert Classic, the Texas Open, the Baton Rouge Open and the Pensacola Open before coming to Augusta.

After he opened with 67, most experts felt a Palmer win was a formality.

That was hardly the case.

After 54 holes, Palmer held a one-stroke lead over Venturi, his friend and challenger from 1958.

Palmer was paired with Billy Casper for the final round, and they went out after Venturi. In typical Masters fashion, the battle for the lead was nip-and-tuck.

Venturi's 33 on the first nine put him two ahead of Palmer, who had played his first nine in even-par 36. Venturi struggled a bit down the stretch, but his final-round 70 gave him the clubhouse lead.

"I haven't won it yet," Venturi cautioned reporters who were eager to interview the winner.

Palmer played even-par golf on the back nine but did not birdie the par-5 holes. When he reached the 17th hole, he trailed Venturi by one and needed a birdie to force a playoff.

Palmer drove safely but hit an indifferent approach to the 17th green. Facing a putt of nearly 30 feet, Palmer's ball crept toward the hole, teetered on the edge and fell in for a birdie.

On the 18th, Palmer lashed a big drive around the corner that left him just a 6-iron away. He played a crisp shot that landed near the hole and stopped six feet left of the pin. With a national television audience watching, Palmer calmly rolled in the birdie putt to become the 1960 Masters champion.

"It wasn't just to beat Ken Venturi, it was to win the Masters," Palmer said. "It isn't something I would have planned that way. Nevertheless, it was something that I enjoyed. The fact that I birdied the last two holes to do it made it even nicer."

The victory was just the beginning for Palmer.

Two months later, he traveled to Denver to play in the U.S. Open at Cherry Hills.

Palmer played indifferently for 54 holes, and his 215 total left him seven shots behind Mike Souchak.

Grabbing a quick lunch after his morning round, Palmer encountered his old friend, Bob Drum, the golf writer for the *Pittsburgh Press.*

As Dan Jenkins tells it in his book Fairways and Greens, Drum's words inspired Palmer to go out and win the Open that afternoon:

"If I drive the green and get a birdie or an eagle, I might shoot 65," Palmer said. "What'll that do?"

"Nothing," Drum replied. "You're too far back."

Palmer did drive the green at the first hole, and he birdied six of the first seven holes. He would go on to win by two shots over a young amateur from Columbus, Ohio, named Jack Nicklaus.

With victories in the first two majors, Palmer drew the attention of the sports world. The British Open, the game's oldest major championship, had been spurned by most American pros for years. But with a possible Grand Slam in sight, Palmer made the trip to St. Andrews.

He made a game effort of it, but fell short by one stroke to Kel Nagle. The next two years, Palmer would win the British Open and receive credit for rekindling American interest in the event.

> "This is the most singularly exciting tournament for me ever. For once in my life, I planned to do something and did what I wanted."
> —Arnold Palmer, after winning the 1964 Masters.

KING OF THE WORLD

Palmer can be credited with taking golf to the masses in the 1960s. He won six of his seven major championships from 1960 to 1964, and he was becoming a spokesman for a variety of products.

Thanks to his alliance with Mark McCormack and International Management Group, Palmer created a business empire that made him the undisputed king of golf, if not the entire sporting world.

Chirkinian, the television producer, recognized Palmer's appeal almost instantly.

"Up until then, golf was considered quite the elitist game," he said. "Then we have this blue-collar guy who doesn't have the prettiest swing. What you saw was what you got. He had this identification with nonprivate club members who are out hacking it around on public courses. They considered him one of them."

After losing the 1961 Masters with a collapse on the final hole, Palmer shrugged off that disappointment the next spring.

He fired three straight subpar rounds to start the 1962 Masters, but he had to rely on some late-round magic (birdies at Nos. 16 and 17) to force the tournament's first three-man playoff.

In the Monday playoff, Palmer made five birdies on the back nine to win easily.

"Maybe it helped me that everybody kept asking me how I made six at the last hole last year," Palmer told reporters.

Before 1964, Palmer had won the Masters in just about every way imaginable. In 1958, he endured the controversial ruling at the 12th; in 1960, he birdied the final two holes to win; and in 1962, he survived a three-man playoff.

He was due for a breather, and he got it in 1964. His six-shot margin of victory was the second best in tournament history, as was his 276 total.

Palmer remembers that tournament for a different reason. He was trying to quit smoking, something he gave up for good later on.

"That was the year there was a lot of question about my game," Palmer said. "The press was on me a little bit about quitting smoking. They thought it was (detrimental). I probably played the best Masters I ever played."

With his six-stroke victory, Palmer became the first four-time Masters winner.

Playing with his good friend Dave Marr, who would wind up tied for second with Jack Nicklaus, Palmer tried to ease the tension as they prepared to tee off on the 18th that Sunday.

"We're bantering a little bit, and I said to David, 'Is there anything I can do to help you?,'" Palmer said. "We were very close (friends), and he said, 'Yeah, you can make 10.' That was kind of funny."

The good times in Augusta, though, were close to being over.

Palmer tied for second in 1965 when Nicklaus ran away from the field, and he would finish in the top four the next two years. Surprisingly, the 1967 Masters would be the last time Palmer would seriously contend at Augusta National.

> "I always like to think there's always a couple more good rounds in my body, and maybe there are."
> —Arnold Palmer, at the 2002 Masters.

GOLF JUNKIE

Make no mistake about Arnold Palmer: He's a certified golf junkie.

The man has thousands of clubs, tees it up every chance he gets and loves the "needling" and badgering that are a part of the daily games at Bay Hill Club and Lodge.

Not even surgery for prostate cancer in 1997 could keep Palmer away from Augusta.

His obsession also explains his decisions to continue playing PGA Tour events and at the Masters well beyond his prime playing years.

"I'm feeling great; my golf game is getting a little better," Palmer said in late February. "It's a little better than it's been."

Palmer shot 88-79 at his Bay Hill Invitational last month and missed the cut.

These days, Palmer takes pride in small victories. The look on his face at Bay Hill after he hit two solid shots to reach the 18th green, and break 80 that day, summed up Palmer's love for the game.

The ovations on every hole didn't hurt him, either.

"The people and those things are the reason I played as long as I have," Palmer said at Bay Hill. "Without the thoughts that they give me and to continue to tell me that they want me to play, I wouldn't be here now. It's nice, and it's been nice through the years."

Palmer, who has not made a cut at the Masters since 1983, still has a positive outlook about his final appearance.

"I'm looking forward to it. I'm trying to make the cut," he said. "It would be a thrill for me. It would be a nice way to end it all."

> "He has said this will be his last year for the past few years now. When you
> have experienced the thrills of Augusta like we have, this is easy to understand."
> —Gary Player.

TAKING A MULLIGAN

Two years ago, Palmer announced his intention to end his streak of playing at the Masters. He claimed that he didn't want to get a letter from Hootie Johnson, the Augusta National and Masters chairman.

Although the comment drew a chuckle, it was not far from the truth. Before the 2002 Masters, Johnson had sent letters to past Masters winners Doug Ford, Billy Casper and Gay Brewer that basically ended their lifetime invitation to the tournament.

By frequently playing a few holes and withdrawing, the three men had not maintained their obligation to the spirit of the lifetime exemption. Johnson and the club also outlined a policy that would end a former champions' playing days at age 65.

Palmer's decision to call it quits was front-page news. He proudly led his fans around a beefed-up Augusta National layout, shooting 89 in the first round. On the second day, Mother Nature intervened and cut off his round with just a few holes to play.

Palmer returned that Saturday morning to finish his round of 85. Several Masters participants lined up outside the scorer's tent to personally bid Palmer farewell.

But Palmer, the golf junkie and leader of Arnie's Army, could not go out like that. In 2003, barely a month before the Masters, Palmer and Nicklaus sent letters of their own to Johnson. They urged him to restore the lifetime exemption. The sweetener on the deal was that Palmer would return to play two more years in order to achieve the magic number of 50 consecutive starts.

"That's something that happened, and I think Hootie has done a great job with the club," Palmer said.

"I'm very happy. I think there is something to be said about competitiveness: When you stop playing competitive golf, you should not play Augusta. Now, I saw the opportunity to play for 50 years, and that was unusual."

Both Nicklaus and Player know how much Palmer and the Masters have been intertwined.

"What Augusta has meant to both our lives, the importance of it to us, is something we've always shared," Nicklaus said. "When we met with Hootie Johnson last year and had the (age limit) rule changed, we were of one mind on how we felt and, obviously, made a pretty good argument. That's been our history together."

Player, who was vocal last year about the age limitation for past champions until the club rescinded it, knows Palmer will have a difficult time letting go.

"It is hard to give it up here," Player said. "Whether this year is it or not, Arnold Palmer has had an incredible impact on the history of this tournament, and we can all thank him for the legacy he leaves and for his part in securing its continued rich traditions for the future."

Palmer is a bit more emphatic about this being his last hurrah. There are no ifs, ands or buts this time around.

"This is definitely it," Palmer said.

> "When I walked on that hallowed ground, if you want to call it that, it was pretty special. It was a privilege. And, of course, I think there is something to be said for the fact that America gives you a chance to earn those privileges."
> —Arnold Palmer, on playing in the Masters, during a Golf Channel interview.

A MAN IN FULL

Although Palmer experienced more success at Augusta National than anyone except Nicklaus, he also experienced his share of disappointments in the Masters and other major events.

Palmer's frailties were never more exposed at the Masters than in 1961.

"It was certainly a disappointment. I made a very bad mistake in the process of playing the 18th hole," Palmer said. "It was something I was taught not to do. I knew better, but my mind was kind of reeling, and I made a mistake."

Palmer let his guard down. Standing in the middle of the 18th fairway that Sunday, he needed only par to win. Instead, he blocked his approach into the bunker at the right of the green. Then he played a loose bunker shot that rolled over the green.

Now he had to get up and down to save bogey and force a playoff with Player. He chipped long and missed the putt to lose by a stroke, one of the most bitter losses of his career.

Palmer would recover to win two more Masters, but his inability to post victories in the other major championships would nag him. Although he won seven professional majors, he is also well known for never having won the PGA Championship to complete the career Grand Slam.

He also lost three U.S. Opens in playoffs.

"Certainly I didn't think (1960) would be the last Open I would ever win," he said. "I had the good fortune to win the Open. There isn't a hell of a lot more I can say about that."

Palmer was 34 when he won the Masters in 1964. He was at the pinnacle of the game. Although Snead and Hogan were past their prime, Player was a worthy opponent and Nicklaus was a rising star.

But no one could have predicted that it would be his final victory in a major.

"I don't really know why it was the last. I hope it wasn't the satisfaction of winning the Masters," Palmer said. "Maybe I lost some of the desire or the courage that I had earlier on. I don't know. I'll accept it."

Bobby Jones once said that if all his life experiences were taken away except for those at St. Andrews, he would have lived a rich and full life. Palmer can say the same about the Masters and Augusta National.

"Everything that has happened and continued to happen has been great memories for me," he said. "The importance has not dwindled at all.

"That's part of what makes it all so great for me. It's been a great trip for me."

Augusta

from *Jack Nicklaus: My Story* by Jack Nicklaus with
Ken Bowden

During my peak years particularly, what got me off the tennis court and
the fishing boat and onto the driving range each January was the thought of
the Masters. In 1963, golf's great spring-time rite had a particularly strong
appeal. Since missing the cut on my first visit to Augusta in 1959, I had finished tied for thirteenth, tied for seventh, and tied for fourteenth. As U.S.
Open champion, I wanted to redeem myself in America's shrine of golf so
badly I could hardly wait to get to the Augusta National again.

It is hard to imagine that there has been a good golfer since the Masters
Tournament began in 1934 who hasn't dreamed of winning it. Most readers
of this book will know about the event, so I'm not going to waste words
describing it. All I want to say is that, for me, it has been a career-long joy.
Young as the Augusta National is relative to how long the game of golf has
existed, it exudes more history and is home to more ghosts than any other
American golfing mecca, to a degree that still pumps me up just driving
down Magnolia Lane each April. Part of the appeal is the way the Masters

has set the pace in providing the finest quality and condition of golf course and the highest standards of tournament organization and presentation. Many of the refinements and special touches we enjoy today all over the world as players or watchers of top tournament golf derive from the Augusta National and the Masters. It would, for instance, be foolish of me to deny that they were and remain the inspiration and model for the golf club and the competition I started in the mid-1970s, Muirfield Village and the Memorial Tournament.

In 1963, there was another reason, beyond my previous poor showings, for my burning desire to win the Masters. I wanted to win it for the man who had given birth to the club and the tournament, and who had been at the forefront of my golfing consciousness almost from the time I had gone out for the game.

I have talked previously about how, in 1926, Bobby Jones came to Columbus and won the U.S. Open at Scioto, watched the entire way by my then teenaged father, for whom Jones immediately became a lifelong idol. The impact of this on me was that seemingly every time, as a youngster, Dad and I talked seriously about some aspect of golf, Bob Jones would come up in one form or another. Also, Jack Grout had known Jones well and admired him greatly and, like Dad, loved to reminisce about both his wonderful golf and his fine personal qualities. The result was that, by the time I first met Bob Jones, he had become a heroic figure to me. So far as I tried to emulate anyone in my early teens, he was the man.

The occasion of our first meeting was the 1955 National Amateur, played at the James River course of the Country Club of Virginia. Mr. Jones had been invited by the United States Golf Association to speak at the traditional prechampionship players' dinner on this, the twenty-fifth anniversary of his Amateur victory at Merion that completed his 1930 Grand Slam. At fifteen, I was the youngest player in the field. During a practice round, Bob had seen me get home in two at the 460-yard eighteenth hole and asked to meet me. Both Dad and I found him easy and pleasant to talk to. Finally he told me, "Young man, there were only a couple of fellas who got home on that hole today and you were one of them. I'm going to come out and watch you play some more tomorrow."

Did that make me nervous? N-o-o-o-o, not a bit. Here I am, a fifteen-year-old, teeing it up in the first round of my first Amateur, against Bob Gardner, one of the best golfers in the country, and all I've ever heard of about golf history is "Bobby Jones this... " and "Bobby Jones that... " And now Bobby Jones is coming out to watch me play. But what was I going to say, other than, "That'll be just fine, Mr. Jones, sir"? All through the first nine the next day I'm looking over my shoulder for Bobby Jones, and finally I see him coming down the tenth fairway in his golf cart as I'm getting ready to tee up at number eleven. At that point I'm one up in the match and feeling pretty good about myself. Half an hour later I'm two down, having gone bogey, bogey, double-bogey. Whereupon Bob Jones turns to Dad, who's walking with us, and says, "I don't believe I'm doing young Jack much good. I think I'd better get out of here." Which he does. Right away I get back to even, but then bogey the last hole to lose the match one down.

As he later explained to my father, Bob felt that his presence might have started me trying too hard, and thus took off as soon as he could without, he hoped, leaving us with the feeling that he had given up on me too quickly. Even at that minimally perceptive age, I was impressed by such sensitivity to and concern for a youngster with whom he had made only the most casual acquaintance. As our friendship deepened over the years, it was for me this kind of thoughtfulness and graciousness to everyone he encountered that continued to shine brightest of his many qualities. As to his golfing achievements, they were stunning to me as a youngster and they have remained that way ever since, particularly when viewed in context with his educational accomplishments, his full family, business, and social lives, and, most of all, how little tournament golf he played even during his finest years.

For Bob Jones by Masters time of 1963, made ever frailer and less mobile by a painful and crippling spinal illness, I think I helped to generate memories of happier years. For me, he was the supreme example of a golfer recognizing, and rising time and again to, the great occasions. The more our paths crossed, the stronger became my determination to show him that I was cut from the same cloth.

In short, what would grow into the dominating force of my golfing career, an endless preoccupation with the game's four modern major championships, was just beginning to crystallize. And there has never been any question in my mind that its chief stimulus was Bobby Jones.

At the pro-am preceding the Lucky International in San Francisco the last week in January of 1963, I had hit an 8-iron into the final green, then developed so sharp a pain in my left hip that I could barely walk off the course. It turned out to be bursitis, and despite regular treatments—I received numerous cortisone injections over the next few weeks—it troubled me to varying degrees right up until the Friday of the week prior to the Masters. As with so many of the minor ailments of athletes, the only real cure was rest. One of the ways I tried to rest the hip was to reduce the number of full practice shots I hit. This eased the physical pain, but didn't do much for my mental condition.

I tied for second behind Bill Casper in the Crosby that winter, then beat Gary Player with a 65 in an eighteen-hole playoff in Palm Springs. Yet, well as I scored at those and other times, I felt like I was playing only half-prepared. Given my kind of temperament, that is a most unpleasant frame of mind. The frustration was worsened during much of this period by the fact that I was also trying to master a new way of flighting the golf ball.

Up until that time I had faded the majority of my full shots—curved them slightly from left to right. When I absolutely had to move the ball the other way—draw it from right to left—for a strategical or recovery reason, I could usually do so, but never with quite the control and confidence of my long-established bread-and-butter fade. In fact, almost from taking up the game, drawing shots consistently had given me fits. I would feel I had the draw under control for a day or two, but the next time out it would turn into a hook for no apparent reason—that low burner to the left that makes good scoring hard labor if not impossible.

Predominantly fading the ball had never really concerned me until I began thinking so hard about the Masters that winter. I was plenty long enough not to need the extra roll that draw spin produces, and the additional height and softer landing of the faded shot had proven a tremendous scoring weapon, particularly with the long irons, my strongest suit since my mid-teens. However, reflecting on my previous indifferent showings at the Augusta National, I now experienced three revelations about the course that seemed to demand a change of strategy.

The first of these was that Bob Jones, who helped Alister MacKenzie with the design, was almost exclusively a right-to-left golfer. The second was that, perhaps because of this shotmaking preference of Bob's, at least half of Augusta National's holes either drifted to the left or doglegged that way. The third revelation was that the majority of Masters winners had been essentially right-to-left golfers, notable examples including Arnold Palmer, Sam Snead, and, before his change to the fade, Ben Hogan. The outcome of all this was that I decided I had no option but to finally force myself to learn to draw the ball controllably and consistently.

Now, anyone who reads more than the headlines of the sports pages knows that all professional athletes are champion rationalizers—the reason being, of course, that they will go to almost any lengths to sustain the high levels of confidence necessary to become and remain top performers. What you have just read was one of my all-time classic rationalizations.

Fading the ball reliably had been getting harder and harder for me because, to fade, you have to aggressively lead with and clear the left side of the body swinging down and through, in order to keep the clubface slightly open at impact. For weeks, pain or the threat of pain in my left hip had inhibited such an action, with the result that, quite involuntarily, I was drawing more and more shots purely as the product of an earlier closing clubface. Thus, although I would not have admitted it at the time, what I'm sure I did was cook up those three "revelations" about the Masters course in order to prop up my confidence in the face of a subconsciously unappealing swing change forced on me by injury.

Mentally upbeat about the upcoming Masters as this helped keep me, there remained the problem of hitting sufficient practice shots to become truly confident with the new flight pattern. What it boiled down to was that, in order not to risk compounding the injury, I had to try to learn a new set of tricks on the golf course itself during actual tournament play. That is no-no number one in Golf 101, and it produced erratic performance right up until the Masters. Mostly I was either very good or very bad—high on the leader board or on down the road.

I'm going to digress for a moment here and return to the hip injury, because I think it offers a good example of how important learning your body is for the professional athlete.

Over the weeks following the injury, each of the doctors who administered cortisone injections asked me the same question: Had I heard any kind of popping noise at the time I first felt pain? There had been no audibles from the hip area in San Francisco, but then, in the second round of a tournament in New Orleans in early March, as I whaled a wedge out of heavy rough, something in my hip went "pow" and almost immediately the pain vanished. Back home in Columbus after that tournament, I could hardly wait to see Dr. Jud Wilson, the orthopedic surgeon who had fixed my dad's ankle and given me most of my injections, and tell him what had happened and get his assessment of the situation. His diagnosis was that, in hitting the shot in San Francisco, I had caused a tendon covering the hip bone to slip out of place, and that the "pow" in New Orleans had been the tendon popping back where it belonged as a result of the hard swing I was making.

Given such information, I imagine most people not dependent on their bodies for their living would say thank you very much and quickly put the matter out of mind. What that first incapacitating ailment as a professional golfer did for me was to get me started on what became a lifelong study of how the human body functions in general and of the workings of my own body in particular.

Over the years ahead, that hip tendon problem would recur more often than I have cared to publicly admit. Eventually, I figured out that it was probably caused, or at least aggravated, by my right leg being about a quarter inch shorter than my left, which exerted added pressure on the left hip during the golf swing. By then I had also figured out a stretching maneuver that for many years popped the tendon back in place (if you noticed me contorting myself strangely on the golf course, that's what I was doing).

In the same way—by listening carefully to my body, then searching out ways of making it and keeping it healthy—I was able to play for a long time with very little serious or game-limiting injury. In fact, thanks to my functional anatomist friend Pete Egoscue and the exercise regimens he began tailoring for me in the fall of 1988, I continue to have avoided back surgery despite a couple of herniated discs. Looking back, I am proud that I had the intelligence and discipline to start along that self-care road as early in life as I did.

Getting back to golf, with the hip pain gone a full month ahead of the Masters, I suppose I could have attempted a return to my old left-to-right shot pattern. If that thought occurred at all, it did not survive very long. The relief of being able to play without discomfort, plus the ability to practice hard again, simply increased my confidence in my commitment to the new shape. Passing up the Greensboro tournament, I spent the week before the Masters at home in Ohio, working on confirming to myself one last time that I now really could draw a golf ball consistently with all of the longer clubs. The next Sunday I flew to Augusta in high spirits even though Barbara, imminently expecting our second child, couldn't make the trip (Steve arrived the following week).

Although I had ingrained the habit of pacing off and noting down tournament course yardages everywhere I played following my introduction to the technique by Deane Beman at the 1961 Amateur, I hadn't done so at Augusta the previous year, dumbly assuming I knew the course well enough after playing in four Masters. I corrected this error in practice, as, drawing most full shots nicely from right to left, I scored 69, 70, and 67, then 32 for nine holes of final tuning.

As at Oakmont nine months previously ahead of my U.S. Open victory, on Wednesday night I felt 100-percent ready for action.

One thing you can generally bet on at the Masters, in addition to all the scenic beauty and the fabulous atmosphere and the fine organization, is some interesting weather.

This being Georgia in the springtime, everyone hopes for four calm and cloudless days with low humidity and temperatures in the mid-70s. According to the old hands, you'll generally get one day like that, sometimes—if the gods of golf are smiling—two. The other two, the veterans maintain, will be either very windy or very wet or very chilly, or a combination of all three.

In 1963, the final practice day, Wednesday, was perfect. By the first tee time Thursday morning there was a gale blowing—one of the windiest days, some Masters veterans said, in the tournament's history. After thirteen holes, I found myself three over par. What with the wind speed and the dried-out greens, I had plenty of company. But I was still a little surprised, because I had struck the ball much better than this score indicated. The right-to-left pattern was holding up well, and although I'd gotten a couple of bad bounces and missed some makeable putts, I was playing pretty tight golf. The results were disappointing after the practice scores, but then I had long ago learned that practice scores are meaningless beyond whatever they may do for your confidence. But there was a long way to go. I decided to hang cool and keep on trucking.

The reward came immediately with the day's first birdie at the fourteenth hole, followed by another at the par-five fifteenth and a great little chip at sixteen to save my 3. I slipped to another bogey at seventeen, but parred the final hole for a round of 74. I would have liked better, but no one had run away and hidden. Mike Souchak and Bo Wininger shared the lead at 69, with most of the scores in the mid to high 70s.

Friday, typically, was perfect again—warm and sunny with the lightest of breezes. I missed the green at the first hole with a wedge, but made par and never missed another putting surface all day until number eighteen, where I chipped dead from the fringe. From the second through the sixth holes all my first putts were for birdies, and they all looked like they would drop until the last moment. The birdies began on the seventh and eighth, and I added to them on twelve, thirteen, fifteen, and seventeen. With no bogeys, it finally added up to 66, my first round under 70 at Augusta playing for real, and by far the best one I had put together in five Masters. At the end of the day, Souchak still had me by a shot, but I was a pretty contented golfer. What pleased me most was that I had been able to capitalize on the ideal scoring conditions better than any of the other contenders.

It has often been said that most major championships are lost rather than won, and that Jack Nicklaus has claimed a number of his by sailing steady while others were blowing backward. There is some truth in that, and if ever there was a round where the importance of bearing down and hoping for the best in adverse conditions seared itself into my brain, it came on day three of that 1963 Masters.

We had gone from perfect weather in practice, to high winds on Thursday, to perfection again on Friday. On Saturday came the monsoon. The rain fell ceaselessly, totaling more than an inch by the end of the day. A lot of the field felt that the course had become unplayable by late afternoon and that the round should have been canceled. I had little sympathy for that view, having adopted the same philosophy toward rough course and weather conditions as I have to health problems or other personal difficulties: Once the gun has gone off, you keep quiet and get on with the job as best you can. The more you let your mind dwell on negatives, of whatever type, the larger they grow and the greater the risk that you will convert them into excuses. I have preferred to save my energy for finding solutions to problematical conditions, rather than waste it on whining.

I will admit that this round tested that attitude to the limit. On the opening hole I hit a horrible duck hook into the trees separating the first and ninth fairways, but somehow scrambled a par. After ten holes, however, I had missed an eighteen-inch putt and a two-footer, along with several more from under four feet. At the eleventh, the driver slipped in my wet glove—I changed gloves eight times during that round—and the ball flew dead right and smacked a pine tree about 150 yards from the tee. I couldn't see where it finished, and nobody in the gallery had either. Walking down the fairway, I experienced the sick feeling known to all golfers who suspect they will shortly be tramping back up it again, then adding two penalty strokes to the score when they leave the green.

Spectators are not allowed down the left side of the eleventh hole during the Masters, but I had noticed a security guard standing all by himself in the left rough. As I began to look around for my ball off to the right side of the fairway, the guard called out, "Is this yours? A Tourney 6?" *Phew*! Again I scrambled a par, and it lifted my spirits sufficiently to keep on matching the numbers on the scorecard.

The Masters invented the system, now almost universal in golf, of using different colors to indicate under-par and over-par scores on leader boards, in its case respectively red and green. I am red-green color-blind and thus unable to distinguish between the two. Coming up eighteen, I looked over at the big leader board facing the clubhouse and saw a "2" next to my name, which I knew had to be red, along with a whole mess of 1's that could have been either color. My caddie at the Masters for many years was a local character called Willie Peterson. I asked him, "Willie, are we leading this tournament by three strokes or by one?" Willie took a quick look then told me, "Them others is all green numbers. You're leading by three, boss."

By not quitting on myself and keeping my composure, I had somehow struggled around in 74. Normally, a score that high would have dropped me well back into the pack. Because of the awful conditions, it had moved me from one stroke behind into a handsome lead. Nothing like that had happened to me before, but it was a lesson I would never forget. I went home exhausted but happy, dried out, ate, and fell asleep the second my head hit the pillow—and stayed that way for about eleven hours.

A little incident during that round further points up the value of patience and perseverance at golf. I was paired with the leader at the halfway point, Mike Souchak, and I am certain he could have finished a lot better if he had not let himself get trapped into making a false assumption. At the thirteenth hole, the entire fairway in the elbow of the dogleg appeared to be flooded, to a degree permitting neither of us to find a lie for our second shots that wasn't casual water. Mike said to me, "You know, I don't think there's any way we're going to be able to finish today. They're certain to cancel the round." After that, he sort of hockeyed his way through the rest of the hole and made a big number, and finally handed in a 79.

The round was not canceled, of course, and I'm sure Mike's assumption that it would be hurt him more than the shotmaking difficulties he and all the rest of us were experiencing. The lesson is a simple one: Hang in hard until you've holed the final putt or someone in authority has told you to stop. Cliché though it may be, this game is never over until it's over. Keeping that at the front of my mind has been as big a factor in my record as any of the shots I've played.

On Sunday, the gods of golf smiled again, clearing away the clouds about the time I arrived at the course an hour before my 1:25 P.M. tee time. The crowds by then were enormous and would get bigger by the hour-to the point, in fact, where people had to be turned away at the gate for lack of parking space, thereby provoking the decision henceforth to sell only all-tournament admissions.

I felt great-increasingly confident with my right-to-left draw, sure I would play well from tee to green. I hit my first good opening drive of the week and put a 9-iron twelve feet from the cup. I missed that putt, plus real birdie opportunities on each of the next six holes, then bogeyed the par-five eighth hole through stupidly forgetting to check the pin position as I left the adjacent first green. The bogey would have hurt more if anyone had been making a run at me, but at that point no one was. Turning for home, I was still a couple of shots clear.

The rush began on number twelve, that lovely little devil of a par three that surely must have decided more Masters tournaments than any other single hole. As I'd looked over a long putt for birdie on the eleventh green, a huge roar had come from the direction of the fourteenth green. A few moments later, the leader board close to the eleventh green indicated the cause—a birdie by Sam Snead, tying him with me at one under par.

Then in his fifty-first year, Sam had gone on a diet during the winter and, for the umpteenth time, retuned the superb golf swing that had already won for him three times at Augusta, and more times elsewhere around the world than anyone except he could remember. He was playing beautifully despite a sore foot, and, sensing it might be a last hurrah, the fans were giving him their all. Unfortunately, and through no fault of Sam's, some were also inspired to let me know their preference. In those days I was usually far too focused on my own play to hear gallery comments, but these were too loud and pointed to ignore. Because the Augusta National during the Masters was the last place I expected golf fans to root openly against a player, this greatly surprised me, and naturally unnerved me a bit.

When the time came to hit at the twelfth, I watched my playing partner, Julius Boros, float a lovely shot to within about twelve feet of the flagstick, positioned this time at its easiest in the front left of the green. I figured he'd hit a 7-iron, and decided to do the same. My intention was to aim a fraction right and play a quiet little draw. I aimed fine, but failed to stay down on the shot long enough. Caught thin and pushed, the ball looked for a moment as though it wouldn't even clear Rae's Creek, but just made it and landed on casual water in the front bunker. I was allowed a free drop, but there was no way to avoid the ball partially embedding itself in the wet sand. Considering the lie, I thought I hit a pretty good sand shot, but the ball came out fast and ran through the far side of the green. From there I decided to putt rather than chip, but, misjudging the slowing effect of the fringe grass, ended up some eight feet past the hole. It was a gut-wrenching moment. Even if I made the putt for bogey, I would trail Sam by a shot with six holes to play.

The bad news then got worse—fast.

As I watched Boros address his birdie putt, a leader board change indicated that Gary Player had birdied the fifteenth hole. Gary had started five strokes back of me. Now, thanks to a great run of four almost back-to-back birdies, he was a stroke ahead—two if I missed the upcoming eight-footer. Also, Tony Lema, playing brilliantly in his first Masters, was now tied with me. Moments later, Julius joined the club as his birdie putt toppled gently over the front lip. From being out in front alone and seemingly unchallenged half an hour earlier, I now had four of the world's finest golfers tearing at my hide. I studied the eight-footer a long time, told myself to hit it firmly whatever, and did so. A surge of excitement ran through me as the ball dove into the cup. It was a very big putt.

By the time I arrived at the thirteenth tee, Snead had also birdied the fifteenth, so was now two strokes ahead of me. That resolved any doubts about gambling. I hauled out the driver and drew the ball perfectly around the dogleg, then went for the green with the 2-iron, knocking the ball about sixty feet beyond the cup. As always on this tree-shaded, sparsely grassed green, the speed was hard to judge, and I left the first putt about five feet short. Then, surveying the line of that little tester extra carefully, extremely aware of how important a birdie would be, guess what I discovered? . . . Growing dead on my line, was a flower—yes, a *flower*. The Masters greens are cut—generally, almost shaved—every morning and evening, so this was difficult to believe. Closer inspection proved it was just what I'd thought—a dandy little flower, probably a daisy. Golf's rules prohibit interfering with living objects, so there were no options. I would have to bang the ball right over the top of the flower. I did just that and found the hole. The birdie reduced my deficit to Snead to one.

Whether one likes it or not, luck is an enormous factor at every level of golf. Even when the breaks have been against me, I have tried to accept them as part of the game's challenge and charm, because I believe it would be a pretty dull affair if it were entirely predictable. Also, I figure the breaks even out over time. If that's true, I made up for a whole warehouse full of bad ones on the fifteenth hole that afternoon.

After a solid par at fourteen, I had hit a big drive at this long par five. When I got to the ball, however, I found it had settled against the raised front of an old divot. Given a perfect lie, the shot would have called for the 1-iron. To be sure of forcing the ball through the tuft of dried turf, I decided to go with the 3-wood and choke down a little. I made a good swing and impact, but the tuft affected the spin imparted to the ball, because it took off left then hooked—dead on line to bounce and bumble into the pond forming the entire left side of the sixteenth hole. "Oh boy, there goes the 1963 Masters," I said to myself, then aloud to the world at large, "Somebody please stop that ball."

Nobody did, and it vanished from sight beyond and to the left of the green. But there wasn't the loud groan that always greets a shot, as Henry Longhurst so graphically liked to put it, gone to a watery grave, and when I got down there, lo and behold, there was the ball—pulled up short of the water by the muddy tracks left by spectators. I took the permitted free drop, blessed Saturday's monsoon, played a great chip from a tight, wet lie, and almost made birdie. About then the adjacent leader board confirmed, as I'd heard leaving the tee, that Snead had bogeyed the sixteenth hole by three-putting. The board also showed that Player had finished his round with two straight bogeys. All was not yet lost.

Sixteen at Augusta National is a 190-yard par three, almost entirely over water. Pumped up, I hit a 6-iron twelve feet short of the hole. As we walked to the green, Willie Peterson, my caddie, glanced at the leader board and immediately got excited. Sam had also bogeyed eighteen. I was in the lead again by a shot. "Boss, all we need is three pars," said Willie. I agreed, but I had a good feeling about the twelve-footer—and it wasn't misplaced. Birdie. A two-stroke cushion with two holes to play.

For some strange reason I felt more nervous setting up on the seventeenth tee than I had been all day, but still managed to hit a solid drive. Climbing the hill after it, I detoured a little left to look at a leader board. Suddenly, I realized we had forgotten all about a gentleman from Oakland, California, by the name of Anthony David Lema. If Tony birdied the final hole and I bogeyed my last two, he would become the first golfer to win the Masters at his first attempt. Then, just as my playing partner, Boros, hit his approach to seventeen, there came an enormous roar from the eighteenth green, indicating that Lema had indeed finished with a birdie. There was no way I was going to play my second shot until I knew for sure whether that was true. I fiddled around until the board changed. Now I *did* know for sure—and also that I must make no worse than two pars to win *my* first Masters that sunny Sunday afternoon.

I hit what felt like a solid 8-iron to the seventeenth green, but heard a fellow in the gallery shout, "Get up! Get up!" even before the ball reached its apex. I sprinted over to the left to see the shot land. It did so on the green. Two putts later, I had the first of those pars.

The entire right side of the eighteenth hole in the driving area at Augusta National is a forest—deadsville. I chickened out a little and drove the ball well to the left. It ended up in spectator territory again, and again I was fortunate and got a free drop onto the fairway because of the mud. However, the lie I gave myself wasn't the best and the green, ten deep with spectators, looked smaller than ever. I did some pacing and some hard thinking. I had 160 yards to the flag, uphill, with the adrenaline on full rush. That computed to a choked 6-iron. I hit the shot exactly as planned, but the ball ran farther than I'd figured it would. The result was a thirty-five-foot downhill putt with a double break, first left, then right. I judged the breaks perfectly, only just missing the hole, but not quite the distance, the ball finishing three feet past. Setting up to that putt, I reminded myself that, even if I missed, I would have another chance to win in a playoff. The thought relaxed me sufficiently to stroke the ball firmly. It broke left faster than I'd expected it to, but slipped into the hole just a millisecond before it caught enough of the lip to spin out.

As I'd walked onto the eighteenth green, the announcer there, Ralph Hutchison, had asked me to save the ball if I won and give it to Bob Jones. When the winning putt dropped, I just had to throw something, so I whipped off my cap and slung it to the crowd.

At the ceremony a little later, Mr. Jones and I made an exchange. After he and the previous year's champion, Arnold Palmer, had presented me with my green jacket, I gave Bob the ball.

It was a small thing, but the look in his eyes remains one of the most emotional memories of my life.

A Master Feat

Lee Elder Had to Hurdle Racial Barriers before Making Augusta History in '75

by Brad Townsend, *The Dallas Morning News*,
April 3, 2000

Lee Elder, dapper in his dark green pants, light green sweater and white visor, looked remarkably composed on that drizzling April 10, 1975 morning.

He wasn't.

"I was shaking," he recalls. "I was very frightened. I could not believe that I was at Augusta National, getting ready to tee off the first tee in the Masters."

Nerves are normal for a Masters rookie, but Dallas native Robert Lee Elder was no ordinary first-timer.

At a shade past 11 that morning, Elder became the first African-American to compete in the Masters. His tee shot split the fairway. The invisible, but long impervious wall tumbled.

Elder's life changed forever. So, it seems, has Augusta National and golf.

This week, a quarter-century later, a 24-year-old of African-American and Thai descent, Tiger Woods, is heavily favored to win his second Masters in four years.

Elder, 65, is returning to Augusta National to be honored by the Golf Writers Association of America. And to watch Woods.

"Time really has passed," says Elder, relaxing over lunch during the recent Legends of Golf senior tour event. "I'm looking forward to that drive down Magnolia Lane.

"The cobblestone driveway. The magnolias and azaleas. The 'Welcome to Augusta National' sign."

Elder's voice imparts no bitterness, although his eyes moisten when discussing the hate mail and death threats that he received leading to the '75 Masters, the obstacles that he encountered while growing up in East Dallas and why he left, gladly, at 15.

Mostly, he is appreciative of the way that he has been treated through the years at Augusta, starting, yes, with that week 25 years ago. He treasures his role in golf history.

"That whole committee at Augusta National is just wonderful," he says. "I really can't say enough about them and that golf tournament."

But Augusta National has no plans to commemorate Elder's anniversary. Understand that in its 65-year history, the club has dedicated four plaques and three bridges. The men honored are Bob Jones, Clifford Roberts, Gene Sarazen, Ben Hogan, Byron Nelson, Arnold Palmer and Jack Nicklaus, all towering golf figures.

Lee Elder played in six Masters and made three cuts. His best finish was a tie for 17th in 1979. In '75, he shot 74-78 and missed the cut.

In the Masters media guide's list of significant dates in the tournament's history, 1975 has one mention: "Jack Nicklaus becomes the first five-time winner."

"Lee Elder will always have a special place in Masters history," Augusta National chairman William "Hootie" Johnson said in a prepared statement. "He has long been a credit to the Masters and the game of golf."

Broach the '75 Masters to most players and fans, and they'll recall Nicklaus outdueling Tom Weiskopf and Johnny Miller in one of the event's most storied finishes. They'll probably describe Nicklaus' 40-foot putt on No. 16. They might note that it was the last Masters in which Palmer was a factor. He tied for 13th.

Elder? He seems an uncomfortable subject for some. Is his an anniversary to embrace, or a reminder of times most would rather forget?

"No," replies Nicklaus when asked if he had any thoughts about the subject. Several other senior tour players, including Elder's second-round playing partner Miller Barber, also declined to comment.

"We just went out and played golf," says Gene Littler, Elder's first-round playing partner in '75. "Nothing happened. Nothing was said.

"Obviously, it was a big deal for him, and we appreciated that. But I think both of us just tried to make it another round at Augusta."

It isn't so much that Elder disclaims Dallas as his hometown. Mostly, it's that he has lived in other places longer.

He spent 19 years in Los Angeles, then 23 in Washington, D.C. He split time between D.C. and Pompano Beach, Fla., until a divorce five years ago left Pompano as his base.

"I consider Washington, D.C. my hometown," he says.

Many of his Dallas memories are pleasant. Some are not.

He was one of Charles and Almeta Elder's 10 children. They lived on Philip Street, within walking distance of Fair Park.

When Lee was 9, the family received a telegram, saying Charles had been killed in World War II.

"My mother left her bedroom," he says. "A couple of months later, she died of a broken heart."

That was the year that Moses Brooks, 13 months older than Lee, took him to Tenison Park Golf Course, where they could caddie for a dollar a day.

Tenison Park, like all Dallas courses at the time, was all-white. But the head pro allowed the caddies to play there on Mondays and Fridays. On other days, they practiced across the street at Samuell Park, on makeshift holes.

"There was no doubt in my mind that he would be a good golfer because he had a lot of confidence," Brooks says.

At Tenison, Elder and Brooks played gambling games with players such as J.W. White, Dick Martin, Arthur Corbin, Dan Gruber, Jimmy Powell and the king of gambling golfers, Alvin C. Thomas, a.k.a. Titanic Thompson.

One year, recalls Brooks, he, Elder and White (who later became head pro at Cedar Crest) went to Fort Worth to attend the Colonial Invitational. Problem was, they had two tickets.

All three got in by passing one of the tickets through the fence, but were caught a couple of hours later. Rather than have one boy left out, all three decided to leave.

"Lee looked down the fairway and said, 'Some day I'll be back and they won't be able to put me out,'" Brooks says. "I wanted to know what he'd been drinking at that age.

"But he proved it to be true."

Elder's oldest sister, Sadie, tried to care for her five brothers and four sisters. Lee says he was fortunate that his aunt, Helen Harris, took him in. During his early teenage years, Lee split time between Dallas and Helen's home in California.

Elder attended Lincoln High School as a freshman. But at 15, disillusioned by the lack of courses available to African-Americans in Dallas, Elder went to California and didn't return.

He says he tried to find someone in Dallas who would sponsor him, but the area was brimming with talented players. White players.

"It just so happened that I had a little more foresight," he says. "I wanted more. I wanted to be more. I wanted to be part of learning the game. Dallas could not afford me that."

Brooks and most of Elder's friends remained.

"I chose the wrong route," says Brooks, who over the years qualified for some mini-tour and senior tour events and now lives in Oak Cliff. "I went for the gambling golf."

Elder also went the gambling route, but did so out of California, where society was more open-minded and playing opportunities more plentiful.

Bill Spiller broke pro golf's color barrier by playing in the 1948 Los Angeles Open. It wasn't until 1953 that the PGA of America (then pro golf's governing body) added a constitutional amendment allowing for "approved entries"—non-members who could play in tournaments if invited by sponsors.

But it wasn't until 1961 that the PGA's "Caucasians-only" clause was stricken from the constitution, formally integrating tournament golf. Even then, cities in the Deep South, where much of the tour schedule was played, more than discouraged African-American participation.

Standout players such as Ted Rhodes (during the '50s) and Charlie Sifford (the '60s) had a difficult time getting into regular tour events, much less the Masters.

Elder credits Rhodes as the person most influential in his development. Rhodes and a one-time Texas pro, Ray Mangrum, convinced Elder to change from a cross-handed grip to a conventional one.

Elder made a living by playing in some West Coast satellite tours, and by barnstorming with Titanic Thompson. It wasn't until 1967, at age 33, that he saved enough money to try tour qualifying school. He made it on the first try.

By then, Augusta National was under increasing heat to invite an African-American to its tournament.

Pete Brown had become the first black to win a tour event, the 1964 Waco Turner Open. In '69, Sifford won the Los Angeles Open in a playoff over Harold Henning. Still, no Masters invite was forthcoming.

Starting in 1972, the Augusta National committee decided to extend automatic invitations to the winners of PGA Tour events.

In 1973, a group of 18 congressmen wrote to Augusta National chairman

Clifford Roberts, requesting that Elder, who they believed was worthy, be invited to the Masters. Roberts expressed surprise and mock flattery that congressmen would deign to help run the Masters.

"We feel certain someone has misinformed the distinguished lawmakers," Roberts wrote back. "Because there is not and never has been player discrimination, subtle or otherwise."

In 1974, however, Elder forced the issue by winning his first PGA Tour title—the Monsanto Open in Pensacola, Fla. A few years earlier, at the same club, Elder and other African-Americans had been barred from the clubhouse.

Roberts, then 80, immediately issued Elder an invitation to the '75 Masters. Two months before that Masters, Roberts invited Elder for a practice round. During the tournament week, Roberts personally met Elder's limousine.

"I had heard several things that were not so wonderful about him," Elder says. "Why the change of heart? I do not know. I think he wanted me to be accepted, just like the other players."

Many, however, were anything but accepting. Elder recalls some of the hundreds of threats that he received, many of which contained racial epithets:

" . . . You're out of place; society is not going to accept you, even though you qualified for the Masters."

"You'll never play at Augusta; I'll get you before you get there."

"If you get to Augusta, you'd better look behind all the trees."

Says Elder: "I took every one of them serious. They were things that really were frightening. Things that you had to walk and think about."

Again, there is no contempt in his voice. He recalls that his friendship with Jackie Robinson, who broke baseball's color barrier in 1947, helped him keep perspective.

Robinson advised Elder that he had to be the bigger person. He reminded, "It's easy to get into trouble and hard to get out of trouble."

"Those kind words have always been with me," Elder says. "I know there have been times when I really backed down in situations where I probably would not have."

Elder had to take precautions after arriving in Augusta during that April week of '75. Because the media was clamoring for his time, he and then-wife Rose rented two homes, one under an assumed name.

They hired a maid and a cook and spent most of the week in the rental home. When they did go out, they made certain it was with a group of 15 or more.

"We had everything we wanted [in the home]," he says. "Chairman Roberts repeatedly asked if there was anything they could do."

Elder says that once inside Augusta's gate, he felt absolutely safe because of the club's tight security. He vividly remembers Augusta National's African-American staff members treating him with reverence and appreciation.

He tried to return the sentiment.

"Most of all, I wanted them to know that I was an Afro-American who cared as about them as they cared about me," he says.

He remembers playing in Wednesday's par 3 tournament with Jim Colbert and Gene Sarazen, then going to the press center for a news conference that lasted three hours.

He remembers the kind, encouraging words from Littler on the first tee the following morning. He remembers seeing former Cleveland Browns great Jim Brown in the gallery.

He remembers that first tee shot, as if it were yesterday. He parred that hole and birdied No. 3 to go 1-under.

Calvin Peete, then a 31-year-old African-American who would play in eight Masters starting in 1980, also remembers.

"It had a definite significance," he says. "That's what inspired me to get to the Masters."

Augusta National changed forever that week. But what about pro golf in general?

Did Elder's presence that week fling open the door of opportunity, or just nudge it a little wider? In terms of African-American participation, has the sport fared better, or worse, these past 25 years?

"I wish more doors had opened," Peete says. "There seems to be a trend. Since 1960, there's only been one prominent black player per decade.

"Lee Elder came up after Charlie Sifford. Then I came up after Lee Elder. Then Tiger Woods came along after me. That's disappointing, very disappointing."

Elder concurs.

"Do you realize that today we have only one Afro-American on the regular tour and only five on the senior tour? That is a low figure. During the time I was on the regular tour, we had 12."

More numbers, these from the PGA Tour's developmental tour. Of the 171 exempt and nonexempt players in the Buy.com Tour's media guide, only one face is black: Zimbabwe native and University of Virginia standout Lewis Chitengwa.

And in this, the LPGA's 50th anniversary season, current player LaRee Sugg joins Althea Gibson (1964-71) and Renee Powell ('67-'80) as the only African-Americans to play that tour.

Elder and Peete say there is no doubt that Woods has drawn countless young African-Americans to the sport. And that the tour's nationwide, multimillion-dollar First Tee initiative will, in time, provide affordable access to courses and facilities.

But it will be years before Woods' impact is evident in the pro ranks.

"It's big business now," Elder says. "During the days we came up, we came out of the caddie ranks. Now you've got them coming out of the college ranks. Our young Afro-Americans do not have that chance."

Elder and his wife of five years, Sharon, oversee the Live The Dream Foundation, a youth golf initiative that soon may expand from five cities to 10.

That door? It's open wider now. But 25 years later, Elder and others are still banging.

"Did I Tell You the One About..."

As CBS' Voice of the Masters, Jim Nantz Has 20 Years' Worth of Stories to Tell

by Craig Bestrom, *Golf Digest,* April 2005

Spend a day, an hour or even a few minutes with Jim Nantz, and you realize that all he needs is an audience. Whether he's speaking to one person, a
few hundred at a banquet or several million from the 18th tower at Augusta
National, Nantz is doing what he always wanted to do. "For me it has everything to do with the words, the voice and telling a story that really captures
people," he says.

What we learned during four sit-downs in four zip codes is that Nantz is the
ultimate fly on the wall. As a result, there are countless stories in his head.
Whether it's a special stock tip from Gene Sarazen, cutting practice with Fred
Couples at the University of Houston, or an embarrassing on-air slip of the
tongue beside Clint Eastwood, Nantz remembers the most minuscule of details.

Nantz's sports savvy goes way beyond golf. He's also CBS Sports' lead play-by-play voice for pro football and college basketball, but from an early age, golf was the key. "The dream for me was always the Masters," he says, "and after my freshman season on the Houston golf team I knew CBS was the only way I'd get there."

Golf Digest: This will be your 20th Masters for CBS. Tell us about your first one, when Jack Nicklaus came to the 16th tee on Sunday, trying to win his sixth green jacket, and you had the microphone.
Jim Nantz: I knew the pin would be backleft that day. Excuse me, the hole location. Before the round I asked Frank Chirkinian [former CBS golf producer] what I should say if somebody makes a hole-in-one.

"Son," he said, "I'll tell you exactly what to say if somebody makes a hole-in-one at 16: nothing! This is a visual medium, you idiot! Now, get out of my office and get down there to rehearsal."

Chirkinian was a tough guy, known as The Ayatollah.
Frank was a stickler about punctuality, and Lance Barrow still adheres to it. If it says rehearsal is at 3 o'clock, you'd better be there at 2:50. At 2:51, you're late.

I was doing the 16th that first year, and I didn't really have a handle on the easiest way to get there—what crosswalks open up a little sooner than others. I remember fearing for my life that I was going to be late for a rehearsal. I was heading down that great valley between Nos. 18 and 8, and I'm in a mild jog, fueled by a fear of being late and maybe being banished forever from the Masters. Suddenly a member came up, a green jacket, didn't know who I was. He stopped me and said, "Young man, we don't run around Augusta, we walk."

So how did you react when Jack's charge began that Sunday?
I ran down to 16. Excuse me, walked down to 16. We're on the air, and he's

birdied 9, 10, 11, makes 4 [bogey] at 12, birdies 13. I'm able from my tower to see Jack make eagle at 15. As he marches to the 16th tee, I know we're going to be live, and the whole world is going to be watching. That might have been the most terrifying moment of my career.

So you called upon the reservoir of Jack Nicklaus facts in your head?
I set it up by talking about him winning his first green jacket in 1963, that he made birdie here that day. Then I talked about 1975 and the Miller and Weiskopf thing [Nicklaus' long birdie putt at 16]. I'm waxing like I'm Henry Longhurst, like I've had all the experience of these culturally literate icons that I so much wanted to be like. I'm 26 years old! The whole time I have chill bumps up and down my arms.

One of the CBS rules to this day is you never talk over a shot, and Jack got right to the point of pulling the trigger when, suddenly, he backed off. Knowing Jack through the years, I knew I had another minute to kill before he hit the shot, and I'm completely out of material.

Chirkinian had been telling all of you to pull in Tom Weiskopf from time to time. So that's what you did.
Exactly. "Tom Weiskopf, what is going through Jack's mind right now? He has not experienced this kind of a streak in a long time." And Weiskopf says, "If I knew the way he thought, I would've won this tournament." A classic.

After nearly making a hole-in-one, Nicklaus makes the birdie putt, and you say …
"The Bear … has come out of hibernation." And as soon as I said it I was completely consumed with self-doubt. I'm thinking, Somebody else has already said that, you idiot. Later on at the CBS compound, Brent Musburger came over and said, "Hey, kid: That was the line of the day."

So what is your most embarrassing on-air moment?

It might've been on Sunday of the 2003 AT&T Pebble Beach National Pro-Am, shortly after Davis Love had won the event. Clint Eastwood was in the 18th tower with me, live on the air, and I told him that Davis' father had been a huge Clint Eastwood fan. "I'll bet you didn't know," I said, "that when Davis was a young boy, one of the first adult films his father ever took him to see was one of yours."

Without hesitating, Clint turned to me on camera and said, "I have never made an adult film in my life."

My first thought was, *What did I just say?* It's a moment I'll never forget, and one that Clint probably hasn't forgotten, either.

Your access at Augusta must lead to some memorable behind-the-scenes moments. What comes to mind?

One of my traditions at Augusta is to take a walk around the course late on Wednesday afternoon. Usually very few people are around, and it serves as a little meditation. I like to get out to Amen Corner, check the green conditions at 12 and stand on the 13th tee for a while all by myself.

While doing this a few years ago, I'm looking from the 12th green back up the 11th fairway, and I see two people walking very slowly. One is leaning on a cane and holding onto a lady. It didn't take long, even from 400 yards away, to realize it was Byron Nelson and his wife, Peggy. I thought, *How special is this?* Byron Nelson is out walking around Amen Corner.

So I scurry up the 11th fairway and pull alongside, and they tell me that Byron is taking Peggy out to the Byron Nelson Bridge [at the 13th tee] for the first time. She'd never seen it. He said, "I just don't know how many more chances in my life I'm going to have to walk Amen Corner."

Trying to be as respectful as possible, I said I'd get out of their way, but Byron says, "No, no, no. Come with us."

About that time, Davey Finch, one of our cameramen, was out shooting some beauty shots for the broadcast. He saw me with the Nelsons, so he came over. Again, not to be an intrusion, I asked Byron, "Would you mind if we recorded this for history? I know the club would love to have it." He said it'd be fine, so Davey got Byron Nelson walking across his bridge for maybe the last time.

Once Byron got across the bridge, he read the plaque that pays tribute to his great record at Augusta. Then, as hard as it was for Byron to do this, he leaned down, kissed his hand and patted the plaque with his hand. It was as touching as anything I've ever seen.

You had a special day with another Masters legend, Gene Sarazen.
Thanks to Ken Venturi's time living on Marco Island [Fla.], he was very close to Gene Sarazen. So I was able to be around Mr. Sarazen quite a few times.

I was host and MC of an event Kenny held at Marco Island in early March of '99. Gene Sarazen came and sat on the first tee all day. As every group came through off a shotgun start—Greg Norman, Ernie Els, Nick Price, Davis Love, David Duval and more—I would ask all of them to make a comment about Mr. Sarazen. It was magic.

As I spent that whole day with him, I had the luxury of getting into the kind of stuff that if you had five minutes you wouldn't go there. I said, "Would you mind giving me an idea of what your day is like? What's a normal day for you?"

He told me about waking up at 8 every morning. He lived in a high-rise. He'd get up, take a shower, shave and usually get very dressed. Always very dapper. At 9 o'clock he'd have breakfast and read the paper. By 9:30 he'd be a little tired, so he'd take a nap. He was 97 years old, I believe.

And after the nap?
Back up at 10:30, and he'd sit on his balcony and watch the world go by. Eventually he'd come back in and have lunch.

"Then you'd go take another nap?" I asked.

"No, no," he said. "Done with the naps by then. Usually from noon until 4, I watch CNBC. You know, the stock ticker."

Sarazen was a stock man at 97?
That's what I said. "You're kidding!"

"Actually," he said, "I haven't bought a stock in 70 years, since 1929. But the best way to know what's going on in the world is to watch where the money is moving. There's a story here, Jim, that I've never told anyone."

He went on to tell me about his rival Jim Barnes, who won the first two PGA Championships. Barnes and Sarazen didn't get along great, but in 1929 Sarazen was on the train when he happened to see Barnes, who was doing investment work on Wall Street.

As Mr. Sarazen was telling me this story, I remember him saying, "I didn't much like Mr. Barnes, but I said, 'Hey, Barnes, how's the stock market?'"

Barnes warned him that key indicators pointed to the potential of a crash. "I give you five days, tops," Barnes told him. "Sell everything you own."

So Sarazen says he sold all of his investments. "The stock market crashed, and I didn't get hurt at all," he said. "Matter of fact, in many ways Jim Barnes saved my life."

Sarazen shared that with you only a couple of months before he passed away.
It was about five weeks before Mr. Sarazen was going to hit what turned out to be the last golf shot of his life, the opening shot at the 1999 Masters. He had told me, "You never know when it'll be my last shot."

What I'll never forget about that last shot is, really unable to generate any speed, he still hit it so flush. It probably flew only 70 yards in the air, right down the middle. He just hit it solid, still one of my favorite golf shots I've ever seen.

As he was leaving, he saw me and said, "Hey, I wanted to tell you today, off our discussion a few weeks back: I've got a stock I want you to buy." I said, "Are you serious?"

What was the stock?

I don't want to tell you; I don't want anybody to get investigated. [Laughs.] He says, "You've got to buy this stock. It's the first stock I've bought in 70 years. I told him, "Coming from you, I'm gonna go buy it no matter what it is." Later that day I called my business manager and said, "I've got a stock I want you to buy. All I know is, Gene Sarazen waited 70 years to buy the right stock, and I'm riding it. Let's load up."

How'd it do?

The stock is worth nine times what I paid for it, and I still own it. Every day I open the paper, look up the symbol and think, Gene Sarazen.

Getting back to Nicklaus' victory in '86, Ken Venturi told you that day that you'd never live to see a greater Masters. But for you, it's hard to envision anything comparing with 1992, the year you and your college suitemate, Fred Couples, lived out your dream.

Freddy had the great start to the '92 season. All year, he and Blaine McCallister, my amigos at the University of Houston, had this goal of coming to the Final Four to serve as runners for me. Fred was No. 1 in the world, the favorite at the Masters that would be starting in a few days, and here he was with Blaine, carrying my briefcase, running stats and hustling for Billy Packer and me during the two semifinal games Saturday.

Eight days later Fred is winning the Masters, and you're calling it.

I was only doing the Butler Cabin then. When he came into the cabin, we're on the air. Jack Stephens [former club chairman] is there, and Ian Woosnam is there as the '91 champion to present the jacket. What are the odds that two kids who talked about this in college, that it was going to come true?

I'd decided long before that I would conduct this as I would if just anyone had won the tournament. But the last question I wanted to personalize a little, bring a lot of guys into that moment. I wanted them to be remembered. Before that I did some general questions about the ball staying up on the bank at the 12th hole.

Fred was answering the questions, I thought, with a tinge of fear that I was going to break into a personal thing. His fear is always that he's going to completely lose it. I know that there are some very tender feelings in Fred that are just barely below the surface. I've seen it many times.

Did the tears ever come?
In the end I said, "You know, Fred. I think about our days at the University of Houston and Taub Hall. I can't help but think of Blaine McCallister and John Horne, Paul Marchand, who is here today."

He turned his head, covered his eyes and looked off to the side. My voice is quivering. I said, "All of us said, 'One day you're going to look great in a green jacket.'"

The only way he could compose himself was to not go there, so he said, "Well, I always thought this was the one tournament I'd have the best chance to win. Always the one tournament I always watched as a kid growing up."

He didn't personalize it at all.
Woosie gave him the green jacket, and I said something like, "A perfect fit," although it looked like it might have been Woosie's jacket, because the sleeves came up just below Fred's elbow. My last sentence was something like, "Fred Couples has won the Masters, and good night from Augusta." At that point, we both totally lost it into a long, sobbing moment, slapping each other on the back. We fell to pieces.

But you were off the air by then?
I thought maybe we were still on the air, because the cameras continued rolling. It's all on tape. In fact, I've often thought it's a shame, from Freddy's

perspective, that it didn't get shown live. People have often said about Freddy, "If he only tried a little harder …" I think they would've seen right there how much Fred, his whole career, wanted it more than anybody's ever given him credit for.

What was your first impression of him when you met in college?
The day all the incoming freshmen arrived on the Houston campus Coach [Dave] Williams put us in a room and asked us to stand up one at a time and introduce ourselves to everyone. I was pretty intimidated just by that because I knew my playing career fell far short. I thought Fred was very bashful, but it didn't take long to find out that we had a mutual passion for sports.

In 1978, the year Bucky Dent hit the home run in the one-game playoff between the Yankees and the Red Sox, we were the only two guys on the golf team who got to see it. That was our sophomore year, and I'm not especially proud of the way we got to see it. Coach had a rule that we had to play and turn in a scorecard every day, and that day was no different. But Fred and I had to see that game. We couldn't possibly go out and play golf that afternoon.

How'd you get out of it?
We feigned sickness. We feigned one of the worst flus to ever strike the University of Houston.

Fred and I went to class that day, but we pretended to have a hard time getting our lunch down. After lunch, Coach would usually walk down the dorm hall where the guys on the golf team lived together, and he'd poke his head into our rooms and make the pairings for that day.

When he came into our rooms that day, I was in my bed with the shivers, fighting a horrible fever—98.6 [laughs], and Fred was in his bed, supposedly trying not to throw up. I don't think coach was too concerned about me missing the day. By my sophomore year we had 18 guys on the team, and I was definitely No. 18. But he went in to Fred, who was one of his star players, and he said, "Fred, you look awful. I don't want you playing today. You need to rest up." He came in to me, and I said, "Coach, whatever he's got, I've got it, too."

I'm not proud of this, but one of our happiest moments together was when we walked down that hall and confirmed that the coast was clear.

Fred spent a week with you in New Jersey during one of your summer breaks from the University of Houston. What do you remember about that week?

That was the summer Freddy was low amateur at the U.S. Open at Inverness. He was coming to the All-America golf banquet at the Waldorf hotel in New York City. I'd go back in the summers and house-sit for a family, and I'd work at Battleground Country Club cleaning clubs, helping around the shop, putting bags on carts. We worked it out that when Fred came to New York I would come into the city to pick him up. I still remember trying to find him that day.

Finally, after about an hour of searching, I spotted him in the enormous lobby of the Waldorf. He's sitting in a far corner, hidden behind a column. You could very easily have looked all day and never seen him. He was kind of sitting there waiting for someone to come scrape him off the carpet and take him away.

After that week you had to get him on a plane back to Seattle.

His mother called and said, "You know, Jim, Fred's coming home tomorrow. Please make sure you get him on the plane, and tell the flight attendants that he has to connect in Chicago. He's going to need some direction and help to get to the gate and all."

I drove him to the Newark airport, and you know how they let you pre-board with small children? Well, I got on the plane with him and put him in his seat. I found the lead flight attendant and told her to make sure he found the gate for his connecting flight in Chicago. I wished him well, told him I'd see him back at school, and he made it home safely. [Laughs.]

Think he'd have made it without you?

The truth is, Fred is a very smart guy. I like to say he's as dumb as a fox. By that, I mean he is completely savvy about everything. A lot of times when he wants to feign that he's not sure what he's supposed to do, or he didn't get your phone call or he doesn't remember his phone number ... I know the deal! It's a great weapon, and he uses it well. And I say that with all due love and respect for my brother.

You mentioned that you put Fred to work at a Final Four. Tell us about the time Nick Faldo and a couple of his friends surprised you at the Final Four in New Orleans.

That was in 1993; the tour was in New Orleans that week. We're in the middle of the first game when Len DeLuca, CBS' vice president of college programming at the time, comes over during a timeout and says, "Nick Faldo, Mitchell Spearman [instructor] and Fanny Sunesson [Faldo's caddie] are at the press gate wondering where their tickets are."

You were supposed to have left tickets for them?

This was the first I'd heard of it.

Was Faldo a friend of yours?

I knew Nick. He went to the U of H. We used to joke that we almost became teammates. He left after a year, and he was a little ahead of me. But it's not like we had a real social relationship.

So, what did you do?

Len asked me how he should handle it, and I told him, "Hey, it's Nick Faldo. If there's a way you can get him in, get him in."

Let me guess: He got in.

All three of them. Mitch and Fanny went up into the stands, and Nick was put to work as a runner. During a break between the two games, Nick came down to say hello, and Billy Packer busted him a little about his shenanigans. Finally, Nick asked if there was anything he could do for us. So I said, "Yeah. Could you go get us ice-cream cones?" Here I was asking the No. 1 player in the world to go get us an ice-cream cone. And he did.

I told him that some day he's going to be on about the 14th hole on Sunday at the British Open, and he's going to have a marshal come up to him and say, "There's a guy named Jim Nantz who's looking for his two passes. What do you want us to do about it?"

That kind of thing happen a lot?
No . . . and I certainly hope this doesn't get something started.

Former President Bush has joined you in the tower a few times. How well do you know him?
I'm blessed to have great friends, and there are a lot of men in my life who've been more than just friends, particularly in the last 10 years with my dad battling Alzheimer's. There's been like a generational thing to where they're almost surrogates.

Who besides the former president?
It's a long list. Obviously "41" would be at the top of the list, along with Ken Venturi, Billy Packer, Frank Chirkinian and Hot Rod Hundley. Hot Rod and I did Utah Jazz games together when I was 23 years old. He did play-by-play and I was the analyst, which was a little weird because Hot Rod Hundley was the No. 1 pick in the NBA draft in 1957 and a two-time All-Star. I was captain of my high school basketball team, and our varsity record was 2-42.

Within five years of that, I'm an NBA analyst making all these judgments, saying things like, "What is Adrian Dantley thinking about? You can't give up the baseline!" Thank goodness no one ever did a background check on my playing career.

How often do you see 41?
My relationship with the president is something I've shied away from talking about publicly, because most people are going to say, "Yeah, right."

George Bush has thousands of friends. He's a warm person. I'm lucky enough, for the last 10 years, to have been able to go up to his house in Kennebunkport [Maine] three or four times a year and stay with him and Mrs. Bush. It's very special. Sometimes it's just for a night and a quick round of golf the next morning.

What kind of golfer is he?
He's always downplaying his ability, but he has a very efficient game. He turned 80 last year. Cape Arundel, where he plays, is a short, old Walter Travis course, and he can go around in the high 80s.

Anything at stake when you play?
We always play a match, and it's always for one dollar. We were partners one time in a match, and we were down on the 16th hole. He comes over and says, "What do you think about maybe pressing these guys?"

I said, "We're playing for a dollar, right?"

He says, "Yeah. What do you think?"

So I said, "It's a dollar. Let's be daring."

I love that spirit.

Are there members of the Secret Service following you when you play?
Always. He doesn't just show up unannounced. We played a public course in Houston once, Memorial Park. The president walks into the pro shop, shakes every hand, signs everything put in front of him and takes out his wallet and says, "OK, we've got four green fees and two carts."

The guy behind the counter says, "No, no, Mr. President. You're our guest."

The president says, "I insist. I want to come back, and if you don't let me pay for it I'm going to be hesitant to come back because I'm going to think that you're going to think I can play for free."

He paid for everyone.

Do you play much with [George W. Bush]?
I've played no rounds with him since he's been in the White House, but we played when he was governor of Texas. We played a match on New Year's Day once, and I've got video of them paying me the dollar. I think we've played three times, and there's always a lot of talk when we play. There's this mock kind of trash talk. It's never blue, never crass, but it's the kind of casual, "I made 4; anybody beat 4? ... I made birdie; anybody else make birdie?" We'll pitch horseshoes, and one of them will say, "I don't know, I guess I had four or five ringers in that game. How did you do?"

Horseshoes?
One time I was in Maine in July 2001. We were in the back yard pitching horseshoes, and Mrs. Bush was upstairs. She opens the window and yells down, "Uh, George. There's a special report on television right now about a mystery car parked in front of the White House. They're evacuating the White House." The president looked up and said, "Don't worry about it, Barbara. I'm sure it's nothing."

A few minutes later she yells down again, "George. It's on all the channels now. They're evacuating the White House."

Again, 41 says, "I'm sure everything's fine."

Did you sense more concern than the president was letting on?
We pitched the horseshoes to the other end and he says, "Would you like to go inside and see this, or do you want to keep playing?" I thought maybe we should take a look. Sure enough, it was on all the channels. All

we're seeing on television is a long-range shot of a bomb-sniffing dog near a car that's been left unoccupied in the White House driveway.

Now 41 is concerned?
Finally he picked up the phone and called the White House. "Hey, Logan [Walters, the president's former personal aide], can I speak to the president?" he said.

He refers to his son as "the president?"
Yeah. So he says, "Hey, everything all right?" He was fine; he was having lunch with Vice President Cheney. "Well, your mother yelled out from upstairs while I was out pitching horseshoes with Jimmy Nantz."

He hands me the phone, and the president, 43, says to me, "How's it going up there? Who's winning?"
I said, "Your dad has already won the first game, he's up 11–6 in the second, and we just wanted to make sure everything was OK. We've had a full day already. We played golf this morning; he beat me at that, too, with some shots. We've already been out on the boat, and now we were pitching horseshoes. He's taking it to me pretty good."

On the other end of the phone, the president says, "It sounds like 41 is having a big day." I said, "He is." And he said, "Let me tell you something: There's nothing that makes me happier than hearing that."

Commentators on almost every network were still speculating about the president's whereabouts. The president's dad turned off the television, and we went out to finish our game of horseshoes.

How's your golf these days?
When it comes to my game, the Houston thing really haunts me. As much as I beam with pride that I was on the University of Houston team with Freddy, Blaine McCallister and some really great players, and the fact that

I earned a varsity letter for it, I'm troubled by the expectations people have for my game. It's truly taken some of the love out of playing for me. My scores, frankly, are an embarrassment. People think that because I played golf at the University of Houston I must shoot 75 every time I tee it up. Well, I don't. You'd be alarmed how many times I don't break 90.

Have you ever played with Nicklaus, Palmer or Tiger?
I got to play with Arnold Palmer for the first time last year. It was at Laurel Valley with a great mutual friend, Jim Rohr. I played reasonably well, but Arnold shot 70 that day, with five birdies. On the last hole, the par 5 where Dave Marr closed out his PGA Championship in 1965, I knocked it on the green in two. I had about a 40-foot putt over a buried elephant, which I knocked about five feet past. So now I've got this five-footer to win the match for our team—Mr. Rohr and I were playing against his brother Tom and Arnold.

As I'm standing over the putt, Arnold turns his putter upside down and starts talking into the handle of the putter and doing commentary, a parody of me. He had dropped the voice and was describing the break in the putt. It was one of those moments you'd like to have recorded.

Did you make it?
Of course I missed it. But I hit a good putt. I think the announcer suckered me into playing a little more outside the right edge than I needed to.

Any checks or cash framed in your office from a memorable golf bet that you won?
No, but I played with Greg Norman and his son, Gregory, once. It was me, Frank Chirkinian and Gregory, who was 11 or 12 years old at the time, in a three-man scramble against Greg's ball. We get to the 16th hole, and the best shot we have is from some tall pampas grass left of a greenside bunker. This was at a time in Greg's career when he was

clearly snakebit. Doggone it if I didn't pitch in, and we ended up winning the match, 1 up.

Greg sheepishly went over and picked the ball out of the hole and immediately drew all the parallels: It's bad enough that Larry Mize, Bob Tway, Robert Gamez are holing shots, but the greatest indignity of all is some hack like Nantz coming to the Medalist, and he pitches up and over a bunker and into the hole. He was a great sport about it, but I felt like I deserved a place right alongside the others.

You also had a memorable round with Jim McKay, who was one of your boyhood announcing idols.
I used to write Mr. McKay fan letters. These men, these voices were huge to me, much bigger than any of the athletes. I got to meet him and play a round of golf with him shortly after I graduated from college. My college teammate Paul Marchand was an assistant pro at one of Mr. McKay's clubs, and it was such a thrill for me. I remember waiting for his limousine to arrive. I had him built up to be 6-foot-5, this giant who's being chauffeured around everywhere. Much to my dismay, McKay pulled up in one of those station wagons with the wood paneling on the side, and he was driving it himself. He was like 5-foot-5.

We had a great day together, played as best-ball partners against Paul. I holed about a 40-footer for birdie on the first hole, and Mr. McKay jumped up and high-fived me. I mean, this was Jim McKay!

During the round I had told him about my admiration not only for him but for others in the business. Told him about my goals and about my great love of Henry Longhurst and his command of the language. Within weeks, a book arrived in the mail, The Best of Henry Longhurst. Inside it said, "To Jim Nance," spelled N-a-n-c-e, "Remembering our day on the windy links. Jim McKay. Sept. 13, 1982."

Three years and one day later, Sept. 14, 1985, I had actually gotten to the place I'd always dreamed of, making my debut on the air for CBS.

Let's talk about being a sportscaster.
Sports commentator.

Why sports commentator?
Sportscaster sounds like the guy who's on the 11 o'clock news and is putting together a three-minute sportscast of the headlines for that day. And by the way, that's a hard job, and a hard job to do well. But I'm not really casting anything; I'm commentating.

You started out as a sportscaster, though.
I started working for the CBS affiliate while I was still in college, living in dorms at Houston.

Is it true that you once worked 541 consecutive days?
That would've been from near the end of my junior year and right through my senior year. I never had a break. And that's not counting school as a work day. I was working at the CBS radio station, the CBS television station, I was narrating films for NASA, I was doing public address at the Astrodome for the Astros and the Houston Cougars basketball team. I was getting invaluable experience, and I never said no. If somebody gave me an opportunity, I took it. Money was never an issue.

After college you hooked on with the CBS affiliate in Salt Lake City.
I became the television voice for BYU football, including the year they won the national championship [1984]. Steve Young was my analyst, which he was able to do because he was playing for the L.A. Express in the USFL, the spring league. Steve and I missed the whole first quarter and half of the second quarter of one game that year because we were stuck in an elevator that blew a fuse as we were heading up to the press box.

By 1985, you were hired by CBS, the network, to do the college football

report. How long until you got to do golf?

All during the fall of '85 I'd been hearing that I was going to become part of the storied CBS golf lineup, which tickled me to death. CBS' golf season started at Pebble Beach, and I flew out there on the day the Challenger went down. They didn't have room for me in the Lodge, but CBS used to rent "Fairway House No. 2," right on the elbow of the first fairway at Pebble. Big sprawling house that used to be owned by Lawson Little [the 1940 U.S. Open winner].

Who else was in that house with you?

I was going to be rooming with Bob Drum, and I was very familiar with Bob Drum's work. Bob was this giant of a man, and he says, "Hey, kid. Let's go down to Club 19. Have an adult beverage or two." For him, that was about 12 Cafe Royales, which is a little bit of coffee and a whole lot of Royale.

What was your role that weekend?

I just observed. I was a little intimidated. I mean, there was Mr. Summerall, Mr. Chirkinian, Mr. Venturi ... all of these legends. I was fascinated by it all.

When did you finally get on the air?

The next tournament for me was Doral in 1986, and for Gary McCord that was kind of his first tournament for CBS, too.

Gary and I worked the 16th hole together.

That's when you and McCord called the final hole of the playoff on tape as if it were happening live.

Andy Bean and Hubert Green were battling. The golf ran long, so they ended up coming back to us after a Donald Curry fight. The playoff had already ended right in front of us on the 16th green, but Gary and I pretended it was happening live. Gary was the analyst, and he called every shot exactly how he knew it would end up.

"Hubert Green's second shot at 16," said. McCord says, "Jimmy, I look for this ball to end up right of the flag; I see this like 18 feet or so." Ball lands, two hops, boom! Right on the spot.

Bean stands over the last putt, and Gary says, "Not a doubt in my mind he's going to make this."

What are you thinking?
It's my first golf telecast, and intuitively I know you can't do this. This is not right. I just knew that someone in the press room was going to out Gary on this. I'm figuring they're watching in the press room, knowing that Bean is already on his way down there for an interview. As we were walking back to the compound I told Gary, "You can't do that." And he's like, "What? Why not?" Thankfully we both survived it.

A month later you and McCord show up at Augusta for your first Masters, and club chairman Hord Hardin calls you in for a meeting. What do you remember of that?
Frank Chirkinian, as a courtesy to Mr. Hardin, walked us down to his office early in the week. I think this has been dressed up a little bit by Gary, saying that he wore a clown's suit or something. That's, of course, not true. We walked into his office, and there was a chair against the right wall and a chair against the left wall. Frank sat right in front of the desk. I felt like we were a full sand wedge apart. Frank made the introductions, and Mr. Hardin basically just said, Guys, we like to think this tournament is a little bit different, a little more special. We hope you enjoy your time." It was really a welcome.

So nothing was said in there that left you feeling like, don't ever say this?
You'd think it would be a list of do's and don'ts, but it really wasn't that at all. I still to this day have never had anybody at Augusta tell me what to do or what not to do.

Come on.

I promise you. That is the most written about, over-exaggerated, over-embellished tie to the Masters and CBS that's ever been discussed. I've never had a guy say, "Now, don't talk about..." Frank Chirkinian, and now Lance Barrow, help to guide our people.

But as far as Augusta coming in to the announcers and saying, "Do this, do that"?

Doesn't happen.

But you use words we don't hear at any other golf tournament. Things like "patrons" and "first cut."

I think Augusta, obviously, is a cut above your week-in and week-out tour stop. If we want to make it sound like just another tournament we would deal in the same language. It's more polished. It deserves to be. It's just ratcheting it up a little bit in terms of grace.

Are you bothered by critics who question your dramatic intros to the Masters?

All I can tell you is I broadcast Augusta right from my heart. For me, it's the best tournament in the game. When I was a young boy, the goal for me was to get to Augusta. I can tell you none of it is disingenuous or contrived. People tell me all the time that they have the same feelings about Augusta. They thank me for the way I broadcast the tournament.

I feel sorry for people who don't have it in them to open up their heart a little bit and celebrate something that's actually pretty good.

Love that Augusta theme song, too.

You'd be amazed how many letters I get in a year about that theme song ["Augusta," by Dave Loggins]. People want it for their daughter's wedding, or they want to get their hands on it for the music: Who wrote it? What's it all about?

Does the whole approach make you cringe at all?

I love it; are you kidding me? I relish it. Wouldn't trade one Augusta for 20 Super Bowls. I think about the Masters every day of my life; I really do. I think about it more than anybody would probably believe.

Maybe too much?

I don't think so. It's all like a great fantasy for me. These professional athletes have the greatest heart in sport today, and it's why I defend them. I hate whenever there's a social issue that comes up in golf and people in the mainstream media who hate golf and who've conjured up all these stereotypes of people who are in the sport, the way they tear it down ... I resent it, and I'll defend golf and people in golf until my dying day.

Give me an example.

It happens all the time. They want to weigh in on all-male clubs, or the Casey Martin issue, whether he should have a golf cart. The issues become bigger than the sport, and general news columnists want to weigh in: Those elitists, those stuck-up snobs who don't get it. Man, they have their heads buried in the sand. Wait a minute! This sport has given more money to charity than pro football, pro basketball and major league baseball combined. This sport is so built on great virtues of the highest integrity. Golf has the greatest collection of writers in sports today. And look at the great ones, when they get later in life, they want to do golf only. Whether it's Dan Jenkins, Bob Verdi ... Jim Murray's greatest writings were golf writings. Rick Reilly. All the great ones. Too often our sport and the people who cover it let others come in and maul the sport and its reputation. We let them kill it. It upsets me.

Somebody has to get up and defend the great integrity of the sport, and I'm nominating myself.

So why at Augusta in 2003, when Martha Burk had created such a firestorm

of controversy over Augusta National's male-only membership, did you not say a word about it during CBS' coverage?

Who had it wrong? CBS or the mainstream media? Was the amount of coverage commensurate with what happened at Augusta? There were 38 stories written in *The New York Times* from when that issue first surfaced until the Masters.

Did *The New York Times* have it wrong?

I don't know; they dedicated 38 stories to it. I know that she had seven protesters out there with her in the end who were not paid.

Forget the protest itself. But to not even acknowledge an issue that had received so much attention leading up to the Masters... even [club chairman] Hootie Johnson addressed it that week.

It had been mentioned all the time. CBS News had covered it. So now you have a finite amount of time to cover a golf tournament. Do we need to go in and cover a story that's been covered, or maybe over-covered? From a news judgment issue, who had it right? Howell Raines [then the editor of *The New York Times*] or CBS?

What's your opinion on the issue? Are you OK with Augusta's all-male membership?

I'm not saying Martha Burk was right or wrong. I'll say this: It's Augusta's right to decide to do what it wants to do. It's their tournament; it's their club; and they're a private club. And that's all I want to say.

I've got to ask you about Ben Wright.

I shouldn't go there.

At least a couple of questions.

You can't win. When Ben Wright came out with his remarks [about women golfers and the LPGA Tour], which were unfortunate, he got slaughtered. By everybody.

Do you regret how strongly you defended him right after his comments went public?
I defended a guy I worked with for 10 years who I happen to know made a mistake and apologized for it. I'll just say Ben's a good person.

You were one of Ben's very good friends.
Still am.

And you, with Pat Summerall and Frank Chirkinian, took part in an intervention for Ben that helped him get help for his alcoholism.
We did. Went down in 1996, a couple of days after the Final Four. We got down there the night before. His wife at the time, Kitty, brought us all together. I went from the Final Four calling the championship game on Monday night to his home in North Carolina on Tuesday. On Wednesday morning, we were in his living room by 7:30. Ben rolled out of bed, had his robe on, and he was shocked to see us in his living room.

How did it go?
Very emotional.

Did he listen to your advice?
He was on a plane that afternoon to the Betty Ford Center.

Let's finish up with the Masters. If there's a dream scenario remaining for you to see, what is it?
People are going to say this is crazy, but if Greg Norman ever got a chance to go back to Augusta and compete, I think he could win the Masters in the next five years.

I'm always thinking of great stories. Good things for good people. For me, I would love to bring Davis Love into the green-jacket ceremony one year, with all the ties with his father, with Davis being born the day after the 1964 Masters. That'd be a great story.

A David Duval comeback would be a great story, too.
I get asked a lot about David Duval. I like him a lot, and I'm concerned about him and what's happened to his game. I was walking through the lobby of a hotel awhile back when I noticed a lone figure sitting and staring at a painting in the corridor.

It was David, who said hello but didn't much care to talk golf at that point. He was absolutely transfixed by this painting. As I walked away, I thought, You could give me the entire list of guys on the PGA Tour, and there's only one who'd be sitting in a corridor staring at a painting. That's David.

Your thoughts on last year's Masters winner, Phil Mickelson.
Phil gets a lot of credit, as he should, for picking the Baltimore Ravens to win the Super Bowl months before it happened. And I'm here to tell you, the man follows football. He can talk two- and three-deep on rosters for every single team in the NFL. I have fun talking to Phil about the NFL, but one time I made the mistake of asking him, "What do you think about the NFL this year?"

Thirty minutes later, after he finally took his first breath, he was still talking. Finally I said, "You know, Phil, I do cover the NFL for a living." We had a good laugh.

Arnold Palmer played his 50th and final Masters last year. How many do you want to do?
This will be my 20th, and I'd like to work 50 Masters. I'd be 75 years old if that happened. I can't think of anything in my profession that would mean as much. You can talk about Emmys or Super Bowls. Fifty Masters Tournaments, that would be the ultimate.

THE COURSE

The World's Wonder Inland Golf Course

from *The Making of the Masters* by David Owen

If the Masters seems older than it is, that's largely because the tournament, alone among the majors, is conducted year after year on the same course. Every important shot is played against a backdrop that consists of every other important shot, all the way back to 1934. Every key drive, approach, chip, and putt is footnoted and cross-referenced across decades of championship play. Every swing—good or bad—has a context.

The history of the tournament is so vivid in the minds of the competitors and spectators that it almost has a physical reality on the course. The four-wood shot that Gene Sarazen holed in the second Masters is as much a part of the fifteenth hole as the pond in front of the green. Players standing by their drives can't help but think about Sarazen's two as they plan their second shots, whether they go for the green or not—and the same is true for ticket holders and television viewers. The double-eagle is more than just a notable moment in Masters history; it is woven into the fabric of the course.

At the eleventh, no player aims at the flag without recalling that Ben Hogan once said, "If you ever see me on the eleventh green in two, you'll know I missed my second shot." At the twelfth, no player watches a tee shot roll down the bank in front of the green and into Rae's Creek without remembering the final round in 1992, when Fred Couples's tee shot rolled down the bank in front of the green—and stopped. When the hole is cut on the back right of the sixteenth green, no player lines up a long putt from below without thinking of Seve Ballesteros's four-putt in 1988. (Ballesteros, when asked what had happened, explained: "I miss. I miss. I miss. I make.")

When Tiger Woods turned a nine-stroke lead into a twelve-stroke victory on the final day of the Masters in 1997, he conquered not only Jack Nicklaus's thirty-two-year-old scoring record but also his own knowledge that in 1996 Greg Norman had turned a six-stroke lead into a five-stroke loss over the same eighteen holes. For Woods, Nicklaus's triumph and Norman's collapse were both parts of the terrain. And now, for every other player who ever competes in the tournament, Woods's record finish will be, too.

The original design work at Augusta National was done primarily by MacKenzie, who more than once referred to his creation as the "World's Wonder Inland Golf Course." He conceived the routing, positioned the bunkers, and blocked out the greens. Jones is sometimes given equal billing, or even first billing, but his role was more nearly that of a junior associate. (As Jones himself wrote, "No man learns to design a golf course simply by playing golf, no matter how well.") Still, the two men had similar ideas about golf course architecture, and Jones's contributions were significant.

Roberts was apt to emphasize Jones's role in the early days, because he knew that in the minds of most people at that time Augusta National was Jones's course, not MacKenzie's. In October 1931, before construction began, MacKenzie wrote a lengthy description of the holes, and Roberts asked him to supplement it with "two or three paragraphs detailing the fact that Bob collaborated with you on all phases of the plans and due to the fact that Bob had studied civil engineering, and due also to the fact that he is of a studious nature and studies carefully each course that he plays on, he was of very genuine and very practical help to you. You might also add that he contributed several ideas that were distinctly original." Roberts may genuinely have felt that MacKenzie hadn't given Jones sufficient credit, but his first concern was probably that Jones's name be firmly attached to any piece of publicity the club might generate. At any rate, MacKenzie happily—and effusively—complied, writing that Jones had made "most valuable suggestions in regard to almost every hole and I am convinced that from no one else in America or elsewhere could I have obtained such valuable help and collaboration."

Roberts's contributions to the original design were minimal, but he nonetheless played a real role in the creation of the course. In his critiques of MacKenzie's plans, which were sometimes lengthy, he was observant and exacting. He noticed, for example, that a promised bunker on what is now the tenth hole had been left out of a subsequent drawing, and that particular clumps of trees did not appear to be accurately positioned. MacKenzie responded to such comments with varying degrees of good humor and alarm. One result of Roberts's insistence on detailed explanations was that MacKenzie spelled out much more of his design philosophy than he might have if his employer had been more compliant. Regarding a plan for the short, treacherous par-three that was then the third and is now the twelfth, for example, Roberts had questioned whether the green had been drawn to scale, since it appeared to him to be disproportionately shallow and wide. MacKenzie, in his response, explained that the unconventional dimensions were the key to the hole's design—as has been borne out in every Masters ever held. MacKenzie's exchanges of letters with Roberts, along with Roberts's correspondence and conversations with Jones, provided Roberts with an education in golf course architecture. He took those lessons to heart, and, as the years went by, he became an able guardian of the ideas of the two men who had first conceived the course.

The most important idea behind the Augusta National design—and one to which MacKenzie, Jones, and Roberts agreed from the beginning—was that the course should be demanding for the expert player yet not intimidating to the average golfer. It was to be, in MacKenzie's words, "a course pleasurable to all." Jones, in a 1931 interview with O. B. Keeler, said, "We are in perfect agreement that a good golf course can be designed and constructed which will be an exacting test for the best competition, and at the same time afford a pleasant and reasonably simple problem for the average player and the duffer... Dr. MacKenzie and I believe that no good golf hole exists that does not afford a proper and convenient solution to the average golfer and the short player, as well as to the more powerful and accurate expert." Jones addressed the same idea in his book *Golf Is My Game* : "We want to make bogies easy if frankly sought, pars readily obtainable by standard good play, and birdies, except on par 5's, dearly bought."

Jones once said that one of the great strengths of Augusta National was that while pros there were always in danger of succumbing to disaster, average members and their guests might well shoot some of their best rounds ever—that an inveterate 90 shooter, for example, might have a good day and shoot 85. That is still true—even, surprisingly, when the course is in tournament condition. (Members and their guests are allowed to play through the Sunday before the tournament, and their scores at that time seldom differ very much from their scores during the rest of the playing season.) The reason for the seeming paradox is that the kind of trouble which tends to defeat an average player is less severely penalized at Augusta National than it is on other demanding courses: the fairways are generous, the trees are widely spaced, the bunkers are few; out-of-bounds is seldom a danger, and the short rough is (for an average player) as likely to be a comfort as a catastrophe, since it can cause a ball to sit up a little higher than it would on a closely mown fairway.* The greens are difficult, of course—but all greens are difficult for an average player. For a twenty-handicapper, three-putting is close to the norm on any course, and the particular perils of Augusta's greens are offset by the reduced likelihood of losing a ball off the tee or hitting into an unplayable lie.

MacKenzie's and Jones's ideas about course design were revolutionary, and they were squarely opposed to the dominant American design philosophy of the time. That philosophy was perhaps most clearly embodied by Oakmont Country Club, near Pittsburgh, which had been built in 1903 and 1904 and was (and still is) viewed by many as the archetypal American championship course. The Oakmont ideal had been summed up neatly in a single sentence by William Fownes, whose father, Henry C. Fownes, had designed and built the course: "A shot poorly played should be a shot irrevocably lost." The fairways were narrow; the rough was thick and deep, and every hole offered numerous unique opportunities for turning moderately wayward shots into disaster. When Tommy Armour won the Open at Oakmont in 1927, his score for seventy-two holes was 301—a total that has been beaten by every Open champion on every Open course since then. (Armour won his title by shooting 76 in an eighteen-hole playoff with Harry Cooper, who shot 79.)

MacKenzie and Jones both believed that such ruthlessly penal design made the game unpleasant for ordinary players and obscured the differences between great golfers and merely good ones. If a course's perils are so severe as to leave no reasonable possibility of escape, the two men believed, then a skilled player's advantage over a less skilled player is greatly reduced. One of

---

* Average players sometimes have more trouble with Augusta's fairways than with its greens. During the Masters, the fairways are cut to just 0.39 inch, and they are kept at close to that height all spring. For a golfer who occasionally makes less than perfect contact with the ball, such naked lies can lead to a discouraging number of fat shots. For the pros, Augusta's short rough is more of a peril than it may appear, since it usually prevents players from generating enough backspin to hold the firm, undulating greens.

the most famous shots Jones ever hit was a blind mashie to the green after driving his ball into sandy scrub to the left of the fairway on the seventeenth hole at Royal Lytham & St. Annes, during the British Open in 1926. Had Jones driven instead into one of Oakmont's bunkers—which in the early years had deep, triangular furrows that were meant to prevent players from advancing their balls—he would have lost the chance to compensate for a poor drive by playing a spectacular recovery. MacKenzie and Jones both felt that Oakmont and other adamantly punitive courses rewarded straight, conservative shooting at the expense of the game's most thrilling elements. A good golf course, they believed, is one that consistently supplies situations in which superior players can demonstrate their superiority. (Houdini thrilled his audiences by escaping, not by being trapped.) On Open courses today, the best players in the world sometimes feel compelled to leave the best parts of their games at home: They hit long irons instead of drivers from many tees, have few opportunities to demonstrate finesse around the greens, and can resort only to brute strength and good luck when they stray into the rough.

MacKenzie and Jones's model, once again, was the Old Course at St. Andrews. In his book *Golf Architecture,* which was published in 1920, MacKenzie suggested that the one golf hole in the world that came closest to perfection was the Old Course's eleventh—a par-three measuring just over a hundred and seventy yards. "Under certain conditions," he wrote, "it is extremely difficult for even the best player that ever breathed, especially if he is attempting to get a two, but at the same time an inferior player may get a four if he plays his own game exceptionally well." MacKenzie said that adding a cross bunker in front of the green—as had sometimes been suggested— would ruin it, by making the hole "impossible for the long handicap man" without increasing the challenge for the expert. This same philosophy guided the design of Augusta National, and it has guided alterations ever since. (It is eerily appropriate that MacKenzie should have chosen the Old Course's eleventh as his epitome. On that hole in 1921—one year after *Golf Architecture* was published—Bobby Jones, who was then nineteen years old, took five shots to reach the green and angrily withdrew from his first British Open. Jones's mature career is sometimes measured from that burst of temper.)

Another feature of the Old Course that appealed to MacKenzie was the absence of clearly defined boundaries between many of the holes. On the Old Course, the area potentially in play for a given shot is often enormous. Players almost always have distinct options to consider, depending on their level of skill and degree of ambition, and they can usually choose among very different routes to the green. MacKenzie's original hope was that the divisions between fairways at Augusta would be similarly vague. The course as constructed did not quite satisfy him in that regard; while work was still under way, he objected (on the basis of photographs) that the boundaries defining some of the fairways had been cut "too straight." But the lines were softened as construction proceeded. Many greens can be approached—either on purpose or by accident—from reasonable lies in very different parts of the course.

The latitude isn't nearly what it is on the Old Course—and never could be, since the two courses occupy entirely different pieces of terrain—but the theme is sustained. Indeed, first-time visitors to Augusta are often struck by the broad expanse of uninterrupted green that extends from the back of the clubhouse very nearly to Rae's Creek, at the far end of the course. The property, when viewed from many vantage points, looks more like a vast park than like a succession of individual holes cut through trees. That is exactly what MacKenzie and Jones had in mind.

Identifying meaningful similarities between the Old Course and Augusta National may seem far-fetched, since on first consideration the two courses seem antithetical. The Old Course is ancient, ragged, treeless, and so irregular as to seem entirely undesigned, while Augusta National is young, manicured, and almost defiantly artificial. Still, the British golf correspondent Leonard Crawley, after playing at Augusta for the first time, in 1947, detected a powerful kinship and deduced correctly that MacKenzie and Jones had been deeply influenced by St. Andrews. "They have not copied one single hole on those maddeningly difficult and infinitely fascinating links," Crawley wrote a few weeks after his round, "but they built eighteen great holes, everyone of which is perfectly fair and provides a problem. It seems to me that each one demands that a player shall firstly and foremostly use his brains and not merely his physical and, in these days, his almost mechanical ability to hit a target from a particular range. It restores the ideas of some of the old original golf links which furnished the world with those great players upon whose methods and tremendous skill the modern game is now based."

More than sixty years after the first tournament, MacKenzie's and Jones's ideas about golf course design continue to define the Masters in ways that modern golf fans may not fully appreciate. During the closing holes of a U.S. Open, a player can often ride a narrow lead to victory by pursuing a conservative strategy based on avoiding disaster. The same approach has never worked at Augusta, where the final nine holes offer so many birdie and eagle chances that a bold player can make up a wide deficit with brilliant play—or self-destruct with a handful of poorly struck iron shots or miscalculated putts. That possibility has been an integral part of the course from the beginning. "We have always felt that the make-or-break character of many of the holes of our second nine has been largely responsible for rewarding our spectators with so many dramatic finishes," Jones wrote in the early fifties. "It has always been a nine that could be played in the low thirties or the middle forties." The dual nature of those holes increases the pressure on an early leader, who, with an eye over one shoulder, can begin to worry that no number of birdies could possibly be enough. As a result, the Masters seldom turns into a war of attrition; the winner is often the player who is bold enough to gamble at the very moment when human nature is urging him to protect what he already has.

That a course can be extraordinarily demanding while yielding tantalizing opportunities for scoring is an idea that many have found difficult to accept.

But it is the essence of Augusta National. In 1998, Greg Norman was quoted in *Sports Illustrated* as saying that the course was approaching obsolescence. ("It's getting close," he warned.) Yet Norman's own performance in the Masters less than two years before had demonstrated the opposite. Over and over during the final round in 1996, which he had entered with a six-stroke lead, he failed to meet the challenge of the course and in doing so turned what had appeared to be an easy victory into the tournament's most devastating defeat. He didn't lose because of the speed of the greens—which sports page pundits often refer to as the course's only remaining "defense." He lost because under the pressure of the final round he mishit or misjudged a succession of crucial iron shots—virtually all of them struck from perfect lies—leading him to play Augusta National's allegedly easy and outdated second nine in four strokes over par. (Two of his poorest shots—his tee shots on twelve and sixteen, both of which he put in the water—were hit under the most benign of circumstances: from tees, with short or medium irons.) Meanwhile, Nick Faldo was brilliantly managing both the course and Norman, who was playing with him, on the way to a virtually flawless 67 and a five-stroke win. It was exactly the sort of epic finish that the course had been designed to provide.

The Other Side: For Starters, Champion Must Master Augusta's Unheralded Front Nine

by Bill Nichols, *The Dallas Morning News*, April 14, 1996

They say the Masters does not begin until the final nine holes on Sunday.

Try telling that to Jose Maria Olazabal, whose title hopes in 1991 ended with a quadruple bogey on the par-3 sixth hole at Augusta National Golf Club.

After watching two of his chip shots from the front of the sixth green roll back to his feet, Olazabal never recovered from his three-chip, three-putt seven, eventually losing to Ian Woosnam by one shot.

Augusta's romantic back nine captures the world's imagination—and all the television cameras on Sunday. But the front side has seen its share of train wrecks, supplying dramatics that often turn contenders into stragglers by the turn.

Amen Corner, Nos. 11–13, is the game's most renowned stretch in golf. Yet those magical holes, lined with pine trees, azaleas and dogwoods, often have more bark than bite.

It is the unseen holes on the front side that administer the most damage. And as for the tournament beginning on the final nine, that adage simply has not held up.

Since 1970, only six players who were leading at the turn on Sunday did not win.

Hubert Green (1978), Ed Sneed (1979), Curtis Strange (1985), Greg Norman (1986), Scott Hoch (1989) and Raymond Floyd (1990) are the only ones to have blown leads on the back side in the past 25 years.

"The key to this golf course is the first five or six holes," leader Greg Norman said. "It's just a shame people don't get to see how difficult they are. We're churning our guts out on those shots because if you don't hit them, you're in no-man's land."

Because the Masters does not televise all 18 holes on Sundays, the viewing public rarely glimpses the front nine, except for an occasional highlight shot.

But while the back gets all the glory, the front is where the Masters is often won—and lost.

Seve Ballesteros broke from the pack in 1983 by going four under par through the first four holes, and the very next year, Ben Crenshaw took control with a 33 on the front nine.

Lee Trevino once said that compared to 3, 4 and 5, Amen Corner was "a pussycat." Scores support that claim.

In 1993, the top 24 finishers were 15 under on Amen Corner and 30 over on 3-5.

And in Thursday's first round, the five leaders went through 3, 4 and 5 at even par while going a combined 10 under on 11, 12 and 13. Their average score was 34.8 on the front and 31.2 on the back.

Norman, who tied the course record with an opening-round 63, did not make a birdie until the seventh hole, then went two under through Amen Corner.

"To me, the meat of the golf course is the front nine," 1979 champion Fuzzy Zoeller said. "I don't think you have as many birdie holes on the front. You just want to get your pars and get out of there. The back is where you make your move."

The front nine may lack glamour because it is more a test of survival. Players do not attack the front. They use patience instead of aggression. Most feel they are ahead of the game if they stay even through the first six holes.

"It's just like starting a car; you want to get it warmed up before you take off," two-time Masters champion Tom Watson said. "There are no gimmes on the opening holes. You can start off and get in a whole lot of trouble real fast. It takes excellent shot-making and real good decisions to get through there."

No. 1, a 400-yard par-4, offers a rude introduction, with its imposing trap about 250 yards down the right side of the fairway and its large, undulating green.

John Huston, who was one shot off the lead entering the third round last year, slid out of contention with a triple bogey on 1 the next day. And Byron Nelson double-bogeyed it to open his 18-hole playoff with Ben Hogan.

Only 16 birdies were made there last year, and only four players have birdied it three times during the tournament.

"The first hole has turned into one of the most difficult driving holes on the golf course because the trees on the left just past the driving area have grown up considerably," defending champion Ben Crenshaw said. "If I get a head wind on that hole, I cannot carry that bunker. So I have to drive to the left, and many times I have a problematic second shot. And you don't want to start the day with a bogey."

The par-5 second is a birdie hole. Most players like to draw their drives, sending the ball downhill to set up a chance to get on in two. But an errant drive presents problems because of a thick grove of pine trees and azaleas, an area that Jimmy Demaret labeled the Delta Air Lines counter. "If you drive in there, you're looking at a quick exit out of town on Friday night," Demaret once said.

The course's most difficult stretch begins at the 360-yard, par-4 third hole. Despite its short distance, its green makes it tough for birdies. The neck of the green is only seven yards wide.

Four is the hardest hole. The green was expanded for the 1995 tournament to make room for a tough pin placement on the back right corner, but Masters officials softened their approach on Sunday by using the forward tee, which reduced the hole to 180 yards. But even that didn't help. Four yielded only 19 birdies and a tournament-high 76 bogeys last year.

Five, a 435-yard par-4, is a sweeping, uphill dogleg left to a sloping green. With its tricky putting surface, 5 ranked behind only No. 4 with 29 bogeys in the first round.

Before Jack Nicklaus holed a 5-iron on Thursday and a 7-iron on Saturday there last year the fifth hole had surrendered only four eagles since the first Masters in 1934.

"It's probably the toughest par four on the course," Nicklaus said.

The downhill sixth hole, with its large mound on the right side of the green, has played a major role in deciding the tournament.

In addition to ending Olazabal's hopes in '91, the wicked par-3 also ruined Phil Mickelson last year. Mickelson's 7-iron flew the green, then his putt from the fringe slid down the green and off the front.

Mickelson followed his double bogey there with a bogey on the 360-yard, par-4 seventh, which ties No. 3 as the shortest par-4.

Though No. 7 usually offers some relief from the previous four holes, Huston, Chip Beck and Payne Stewart all double-bogeyed, and Loren Roberts triple-bogeyed it last year.

No. 8, a 535-yard par-5, is a potential swing hole. During the two Masters that Watson won, in 1977 and '81, he birdied the par-5 eighth every day. And Zoeller played it at five under to claim his title.

Nine, a 435-yard par-4, seems like a simple hole because drives roll downhill, setting up short approaches. But it is no bargain. Players often are faced with downhill lies to the elevated green. Last year, John Daly hit a gentle putt, but it slid off the green 30 yards back down the fairway for an eventual double bogey.

Despite its tales of woe, the front side remains a hidden jewel. Irving's Paul Stankowski, a Masters rookie, said he had memorized the back nine from watching it on television so many times.

But when he stepped to the first tee for his first practice round Tuesday, Stankowski almost needed a compass to get around. He had no idea what adventures awaited him.

"I stood on the first tee and thought, 'This is No. 1'?" Stankowski said. "It was a great feeling. But I had a better time at No. 12 because I was familiar with it."

The Fateful Corner— Amen Corner

A Reflective Look Back at the Masters Confirms History's Affinity for the 12th and 13th

by Herbert Warren Wind, *Sports Illustrated*, April 21, 1958

On the afternoon before the start of the recent Masters golf tournament, a wonderfully evocative ceremony took place at the farthest reach of the Augusta National course—down in the Amen Corner where Rae's Creek intersects the 13th fairway near the tee, then parallels the front edge of the green on the short 12th and finally swirls alongside the 11th green. On that afternoon, with Bob Jones investing the occasion with his invariable flavor, two new bridges across the creek were officially dedicated: one (leading to the 12th green) to Ben Hogan, commemorating his record score of 274 in the 1953 tournament; the other (leading back to the fairway from the 13th tee) to Byron Nelson, commemorating his great burst in the 1937 Masters when, trailing Ralph Guldahl by four strokes on the last round, he played a birdie 2 on the 12th and an eagle 3 on the 13th, made up six strokes on Guldahl (who had taken a 5 and a 6 on these holes) and rolled on to victory. While Nelson's exploit is certainly the most striking illustration of what can happen at this particular bend of the course, history has had a way of "affixing" itself to these two holes and especially to the 13th, a 475-yard par 5 which doglegs to the left, a beautiful hole scenically and a triumph of strategic design since a first-class golfer must always choose between attempting to carry with his second shot the arm of Rae's Creek that guards the green or playing safely short on his second and settling, in most cases then, for a fairly modest par. Rebounding from his disappointment in 1937, Gudahl virtually clinched the 1939 Masters when he gambled on carrying the creek with his second and picked up an eagle for his intrepidness when his superb spoon finished four feet from the flag. In more recent years, it was on the 13th that Billy Joe Patton met his Waterloo in '54 when he caught the creek with his perhaps over-bold second and ended up with a 7; it was there the same season that Sam Snead may have won his playoff with Hogan when he birdied the hole and took a lead he never relinquished; and it was there in '55 that the eventual winner, Cary Middlecoff, nursing a very hot streak on his second round, brought it to a roaring climax by getting home in 2 and then holing a putt from the back of the green that could have been no less than 75 feet long. What a player does on the 17 other holes— or, if you will, on the 68 other holes—is always significant and often critical, but the point is that no one is pushing the facts around when he remarks that the events which take place on the 13th have an odd way of proving to be strangely conclusive in the Masters. They were this year once again.

On the final round, the new champion, Arnold Palmer, the co-leader with Sam Snead at the end of the first three rounds with a total of 211, was paired with the bona fide sensation, Ken Venturi (214). The two young men were the first contenders to go out, which is important to keep in mind. Although a dozen players were grouped between 211 and 215 as the final day began, by the time Palmer and Venturi came to the 12th hole it seemed fairly certain that the winner of their duel might well turn out to be the winner of the tournament. I limit this to fairly certain for—though many of the contending dozen had ruined their chances on the first nine—Stan Leonard (215), Doug Ford (215), Fred Hawkins (214) and Bo Wininger (213) were working on the subpar rounds at that moment in the long afternoon and were very much in the picture. Arithmetically, however, Palmer was still out in front when he and Venturi prepared to play the 12th, and it looked like they would be pushing one another on to tremendous golf. Venturi had cut one stroke off Palmer's three-stroke lead by going out in 35 and had cut a second shot off it on the 10th (where Palmer went one over). With seven holes to go, then, only one shot separated them.

THE STAGE IS SET

The 12th at the Augusta National, 155 yards long, can be very delicate and dangerous affair when the pin is placed at the far right-hand corner of the green (which it was) and when there is a puffy wind to contend with (which there was). You've got to be up, over Rae's Creek—that's for sure. But you can't take too much club, because the green is extremely thin and on the far side a high bank of rough rises abruptly behind the apron—and you don't want to be there either. Venturi and Palmer both hit their tee shots over the green and into the bank. Venturi's ball kicked down onto the far side of the green, presenting him with a probable 3 (which he went on to make). Palmer's ball struck low on the bank about a foot or so below the bottom rim of the bankside trap and embedded itself. It had rained heavily during the night and early morning, and parts of the course were soggy.

Now the drama began to unfold, and because of the unusual setting it was indeed charged with the quality of theater: only the players, their caddies and officials are allowed beyond the roping around the 12th tee, and one could only watch the pantomime activity taking place on the distant stage of the 12th green and try to decipher what was happening. To begin with, there was an animated and protracted discussion between Palmer and a member of the tournament rules committee, obviously on the subject as to whether or not Palmer could lift his ball without penalty. Apparently the official had decided he couldn't, for Arnold at length addressed the half-buried ball and budged it about a foot and an half with his wedge. It ended up in casual water then, so he lifted and dropped it (patently without penalty) and then chipped close to the pin on his third stroke. He missed the putt and to a 5. This put him a stroke behind Venturi.

Then the situation became really confusing. Palmer did not walk off the green and head for the 13th tee. He returned to the spot in the rough just behind the apron where his ball had been embedded and, with the member of the rules committee standing by, dropped the ball over his shoulder. It rolled down the slope a little, so he placed the ball near the pit-mark. Apparently, now, the official had not been sure of what ruling to make and Palmer was playing a provisional or alternate ball in the event it might later be decided he had a right to lift and drop without penalty. He chipped stone-dead again and this time holed the putt for a 3. Now the question was: Was Palmer's score a 3 or 5?

This question was still hanging in the air heavy and unresolved when, after both players had driven from the 13th, Palmer played the shot that, in retrospect, won the tournament for him. A bit shorter off the tee, Venturi, playing first, had elected to place his second short of the creek with an iron and to take his chances on getting down in 2 from there for his birdie. Palmer, a very strong young man who drives the ball just about as far as anyone in golf (always excepting an on-form George Bayer), was out about 250 yards on his tee shot, a much longer poke than the mere yardage would indicate, for the fairways at Augusta are extremely lush to begin with and the heavy rains had added to their slowness. In any event, Palmer was out far enough to go for the green on his second shot. Earlier in the week, after good drives on this hole, he had played his second with his two-iron. This time, while he probably could have reached with a four-wood, to make sure he carried the creek he took a three-wood, going down the shaft a half-inch or so with his grip. He settled into his stance for the slightly sidehill lie and moved into his swing, very smoothly. He came through with a really beautiful shot. It started out a shade to the right of the pin and, as it rose in its fairly low trajectory, you could see there was a helpful little bit of draw on it that was carrying it away from that twist-back in the creek that hugs the right side of the green. The ball landed comfortably over the hazard and finished hole-high, 18 feet to the left and slightly above the cup.

ACT TWO, SCENE THREE

Then another scene in this unusual and now contrapuntal drama took place. Bill Kerr, a member of the Augusta National Club who is very experienced in rules, although he was not serving on the rules committee this year, had been hurried down to the 13th to lend what assistance he could in clearing up the controversy over Palmer's proper score on the 12th, a terribly important factor at this stage for Palmer, for Venturi, and for everyone in contention. After Palmer had hit his second, Kerr ducked through the ropes onto the fairway, and Palmer related the facts to him. They talked it over for two or three minutes. In Kerr's unofficial opinion, Palmer had had a right to lift—it would still have to be officially decided. As Palmer headed for the green, shouts broke out all along the line as the grapevine communicated the news to the thousands clustered along the hillside that Palmer had been given (however unofficially at this point) a 3 and not a 5.

Palmer is a very resolute customer. From the beginning, believing himself to be entitled to lift on the 12th he had argued his opinion forcefully but not to the point where he had allowed it to upset him. He had hit his great second on the 13th with no particular show of bellicosity but perhaps with a visible pinch more of his always formidable determination. On the green, he proceeded to cap the absorbing crescendo of excitement by holing his 18-footer for and eagle 3. Venturi, having pitched eight feet from the cup on his third, made a very gallant effort to hole for his birdie—and did. However, instead of being a stroke ahead as had appeared to be his position on the 13th tee, he was now two strokes behind with five holes to play.

On the 14th—both players talked the rules question over on the tee with Bob Jones—Venturi fell another shot behind when he three-putted. On the 15th hole Palmer and Venturi were officially notified that Palmer's score on the 12th was a 3. Down the stretch both of them wobbled a bit. Venturi three-putted both the 15th and 16th, though he finished with a fine birdie on the 18th for a 72 and a four-round total of 286. Palmer went 1 over par on the short 16th and three-putted the 18th for a 73 and a total of 284. Palmer's somewhat loose finish ultimately presented two of his pursuers, Fred Hawking and Doug Ford, playing together, incidentally, with a chance to tie if either could birdie the 18th. Hawking, who had come sprinting down the stretch like Silky Sultan with birdies on the 15th and 17th, missed the 16-footer he had to get on the home green. Ford, the defending champion, missed from 12 feet. Ford had previously failed to hole a five-foot putt for a birdie on the 17th, but his best chance, ironically, had come back on the portentous 13th. Nine feet from the cup in 2, the man who is perhaps the finest clutch putter in golf had taken three to get down on the breaking surface of this fast, subtly contoured green. Ford's first putt was running dead for the cup when, a foot from the hole, it slid a hair off the line to the left. The putt he was left with coming back couldn't have been over 16 inches. It broke like a whip, caught only a corner, stayed out.

The Rules of golf are very touchy and troublous things to administer, and my own feeling on the subject is that if a man is notified he has been appointed to serve on the rules committee for a certain tournament he should instantly remember that he must attend an important business meeting in Khartoum and tender his exquisite regrets to the tournament committee.

Granting the difficulty of the job, it was nonetheless unfortunate that the member of the rules committee working the 12th hole sector didn't know his job well enough to make an immediate and proper decision on the buried ball. In truth, as rules go, it wasn't a really tough one or an involved one. Because of the soggy condition of parts of the course after the heavy rains, the tournament committee had involved for the final day of play a local rule permitting the players to lift, clean, and drop without penalty any ball which became embedded "through the green" in its own pit-mark. (You will find this explained under "Local Rules" on page 58 of the 1958 USGA Rules Book.) Since the term "through the green" takes in all parts of the course except trees, greens, sand traps, and water hazards, it clearly applied to the rough in which Palmer's ball pitched and stuck. One possible explanation of the indecisiveness of the official who was handling the 12th was the fact that the ball was embedded only a foot or so below the bankside trap and, since some of the sand had been washed out of the traps by the rains, he may have been uncertain whether or not the area in question was rough or part of the hazard. However, the ball clearly lay below the well-defined outline of the trap.

All in all, it was unfortunate that the rules question arose at such a crucial juncture of the tournament, and it was extremely fortunate that the confusion which developed did not untowardly affect the play of the contenders or the ultimate winning and losing of the tournament.

The 12th

by Rick Reilly, *Sports Illustrated*, April 2, 1990

Don't give me the 18th at Pebble Beach. Or the 8th at Pine Valley. The 17th at Sawgrass? *Pleeeeease*. Don't tell me about number 1 at Merion. O.K., the pins have baskets instead of flags. Call the weavers' union. You can keep the 16th at Cypress Point, too. I don't know anybody who has made a par at the 16th at Cypress Point in my lifetime, and I won't in the next one, so why discuss it? If that hole is a par-3, how come you have to hit a driver?

No, the *best* hole in the country is a hellacious, wonderful, terrifying, simple, treacherous, impossible, perfect molar-knocker of a par-3. It's a hole you play with a seven-iron, a sand wedge and eight weeks of scuba lessons. The best hole in the country is the 12th at Augusta National. Everything else is the front nine at the Sturgeon Bay Night Links.

Lloyd Mangrum called the 12th "the meanest little hole in the world." Jack Nicklaus calls it "the hardest tournament hole in golf." Fuzzy Zoeller calls it "the spookiest little par-3 we play."

More green jackets have been lost at the 12th than at the Augusta City Dry Cleaners. When the Masters comes to shove next Sunday, you can bet somebody is going to walk away from 12 looking as though he had just heard from the IRS. Or *60 Minutes*. Tom Weiskopf made a 13 there once. He bounced back the next day with a 7. That was the last time anybody saw him with hair.

Sam Snead once made an 8 there and withdrew. Toney Penna hit the flagstick and *still* made 5. Gary Player putted off the green twice—on consecutive days. Twelve could drive a Baptist to drink.

Don't come to the 12th tee with a little fear hidden in your sock. Or a loop at the top. Or the Sunday Masters lead. You'll end up with a wadded acceptance speech and a wet Foot-Joy.

In 1973, J.C. Snead doubled it in the final round and lost by a shot to Tommy Aaron. In 1977, Hubert Green was four under par through 11 holes on Friday when he buried his tee shot in a back bunker, beat his bunker blast across the green and into the creek, dropped another ball in the bunker, chipped out to 20 feet and made it for double bogey. He took himself out of the tournament on that hole, but it was a hell of a nice putt.

Jack Nicklaus might have a green coat for every day of the week right now if he hadn't double-bogeyed 12 on Saturday in 1981. He lost by two shots to Tom Watson. You'll recall that when Nicklaus did win again (1986), his drop-dead 30 on the back nine Sunday included a bogey on 12. If he just makes a par there, he shoots 29 and is immediately given the southeastern quadrant of the United States.

Gary Player had the Masters won in 1962 until he bogeyed 12 on Sunday and fell into a three-way tie. In the 18-hole playoff the next day, he came to 12 with a three-shot lead and bogeyed it *again*. Bye. In 1964, Dave Marr was three back and on a run when he skipped one off the water, onto the bank and back in the water. Glory has a funny way of going glug, glug at 12.

In 1982, Seve Ballesteros bogeyed it Sunday and lost by one. On the last day in 1984, Larry Nelson came to the 12th nipping at Ben Crenshaw's spikes. Nelson was within one shot, but couldn't decide between a six-iron and a seven-iron. He should've chosen a waffle iron. "I hit it so bad I didn't know whether to tell it to get up or get down," says Nelson. It bisected the creek perfectly. Nelson made a 5 and finished fourth. In 1987, Jodie Mudd bogeyed the hole twice and doubled it once and lost by a shot.

This is a hole that proves you don't need 230 yards, six miles of railroad ties and an island green surrounded by alligator purses to be great. "If holes were cars," says Peter Jacobsen, "the 12th would be a Cadillac and the 17th at Sawgrass would be a Yugo." Says Robert Trent Jones Jr., a golf course architect, "It's the perfect example of less architecture, more golf."

The funny thing is, from the tee it looks like a Twinkie. It's just a friendly little 155-yard par-3 with a babbling brook running in front of the green and a happy grove of pine trees swaying behind it. And it'll rip your lips off. It has broken more men than bad whiskey and the over-under put together.

It's a pampered little par-3. It even has a thermostat. Since its green gets very little sunlight, it can be ruined by a frost. In 1981, they meticulously dug it up, installed water pipes 10 inches underneath the surface and put it back together. Now, if it gets too cold, they run 60° to 80° water through the pipes.

What they ought to do is bronze it. The 12th hole has more history behind it than Helen Hayes. For one thing, the bridge that crosses Rae's Creek is known as the Hogan bridge. A plaque there commemorates Ben Hogan's thrilling 274 in the Masters in 1953. Just try to walk across that thing without getting goose bumps the size of Pinnacles. It was on the tee at the 12th in 1964 that a nervous Nicklaus cold-shanked an eight-iron. Bobby Jones, his idol, was watching.

The green is about as big as the Des Moines phone book—only nine yards deep in some places, and 35 yards wide. There are three bunkers guarding it: two in back and one in front. Better to have died as a young boy than to get stuck in one of those back bunkers. You'll be faced with a downhill blast to a downhill green that is only slighter faster than the roof of the Transamerica building.

Jones, who designed the course with the Scottish architect Alister MacKenzie, once wrote about the 12th, "Here the distance must be gauged very accurately, and the wind sweeping down along Rae's Creek is often deceptive to the player standing on the tee about to hit.... Once the tee shot has been played into the creek, the short pitch to the shallow green is terrifying indeed."

What's even more terrifying, indeed, is that it's all tucked back into a nook of pines that makes the wind swirl in, out and around the hole. As such, it tortures the best golfers in the world. There are more theories about how to play the wind at 12 than Ping has lawyers. Hogan once said, "Never hit on 12 until you feel the wind on your cheek." Ken Venturi says to look at the flags on 11 and 12, because they're never up at the same time. Don't hit when the flag is down at 12, he says. Player says, "If the flag on 11 is blowing left to right and the flag on 12 is blowing right to left, pay no attention to what's happening at 11." Zoeller watches the trees on the far side of the 13th tee to see where the wind is coming from. Jacobsen says he looks at everything, including the fans behind him. Curtis Strange looks at the water and at the flags. And then there's Green: "They say if the dogwood tree on the right of the 13th tee is moving, then the wind is blowing over the 12th green, and when the dogwood stops moving, there's no wind. I don't believe it."

Bob Rosburg, in the days before he had an antenna growing out of his ear, came to the hole on a windy day and hit a four-iron. Now, Rosburg was never known as the Arnold Schwarzenegger of golf. In fact, it was said that nobody hit more frog hairs in regulation than Rosburg. But on this particular hole, the wind died just as he hit, and Rosburg's ball didn't just clear the water, it cleared the green, the back bunkers, the terraces behind the green and the fence behind the terraces. It ended up on the 9th hole of the bordering Augusta Country Club. *You got a line on that, Rossi?*

So Rosburg had to retee. The wind came up again. What to do? Rosburg swallowed hard and kept the very same club in his hand. This time, his ball landed 15 feet from the pin and he made the most maddening 5 in the history of golf.

Playing with Rosburg that day was Arnold Palmer, who could sympathize. The wind at 12 probably cost him the 1959 Masters. Leading the tournament the last day, Palmer hit a shot that the wind knocked into the creek. He dropped, pitched over the creek and the green, chipped back again and two-putted for a 6. Palmer finished third, two shots behind the winner, Art Wall Jr. Cold-blooded little hole, isn't it?

Nicklaus has a rule for the 12th: Don't go for the pin if it's on the right. Hit for the middle of the green, make your par and get out while you can. There is not enough room, and too much wind, sand and water to go for it. "It comes down to whether you want to keep it in play, or go for a 2 and come away with a 5," Nicklaus says. He must know what he's doing. Until he turned 40, his cumulative score on 12 was even par.

Only three men have made a hole in one at 12 in the Masters—probably because everybody is so scared of it—and each ace comes with a story.

In 1947, Claude Harmon was playing with Hogan. Now, to find two more opposite personalities would have taken six engineers and three computers. It would be sort of like pairing Gary McCord with J.C. Snead. On the golf course Hogan had all the personality of magnesium. Harmon, on the other hand, was a prince among club professionals and was renowned as a charming teacher. He taught four presidents—Eisenhower, Kennedy, Nixon and Ford—not to mention King Hassan II of Morocco.

Anyway, Harmon was your basic hail-fellow-well-met. Hogan was not. On that day Harmon had the honor at 12. He stepped up and knocked the ball into the hole for the first-ever ace there during the Masters. Hogan didn't say a word. Not a shake of the hand, not a "well done," zip. Instead, he took one last puff of his unfiltered cigarette, stepped up to the ball and hit it a few feet past the cup.

As the crowd continued to roar for Harmon, Hogan's eyes never wavered. Harmon retrieved his ball from the hole, accepted the plaudits due him, then moved out of the way. Hogan paced around his putt, stared it down, then stroked it in for a birdie.

As the two made their way to the 13th tee, Hogan finally spoke up.

"You know, Claude," Hogan said. "That's the first 2 I've ever made on that hole."

Oddly, the two were close friends.

In 1959, William Hyndman III, an amateur, made the second ace at 12, thanks to the help of his caddie, who went by the name of First Baseman.

"What's it going to take, First Baseman?"

"Six-iron," said the caddie.

"Six-iron? That's too much," said Hyndman. "Nope. Got to step up and get it all."

And that's exactly what Hyndman did. The ball took one hop past the pin and spun back into the hole. Touch 'em all.

When Curtis Strange came to the tee in 1988, he was lousy a bet to make 1. He had four-putted the unforgivably slick 9th green and was heard to say as he left, "And you people are paying good money to watch this—." The pin on 12 that day was in the one place where you're not *supposed* to make a hole in one—far right. But Strange was going so bad he needed to make some birdies just to make the cut. He aimed slightly left of the pin—still a dicey idea at best—and let fly. "I pushed it perfectly," Strange remembers. It hit the green and rolled six or seven feet into the hole for an ace.

But that's when Curtis did something strange. He picked up the ball and threw it in the creek. "I don't know why I did it," Strange says. "I just thought, This'll do something for the people. It was spontaneous. I didn't think about it. It had nothing to do with what I'd done the rest of the day."

Some sportswriters thought Strange impudent. "He could've given it to his grandchildren," they said. Says Strange, "I hope I have something better to leave my grandchildren than a golf ball."

Some people think it made perfect sense. "All the gods of golf are down there in that corner anyway," says Zoeller. "If you beat that hole, you *better* give them something."

It was such an odd thing to do—to throwaway a museum piece—that people got suspicious. One rumor went that when Strange got the ball out of the hole, he realized he'd been playing the wrong one. *That's* why he threw it in the water. So nobody could tell on him. There was also the story that Strange didn't want the standard golfer-kisses-golf-ball picture in the papers the next day, because he wasn't playing the brand of ball he was paid to play. Bull pucky, says Strange. Go find it yourself, and you'll see.

If you ever get a wild hair and an oxygen tank and decide to go looking for Strange's ball—a Maxfli DDH, he thinks—pick up half a dozen or so of Tom Weiskopf's while you're at it, will you?

The 12th was to Weiskopf what the *Exxon Valdez* was to shrimp. Weiskopf loved the Masters. "Every year, after I open my Christmas presents, I start thinking about the Masters," he used to say. On Thursday in 1980, the pin was, typically, front left, the easiest of all pin placements because you can shoot for it. Better yet, there was no wind. Weiskopf took an eight-iron and sailed it to the front fringe, where it hit, took a little skip-hop forward toward the pin, then spun rapidly and cruelly back into Rae's Creek.

Bad break. Time to drop a ball on the far side of the water and try again, hitting 3. Only Weiskopf didn't lay up next to the creek, he went farther back—about 60 yards from the hole. "I didn't want a little wedge. I wanted a half or three-quarter wedge."

He hit the exact same shot. Fringe. Skip-hop. Spin back into Rae's Creek. Hitting 5. "Now I'm pissed," he recalls.

Weiskopf decided to drop again in the same place—60 yards back. Even Weiskopf is not sure why. "You're embarrassed," he says. "You're in a fog. You're standing in front of the world, and it's like you're playing the hole naked."

This time his drop rolled into a barren spot and his wedge shot did a little Greg Louganis dead into the water. Hitting 7.

Weiskopf wasn't moving an inch. He was determined to drop in the same place, 60 yards from the hole. Who knows what happens to the mind in situations such at these? My theory is that some madness chemical fires in the brain and reason gets cleat marks in its head.

Madness: *We are going to prove to the world that this was the place to drop! I don't care if we blow the tournament and the next six tournaments after this and we have to go back to frying burgers at the Dairy Queen!#!&!*

Reason: *This is crazy. Let's go up and drop right next to the creek like we should have the first time. Whaddya say, fellas?*

Madness: (Cleatstomp.)

Another drop. Another terrible shot. Another sinking feeling. Hitting 9.

There was absolute and funereal silence now. It's quiet at Amen Corner, anyway. The fans are kept about 20 yards behind the 12th tee. But now there was nothing. No groans, no tears, no muttering, no go-get-'ems—just dead, cold silence, the kind you would get in the car for about three miles after your dad blew up.

Weiskopf's forehead was so hot you could stir-fry on it. Drop again. Same spot again. Splash again. Hitting 11.

One person in the crowd began crying. It was Weiskopf's wife, Jeanne. You make big plans, rent a house, bring the kids, hire a nanny, fly to Augusta, go to all the pretournament parties, and then, in one two-minute span of golf, it all goes *splerch*. Standing next to Jeanne was their close friend Tom Culver. Culver hugged her and said, tenderly, "Jeanne ... "

"Yes, Tom?" she said, choking on the heartache. "You don't suppose he's using new balls, do you?"

Finally, Weiskopf hit his sixth ball to the back edge of the green, where, somehow, it stayed, and he two-putted for a 13, the highest score ever taken on any par-3, or par-4, in the history of the Masters. Tommy Nakajima had a 13 on number 13 in 1978, but at least that hole is a par-5.

If I were Weiskopf, here is how I would handle the obvious question the rest of my days. It's the way Palmer explained a 12 he made in the 1961 L.A. Open.

Q: "Thirteen? How the hell did you make 13 on a par-3?"

A: "Missed a 20-footer for 12."

When Weiskopf came to the hole the next day, he was mostly killing time until his plane left town. He had no choice but to go for the pin and try to make an eagle. He hit his first shot off the bank and into the water, and he chose not even to walk anywhere near the creek. He simply put another tee in the ground and hit again. "I thought my chances were better."

Reason: *"Look, this is ...."*

Madness: *"Just shut the hell up."*

He hit another one in the creek, his seventh surly contribution to the Augusta waterway system in two days. He teed it up again. This was now becoming a scientific quest: Could a lofted metal club send a spheroid over an active body of water? This one he knocked on and two-putted for a 7. He finished with a 79. His two-day average for the 12th: 10. If they ever build a memorial to Weiskopf, it had better be waterproof.

If there was one man who allowed himself a slight grin at Weiskopf's 13, it was Dow Finsterwald, who made 11 there in 1951 and has been walking around having to answer for it ever since. Finsterwald was 21 when he washed four balls in Rae's Creek. His playing partner that day, the late Denny Shute, made a birdie 2. As they were walking off the green, Shute said to Finsterwald, "Well, son, we had a good best ball, anyway."

What's to be ashamed of? This hole has taken a mouthful out of some of the most famous hindquarters in golf. Consider: Deane Beman (two 7s), Billy Casper (8), Ray Floyd (two 7s), Bob Murphy (8), Sam Snead (8), Royal and Ancient secretary Michael Bonallack (a 6 and a 7), David Graham (7), Charles Coody (two 7s), Bruce Crampton (7), Ben Crenshaw (7), Lon Hinkle (7), Craig Wood (8), Al Mengert (8), David Edwards (8) and Graham Marsh (8). And you thought you would never see a snowman in Georgia.

Payne Stewart is the latest famous notch 12 has cut in the Hogan bridge. It was 1985, the final round, and Stewart was in contention to win the tournament. He hit an eight-iron on nothing but the sweet spot, and the ball flew into the right back bunker. His bunker shot rolled just past the pin. And just past the green. And just past the fringe, just past the rough, just past the bank and down into Weiskopf's Creek.

Having dropped another ball on the tee side of the creek, Stewart hit a pitch that landed right next to the hole, then spun back into a liquid home. Now he was hitting 6. It was not a good time to ask him if he still felt he had a chance to win the tournament.

"All I could see was that green jacket getting ripped right out of my closet," Stewart remembers. What to do but try it again? This time Stewart was too conscious of the water, and he hit the ball right back to square one—the bunker. He chopped it out of there like a man might chop at a radioactive weed, with more fear than hope. The ball trickled onto the green and stayed, and he two-putted for a 9, more than enough to cost him the championship.

A chip out of that bunker can give you a facial tic. If you don't hit it just tenderly enough, you can easily watch your Titleist do a little 23 skiddoo over the green and into the water. In 1966, Player hit a Thursday tee shot that slammed down so deep into the bank behind the back bunkers that you could barely see the ball. Player considered taking a drop and hitting 3, and he probably should have, but he was no doubt overcome by the madness secretions. He decided to try to slap it out, let it run feebly into the bunker below and hit it again. But Player goofed. He hit too hard, and the ball scooted across the bunker, over the fringe, onto the green and into the cup for a 2. "One hundred percent luck," says Player.

But there have been a whole lot more tears at 12 than laughs. Take what happened to Bobby Mitchell. He lost more than a few balls and a tournament at 12. He might have lost a career.

It was 1972, and Mitchell was a promising 29-year-old on the Tour. He played brilliantly at Augusta that week—17 holes a day. His week at 12 only Stephen King could love: 5-5-5-4, seven over par. Yet he lost the tournament to Nicklaus by only three shots. "I made double bogey every way you could think of," says Mitchell, who is aiming toward a comeback on the Senior tour. "I got stuck up in the honeysuckle one day, hit it into the water the next and got buried in the bunker another day. That dang hole cost me the tournament." He won the Tournament of Champions two weeks later and finished 11th on the money list that year, but after that he never won another tournament and never finished in the top 60 on the money list again.

Twelve has been a thorn in golfers' Sansabelts since the first Masters, in 1934, when Ed Dudley made four 4s there and lost the tournament by three shots. Three years later, Ralph Guldahl was running away with it when he came to 12, plunked his shot into the creek, chipped too far and carded a little 5. That left Byron Nelson to go on such a tear—a 2 on 12 and a 3 on 13—that he not only won the tournament, but also they put up a bridge in honor of his run. It spans Rae's Creek between the 13th tee and the fairway.

Sam Snead never lost a tournament at 12, but he almost did. In 1952, he and Hogan were tied starting the final round. Snead led by one as he came to 12. His tee shot, though, flew dead into the creek. Unluckily, the ball he dropped on the tee side of the creek landed in a depression. He flailed at it and plopped it barely over the water onto the grassy slope short of the green. He was lying 3, and still he wasn't on the green.

In those days, Snead had a caddie named O'Brien, nothing else, just O'Brien. O'Brien caddied for Snead in the Masters he won in 1949 and would again when he won in 1954. But this time victory looked impossible. Snead would make 6 at the 12th, sure as azaleas bloom in March. But that's when O'Brien looked at him and said, "We ain't out of this tournament yet, Sam." At which Snead chipped the ball, only to discover it had a lump of mud on it. Nevertheless, the ball wobbled across the green, mud and all, right into the cup. He went on to birdie 13 and 16, and beat Jackie Burke Jr. by four shots. "That was the best 4 I ever made in my life," Snead says.

But nobody lost and won more at 12 in one year than Venturi and Palmer in 1958. You could say entire careers were at stake.

Venturi was the talk of the Tour. Two years earlier, playing as an amateur in his first Masters, he had led until the final day, when he shot 80 and finished second to Burke. In a lot of ways, Venturi was like Palmer himself—handsome, rugged and preposterously talented. In fact, sportswriters considered Venturi more likely than Palmer to win that year.

On Sunday, Venturi was one shot down to Palmer. His tee shot on 12 landed in the middle of the green and stayed there for what looked like an easy par. Palmer's ball, though, sailed over the green, hit in the grass between the right back bunker and the green and plugged.

When Palmer got to the ball, he told the rules official there, the late Arthur Lacey, that he would be playing the embedded-ball rule and would take a free drop. It had rained the night before and again early in the morning, making the grounds sodden and squishy. A local rule at Augusta National allowed relief from an embedded ball "through the green," which means damn near anywhere you want except the tee, the green and the hazards.

Lacey, wrongheadedly, was having none of it.

"Not at Augusta you don't," Lacey is supposed to have said. Lacey was a fine British golfer from Buckinghamshire who had played on two British Ryder Cup teams.

"I will too," said Palmer from Latrobeshire, getting his fur up. "It's my right."

The two argued a bit more, but neither was to be swayed. Now, here's where things got cloudy. Palmer says he announced then and there to Lacey and anybody else around that he was going to play a second ball and record both scores, to be figured out by somebody bigger than Lacey as the day went on.

Palmer slapped at the embedded ball and moved it only about a foot and a half. Palmer chipped it close but missed the putt and took a 5. Venturi took 3.

Palmer then went back to the scene of the crime—the site of the original embedded ball—and dropped a new ball. Across the green, Venturi sat on his golf bag and whispered to his caddie, "We're going to win this tournament."

This time Palmer chipped it dead stony and made the putt for a 3. So which was it, a 3 or a 5?

Palmer must have thought it was going to be ruled a 5, because he nearly came out of his shoes with his drive on the par-5 13th. In fact, he hit it so far that he was in a position to go for the green in 2. Venturi recalls that as the two walked along the 13th fairway, Palmer said, "I know they're going to give me a 5."

In fact, Venturi says that's why Palmer went for the green with his second shot on 13—to make up ground. He hit a gorgeous three-wood that checked up nicely on the green, and he sank the 18-foot putt for an eagle 3. Venturi made a birdie 4.

As they were playing the 14th, there suddenly were war whoops from the crowd—Armyish whoops. The scoreboard showed that Palmer's 5 on the 12th had been changed to a 3. Now, instead of the two being tied, Palmer led by two. Venturi was so rattled that he three-putted the 14th green, and after Palmer was given official word of the ruling on the 15th fairway, Venturi also three-putted the 15th and 16th. Palmer won by two, 284-286.

Venturi agrees that Lacey blew the call—Palmer was allowed a drop there—but he says the balls should have been played concurrently. "Suppose you sink the first ball," says Venturi. "You're not going to go back and play a provisional then, are you? You declare and then you finish with the farthest ball out and work in. If you were on a par-5 and decided to declare a provisional, you wouldn't finish out with the first ball and then walk 350 yards back and play the next one, would you?"

The rule book for 1958 seems to support Venturi. For one thing, you definitely do have to declare *before* playing either ball, as Palmer did. For another, it reads, "When a competitor is doubtful of his rights or procedure, he may play out the hole with the ball in play and, at the same time, complete the play of the hole with a second ball." Oops. Palmer, who seldom involves himself in controversy, didn't want to touch this one with a 40-foot two-iron. He insists that he played everything exactly by the book.

Palmer eventually won eight majors. Venturi never did win the Masters, and his only major victory was the 1964 U.S. Open. Who knows how different things might have been if Palmer had been stuck with 5 at number 12 instead of 3?

Venturi isn't stewing about it. "I like my position in life now," he says, currently in his 23rd year as a CBS golf analyst. "There were a lot of guys who wanted to beat me back then. And now there are even more guys who want my job."

And Palmer isn't exactly destitute, either.

Here's one last story about the 12th. It was 1963, and the late Champagne Tony Lema was having a rocky Sunday. He had missed a short putt on the 10th hole and three-putted the 11th. Now on 12 he hit a good shot, which left him eight feet from the cup, but his putt just missed. Lema couldn't stand it. He let go a string of oaths that would make a Jersey longshoreman blush. Just then he realized that his playing partner, a Nationalist Chinese named Chen Ching-po, was looking at him curiously.

Embarrassed, Lema apologized for using such language "in front of a visitor to our country."

"Is all right," said Chen. "If I knew those words I would use them myself."

The Masters Look

Flowering Fairway Suits Premier Golf Course to a Tee

by Mark Stith, *The Atlanta Journal Constitution*, April 3, 1988

Tommy Crenshaw, nurseryman for the Augusta National Golf Club, is sitting in a golf cart and looking out onto the broad, glistening green fairway sloping towards Rae's Creek. A stiff, cold wind buffets the branches of tall pines bordering the fairway in the distance. Were it not for the wind, it would be an absolutely first-rate day for golf.

On the hilltop behind Crenshaw sits Fruitlands, the historic white-columned clubhouse, framed by a cloudless, ice-blue sky. The panorama brings to mind Atlantan Bobby Jones' account of his first visit, some 60 years ago, to what was to become—with his guidance—one of the premier golf courses in the world.

"The networks don't get here until the last minute," Crenshaw says, with a bit of nervous anticipation. Crenshaw, golf course supervisor Paul Latshaw and their crews are responsible for making certain that the legendary

"Masters look" will be at its prime when the nation tunes in April 7-10 to watch the 1988 Masters Golf Tournament, the most popular golf tournament on television.

The tournament Jones started in 1934—then modestly titled the Augusta National Invitational—is just around the corner. Right now in Augusta, it's peaceful and quiet, the proverbial calm before the storm of players, fans and media that will soon converge on this pastoral setting.

This is a special place. The world of golf knows it; the Masters, as the tournament would soon become known, has been called the most prestigious tournament on the Professional Golfers' Association (PGA) tour, and is one of four "Grand Slam" events. (The others are the PGA, the U.S. Open and the British Open.) It's somehow fitting that the only person to win golf's Grand Slam (at that time the U.S. Open and Amateur, and the British Open and Amateur) was Bobby Jones.

But the coveted green champion's jacket isn't the only greenery worth noting at the Augusta National. Part of the rich tradition of the Augusta National comes from the beautifully landscaped grounds, and it seems that every golf course—new or old, North or South—is compared to Augusta National's often-imitated layout and appearance.

In fact, if you have azaleas, camellias, privet or other popular plants on your property, you may have a bit of the "Masters look" in your own yard, thanks to the pioneering efforts of a previous owner of Fruitlands, one Baron Prosper Julius Alphonse Berckmans. The Belgian-born Berckmans converted the 365-acre property into one of the South's largest nurseries from an indigo plantation in the mid-1800s.

From its modest, hedge-lined members' entrance off strip-developed and noisy Washington Road (a small wooden sign and guardhouse could be easily overlooked), the Augusta National's narrow, magnolia-lined road leads to the clubhouse and begins a horticultural history lesson.

It's a lesson nowhere near as well-known and certainly less dramatic than the landmark golf played here by Snead, Hogan, Nicklaus, Palmer and other golf superstars past and present. But it's a story that's just as impressive and certainly as influential.

The late H.H. Hume, a noted expert on azaleas, stated that azaleas probably would not have become popular in America had it not been for Berckmans' efforts. By 1861, he had imported over 40 varieties of this popular flowering shrub, and brought in camellias from Japan, France, England and Belgium.

Some of the original plants grown by Berckmans exist to this day on the Augusta National. Magnolia Lane's rows of namesake trees began as seeds planted around 1858 by Berckmans: slight variations among them, such as leaf and flower traits, indicate the variation in seed-grown magnolias from the parent.

A hedge of amur privet on the premises, called the "Mother Hedge," began from 10 plants imported from France about 1860 and is said to be the source of all the innumerable amur privet in the South. A Japanese wisteria, recognized as the first wisteria to be grown in America, has matured to a massive, over-30-inch-diameter trunk growing near the clubhouse.

Two types of arborvitae, 'Berckmans Golden' and 'Berckmans Golden Spire,' were developed at Fruitlands in 1887. Chinese holly, Fortune's osmanthus and a variety of trailing juniper, all used in residential landscapes today, were imported from Japan between 1860 and 1880.

To say that Berckmans planted fruit trees is like noting that Coke makes a diet drink. No less than 1,300 varieties of pears, 900 of apples, and 300 varieties of grapes were offered by Fruitlands Nursery in its 1860s catalogs, which brought in orders from all over the world.

Because of his pioneering work in developing and marketing suitable varieties of peach trees for the South, Berckmans has been called "the father of peach culture in the South." At one time, three of the five major types of peaches grown in the South were introduced or improved by Berckmans.

When Berckmans died in 1910, he left the estate to his young widow, who let the nursery business founder. Berckmans' three sons promptly left Fruitlands, and the abandoned property was sold in 1925 to a Miami hotel owner, Commodore J. Perry Stoltz, who planned to level the mansion and build a 15-story luxury hotel.

But the hotel plans went sour, and Jones and some business associates, including Clifford Roberts, a New York investment banker, purchased Fruitlands in 1931 from the bankrupt Stoltz for $70,000 (less than $200 an acre).

Jones wasted no time in seeing his dream course take shape. He enlisted the help of a master golf course physician-turned-architect, Dr. Alister MacKenzie, and work began on the course that same year. Two of Berckmans' sons, P.J.A. Jr. and Louis Alphonse, returned to the estate to give expert guidance and care for the treasure of valuable plants that remained.

Berckmans' plant legacy was to play a key role in the success of the course design. Some 4,000 trees and shrubs were saved and relocated during construction. L.A. Berckmans suggested to Jones that each hole be named after a distinctive plant grown at the old nursery. Concentrating plants around holes named for them would further reinforce the theme.

For example, around hole No. 13, appropriately named "Azalea," 400 2-year-old azaleas were planted in 1932. Today, they provide waves of color, just in time for the golfers—and the television cameras. The other 17 holes took their inspiration from such beautiful trees and shrubs as dogwood, redbud, crabapple, camellia and peach.

Cuttings taken from other azaleas and camellias on the property yielded 5,000 plants installed throughout the course. Seeds from the citronella (lemon hedge) growing on the northern edge of the property produced 10,000 plants used along the eastern and southern property lines. Over 75,000 plants and more than 350 different varieties have been installed since 1935.

The beautification efforts continue to this day at the Augusta National. Nurseryman Crenshaw and course supervisor Latshaw are well aware of the high reputation the Masters has achieved in its short history (it's the youngest of the Grand Slam events and the only one played on the same course year after year).

"No doubt about it," said Latshaw, who came here two years ago from Oakmont Country Club in Pittsburgh and had seen that course through a U.S. Open and a PGA championship. "This club has set standards for the whole country as far as golf is concerned . . . the beauty aspect, and the fact that all the knowledge they've had with tournaments. A lot of things you see at other golf courses during tournaments have been copied from Augusta National."

The course is designed for winter play—most of the club members are from the North, and the course is closed from June to mid-October. The Bermuda grass used for the fairways goes dormant and turns brown in winter, and is overseeded with ryegrass for a lush green look. Putting greens are bentgrass, and during tournament time will usually be cut daily. Latshaw maintains an armada of some 30 mowers of all types to keep the living green carpet from becoming a shag rug.

Crenshaw and crew (Latshaw and Crenshaw have a staff of 22) maintain the extensive ornamental plantings as well as implementing new landscape plans, which have recently included areas around the nine-hole par 3 course that borders the Masters' course.

And what if it appears that the azaleas will flower a bit late for tournament time? "There are rumors that we cover the azaleas in plastic to force them to bloom early, but that's not true," Crenshaw said. "We will add some flowers here and there for a little color, though."

Even grand old ladies like the Augusta National aren't above dolling up a bit for the television cameras.

Hole number, name and maximum distance.
1. "Tea Olive." Par 4, 400 yards.
2. "Pink Dogwood." Par 5, 555 yards.

3. "Flowering Peach." Par 4, 360 yards.
4. "Crabapple." Par 3, 205 yards.
5. "Magnolia." Par 4, 435 yards.
6. "Juniper." Par 3, 180 yards.
7. "Pampas." Par 4, 360 yards.
8. "Yellow Jasmine." Par 5, 535 yards.
9. "Carolina Cherry." Par 4, 435 yards.
10. "Camellia." Par 4, 485 yards.
11. "White Dogwood." Par 4, 455 yards.
12. "Golden Bell." Par 3, 155 yards.
13. "Azalea." Par 5, 465 yards.
14. "Chinese Fir." Par 4, 405 yards.
15. "Firethorn." Par 5, 500 yards.
16. "Redbud." Par 3, 170 yards.
17. "Nandina." Par 4, 400 yards.
18. "Holly." Par 4, 405 yards.

Bentgrass Greens Hit Milestone

Faster Strain Has Been Keeping Augusta National's Greens Speedy for 20 Years

by David Westin, *The Augusta Chronicle,* April 5, 2001

It was 20 years ago today that the fire returned to the Augusta National Golf Club's greens.

The introduction of the ice-slick bentgrass strain of grass on the greens has helped give Augusta National the reputation of having among the fastest, if not the fastest, greens in the world.

Before the change from Bermuda grass greens, the Augusta National's greens were fast, but had been losing some speed because of a healthier strain of Bermuda grass.

The bentgrass not only brought the greens back to their former slickness, it also added even more speed.

Other courses might have greens that are as fast, but they don't have the undulations and humps that the Augusta National does. Because of that combination, most golfers give the nod to Augusta National when it comes to speedy greens.

"They have a lot of slope, and they're hillier here and faster," said Davis Love III. "They are probably the most severe we play."

As expected, the bentgrass greens made putting tougher, and scores rose. In the first round of the 1981 Masters, the low score was 69, three shots higher than the previous years' opening round on Bermuda grass greens. The winning score in 1981—8-under-par 280 by Tom Watson—was five shots higher than in 1980.

Just how fast are the greens today? In 1981, they were a 9.9 on the Stimpmeter, the device that measures the average number of feet a ball rolls after being released from a chute.

At the time, Hord Hardin, the Augusta National Golf Club Chairman at the time, said "20 years from now, you'll be able to say that the greens in 1981 were 'x' and now they're 'y.'"

Hardin, who made his comments during the annual chairman's news conference on the eve of the 1981 Masters, had no problem with publicly revealing the speed of the greens.

The philosophy has now changed. Will Nicholson, the chairman of the Augusta National competition committees, said Wednesday that information on the speed of the greens is a club matter.

"It's because we want to concentrate on the course at this time," Nicholson said. "We want the publicity to be on this course and these players. When I give a number about the greens, there's suddenly a bunch of stories about them, and it takes away from the players."

The consensus among the players is that the Augusta National greens read at between 12 and 15 on the Stimpmeter.

"The greens are by far the biggest defense of the golf course," Phil Mickelson said of the Augusta National. "When they get to be very firm, as they have been in some years past, it is the only place that I have ever experienced where I'm trying to two-putt a majority of the 15–20 footers as opposed to making them. I'm just trying to get the ball to stop rolling somewhere near the hole, and it is not always easy to do."

Defending champion Vijay Singh said, "You're always concerned where your next putt is going to come from. You can't just go up there and say, 'Well, I'm just going to have a good run at it' because the next thing you know, you have another 10-footer coming back.

"So it's always in the back of your mind," Singh added. "I think pace on these greens is more important than anything else. I think if you get the pace right, putting is a lot easier."

Golfers these days should be putting the Augusta National greens better than ever. According to Love, more and more fast bentgrass greens are showing up at tournaments on the PGA Tour.

"It used to be this was the only place that had really fast greens," Love said. "But we do play a lot more tournaments that do have them like this. More and more golf course superintendents at clubs have figured out how to do it and have the wherewithal to do it."

They just don't have the slopes and contours that Dr. Alister McKenzie and Bob Jones built into the greens when they co-designed the Augusta National in 1931.

A Crack in the Code

Past Champions End Their Silence and Criticize Course Changes

by Ron Whitten, *Golf Digest*, April 2006

The problem with Augusta National is that it's a national treasure, but those involved with it act as though it's a state secret.

Consider all the changes to the course, the lengthening and tightening during the past eight years. Last summer alone, the club changed six holes, with new back tees, new trees and some bigger, deeper bunkers. Some of those holes had been changed just two years before.

But the club won't divulge the thinking behind such constant course tinkering. Not even to past Masters champions.

Some past champions are frustrated about that, but they won't go on the record. Call it the Code of the Green Jacket: Thou shalt not speak ill of Augusta National in public.

In private, more than one has complained that the course has been stripped of its unique personality, its ebb and flow. Players could thrust and parry, expect birdies on some holes and accept pars on others. But now the course makes everybody play defensively, they say, from the first tee onward. A couple of former champions have suggested that the club keeps changing the layout to hasten their departure from the event entirely, and one even grumbles about the new "butt-ugly bunkers, all shaped like bathtubs."

But stick a microphone in front of them, and they clam up.

The only cracks in that code have come from Arnold Palmer and Jack Nicklaus, both Augusta National members now instead of Masters competitors.

"I think they've ruined it from a tournament standpoint," Nicklaus says. "Augusta has meant a ton to me in my lifetime. It's a big, big part of my life, and I love it. That's why I hate to see them change it."

"I love the place, just love everything that happens there," Palmer says. "But now, I'm not so sure. It's changed dramatically from the course I knew the last 50 years."

These two men, with 10 Masters titles between them, are disappointed that they've not been consulted on any of the changes that have occurred to the course since 1998, despite the fact that (or maybe because) they're both golf course architects. Nicklaus has even been a bit catty about it. He says some changes, which were supervised by consulting golf architect Tom Fazio and his team, looked as if they were done "by somebody who doesn't know how to play golf."

When co-founder Clifford Roberts ruled Augusta, in the club's first 42 years, he still entertained suggestions from past champions. Horton Smith recommended moving the seventh green up the hill, so it was moved. Gene Sarazen suggested a fairway bunker on the second, and it got built. But now, Masters champions have no voice. No one knows who is behind recent design changes. The architect? The Masters chairman? A committee? Who knows? Everything at Augusta seems classified.

Even Fazio, given an opportunity to respond to Nicklaus' comments at a public forum last fall, declined to do so, saying that he defers all comments regarding the course to the club.

Club officials say that statements issued by Augusta National chairman Hootie Johnson should suffice. Johnson assumed his role in 1998, the year Tigerproofing began. The trouble is, Johnson's explanations have been superficial and rote. Here's what he said about changes in 2001: "We're always trying to keep the golf course current with the times ... and maintain its integrity."

And here's what he said last year about the most recent changes: "Our objective is to maintain the integrity and shot values of the golf course as envisioned by Bobby Jones and Alister MacKenzie. ... We will keep the golf course current with the times."

A request for anything of substance regarding the Masters—What's the speed of the greens? Is a former football coach on the tournament committee? Who thought it was a good idea to plant yet another row of trees down the right side of 11?—is met with a resounding refusal to answer.

A lot of this secrecy is just plain silly. For instance, the club has long conducted stealth architecture, adding new features, such as tees and bunkers, while obliterating all traces of the old ones. Back when the club first lengthened the par-4 opening hole, officials still listed it at 400 yards on the scorecard, which led to a joke among players that either the back tee had been moved or the golf shop had.

To the credit of the present administration, the club is frank about the most recent increases in yardage. The course will play 7,445 yards, par 72, this year. That's 155 yards longer than it played in 2005, and 520 yards more than in 1997, the year Tiger Woods won his first Masters.

The first has been stretched to 455 yards. The par-3 fourth is now 240 yards, the former drive-and-pitch seventh is 450 yards, the par-4 11th is 505 yards, the par-5 15th is 530, and the uphill 17th is 440. But don't bother asking for details on why the first hole keeps getting longer, or why the 11th hole has had three new back tees since 2001, or why the 17th tee was shoved over to the left tree line, or whether the club has devised an exit strategy in this escalating war against ever-advancing club and ball technology.

LENGTH ISN'T THE ISSUE

Past champions are on shaky ground when they privately gripe about the new length of Augusta National. No one is forcing them to play the course with persimmon woods and balata balls. If their games can't take advantage of modern technology, and Augusta is just too long for them these days, then their beef is with Father Time, not the Masters chairman.

With the exception of a couple of holes, the yardage added to Augusta National makes perfect sense, given how far many competitive players hit the ball these days. Whether the proper holes have been lengthened is another matter.

But sheer yardage is not what has gotten Jack, Arnie and others of the Old Guard riled up. They're mostly upset about the tightening of many holes, through the use of expanded bunkering, transplanted trees and the introduction of rough, what Augusta National calls, in delusional parlance, "a second cut of fairway."

This is where Jack and Arnie are absolutely right. Far from maintaining the integrity of the design that Jones and MacKenzie envisioned, the changes undertaken since 1998 have abandoned their philosophy of multiple options and different lines of attack.

"They've totally eliminated what Bobby Jones tried to do in the game of golf," Nicklaus says. "Bobby Jones believed golf was primarily a second-shot game. He believed that you should have enough room to drive the ball onto the fairway, but if you put it on the correct side of the fairway, you had an advantage to put the ball toward the hole. He wanted to give you a chance to do that shot."

Gone are Augusta's wide corridors that allowed every competitor to play his own game off the tee, to pick the spot he thought provided the best angle of approach for his trajectory and shot shape. Squeezed-in fairways now dictate the manner of play on every hole. It's as if the Masters Committee thinks it's now running the U.S. Open.

Which makes one wonder just how much research Augusta National has really done regarding the original MacKenzie-Jones design. MacKenzie believed that if a good player hitting good shots couldn't post a good score on one of his courses, then there was something wrong with his design. Jones once wrote that he never intended Augusta National to be a punishing golf course.

Jones and MacKenzie believed in rewarding risk on the golf course. Most of that is gone now. Consider the par-4 first. The optimum angle, particularly when the flag was on the left, had long been from the far right of the wide fairway. Today, that area is rough—not particularly nasty stuff, but enough to affect the spin of the ball.

When the hole measured 400 yards, it took a carry of 247 yards to clear the bunker on the right and gain the best angle. Even in Jack's day, that wasn't much of a carry, not much of a risk. But it was the opening hole. With the tee moved back 55 yards, one would think the carry over the bunker would have increased 55 yards, to 302 yards. But the fairway bunker has been enlarged (and deepened), so it takes a carry of 331 yards to clear it. That's not a carry most players will attempt for their first shot of the day in the Masters.

It's as though, in establishing its new yardages, the club used as its benchmark not the average carry of tour players but the maximum carry of a select few. It has targeted very specific golfers. The carry to the fairway bunker on No. 2 is 319 yards. To clear the second bunker on the fifth hole is 319 yards. To clear the bunker on No. 8 is 319 yards. To reach the second bunker on 18 is 317 yards. It doesn't take much imagination to realize that not much imagination went into establishing these distances.

The best course designs challenge different golfers on different holes. Augusta National used to do that. It no longer does.

It's a shame, too, that the club has eliminated all but one short par 4 on the course. When it measured 360 yards, the seventh was a short 4 for everyone. Short hitters could hit a full-out driver and a wedge, and big hitters had to throttle back with an iron off the tee to leave a full wedge into the green. Now, at 450 yards, the seventh might still be a driver and short iron for

Woods, Mickelson and a few other monster hitters, but many in the field will be hitting long-iron approaches or even hybrids into a tiny green designed to accept high, short-iron shots, not low-trajectory ones.

Last summer, the club also eliminated the old backstop slope on the right side of the seventh green, the one players could rely upon to spin a shot back down toward front-right pin positions. Shots hit to that area will bounce over, into the bunker. The seventh was never that easy. Statistically, it played around par during every Masters. That could go up a half stroke this year.

The club planted many mature loblolly pines along the left of No. 7, too, just because it can, I guess. The club added more trees on the 11th and 17th, to go with ones added during the past four years. Given years of sprawling growth, those trees could make those holes look as narrow as the tee shot on No. 18. Unless some are eliminated. But it's hard to think of trees Augusta has cut down. The Eisenhower Tree at the 17th became famous for the club's refusal to cut it down.

The irony, of course, is that Augusta National used to be the trendsetter in matters of course design. But now it's well behind the curve. While Augusta is on a tree-planting splurge, most other prominent clubs are removing trees, having finally recognized their adverse effects on strategy, playability and turf quality.

Palmer found the new trees an irritation when he recently played the 11th.

"All the area on the right, which had afforded the gallery the opportunity to see, it's totally filled with trees. I was surprised," he says. "And I asked the chairman, who's a friend of mine, 'What are you going to do about the people? Those fans are what make Augusta great.'

"'Well, we can't make everybody happy.' That's what he said. Well, that affects me, and my thoughts about it."

The older pines at Augusta traditionally had a bed of pine needles beneath them, which allowed players to attempt all sorts of recovery shots. The newer pines have rough underneath, deeper than the "second cut," and are planted so close together that the only recovery available is usually a pitch out. It's one more example of how Augusta has stifled some playing options.

RELICS OF HISTORY

For a club that takes immense pride in its history, it certainly has a cavalier attitude toward certain parts of that history. From the time Arnie won his first Masters in 1958 to Tiger's first victory, in 1997, the course measured, officially at least, 6,925 yards. But nearly all those tee boxes have been bulldozed away.

What's worse, members and their guests can't try their skills at that old classic length. There are just the 7,445-yard championship tees, overwhelming for average player, and the member tees, at 6,365 yards.

Fortunately, someone at Augusta National had the presence of mind to record all those old tee-box locations with a global positioning device. So they have the data on file. At the very least, the club ought to install small plaques in the old locations, for posterity's sake. Even better, they should construct small tee boxes on those locations, for the benefit of their members. Who wouldn't want to play Augusta National from the tees where Arnie and Jack once reigned?

THE
BACKGROUND

Masters Hardly Defines Augusta

Another City: Each Spring when the Golfing World Turns to Augusta for the Masters Tournament, Many Local Residents Flee. They Don't Mind the Publicity. But This Deep South River City is More Comfortable at the Stock-car Races or Fishing

by John Eisenberg, *The Baltimore Sun*, April 12, 1996

This river city in the belly of the Deep South is synonymous with the Masters, the historic golf tournament played this week and every spring amid the azalea bushes and magnolia trees of the Augusta National Golf Club.

Augustans tend not to quarrel with the regal image of their city that the Masters presents. Good press is good press.

But other than the splendid flowers and trees lining the rest of the city as well as Augusta National, the Masters' image has little in common with the reality of life in Augusta.

"The Masters and the golf club aren't really even part of Augusta," said Tom Moraetes, a lifelong resident of Augusta and director of the Augusta Boxing Club. "The Masters is like a special island unto itself within Augusta, entirely segregated from the citizenry and the city."

Augusta is a laid back workingman's city with a long history of political bickering and racial division. The mayor runs a barbecue joint. Soul singer James Brown is a lifelong resident. College football, stock-car racing and fishing are almost as popular as golf during the other 51 weeks of the year.

It is a town with a large medical community and a river-walk development of restaurants and shops. The local economy relies mostly on the Savannah River Site, a nuclear plant located across the river in South Carolina; the Medical College of Georgia, near downtown; and the military presence of nearby Fort Gordon.

The Masters exists in a different realm, if not in a different city.

For many Augustans, the tournament is just a traffic jam to get through on the way to work.

Masters crowds are composed largely of tourists making a pilgrimage to one of golf's meccas.

The host club is a reclusive sovereignty with a membership including mostly powerful business executives from around the country, not locals.

The tournament field didn't include an African-American golfer until 1975.

The club itself didn't have an African-American member until 1990. Now it has two.

Although hundreds of black golf fans will attend the tournament this week, the Masters remains an emblem of the segregated South to more than a few observers.

"The Masters is ostensibly open now, but there still aren't many blacks around it," said J. Philip Waring, a retired Urban League executive and founder of the Augusta Black History Committee. "Blacks and whites alike understand that the Masters is the biggest and best thing to hit Augusta as far as the economy, publicity and recognition. But there isn't a lot of interest in the black community."

In a sense, a major sporting event with elitist underpinnings is an appropriate symbol for a city that was slow to respond to the civil rights movement.

"This was a tough place to live for a long time," said Robert Law, 60, an African-American cab driver waiting for a fare in front of Augusta National earlier this week. "Things are a little better now."

Changes began to occur after race riots in May 1970 that left six dead. The riots began after several blacks were killed in jail. The National Guard was called in. President Nixon asked James Brown to help restore order.

"Prior to the riots, people here were slow to recognize that there were cultural differences," Mr. Waring said. "The investigations that followed shocked the people here. They had to start looking at themselves as far as their overall fairness to minorities. Black people had just been treated so badly for so long."

Political changes came first. Black city councilmen and state assemblymen were elected. The city's first black mayor was elected in 1981.

There also were social changes. "More opportunity, more black businesses, more black successes," Mr. Waring said. "Just a general awakening compared to what had existed before. There has been improvement."

Still, this city is no different from the rest of the South in the '90s. As Augusta grows, caught in the tide of general migration to the Sun Belt, it struggles to reconcile its divided past with a multicultural present.

Confederate hats and Kwanzaa calendars are for sale in the gift shop of the new Augusta-Richmond County Museum.

"The city is changing a lot," said Elbert Maddox, a construction worker with a son in the Augusta Boxing Club. "There are more things to do, more types of people, just more people period. Where I grew up used to be the country. Now there are houses all around me."

The boxing club is an appropriate symbol. In a small, sweaty gym near downtown, young African Americans, whites and Hispanics learn to box side-by-side in a positive, tolerant atmosphere. Mr. Moraetes began the club with one boxer in his basement 20 years ago. Now he has close to 100. The club has won three national Police Athletic League championships. Two former members have become world champions—Vernon Forrest and Pancho Carter.

"People can be so segregated in their minds," Mr. Moraetes said, "but there are no different cultures in here, just boxers."

Not that all of Augusta is living in happy harmony. The town is still predominantly segregated, with the black community living mostly east of town.

The lingering polarization was symbolized recently by a gridlocked debate over the hiring of a new school board president. An interim president ran the school system for almost a year while the school board remained split along mostly racial lines.

There was a racial component to the biggest issue to hit Augusta in years: whether to consolidate the Augusta city government with that of surrounding Richmond County.

For decades the two bodies competed for grants, programs and authority. "It hindered progress," said Mr. Moraetes, who worked for the county juvenile court.

Some leaders in the black community were opposed to consolidation because the black percentage of a combined city/county electorate would be reduced. In the end, the pro-consolidation forces won a small majority among black voters and a large majority among white voters, Mr. Waring said.

On Jan. 1, the two municipalities merged into a new entity known as Augusta-Richmond County. Augusta's population increased from 44,000 to 202,000, making it the second-largest city in Georgia and 75th largest in the United States.

Elections were held, mostly between city and county politicians who had held similar jobs. County voters dominated thanks to a 4–1 advantage in numbers.

The new mayor of Augusta, formerly the county commissioner, is Larry Sconyers, known mostly for running one of the city's best barbecue restaurants, located behind the Wal-Mart.

"He's a fat guy with no agenda other than to do what's best for Augusta," Mr. Moraetes said.

Thus is Augusta entering a new phase of its long history, which stretches back 260 years.

"I'm not down here to make a name for myself," Mr. Sconyers said. "My goal is to make government services better "

The city came into existence as a navigation point along the Savannah River, which was a major artery in the Southeast during the settlement of the country.

During the Civil War it served the Confederacy as a railroad transportation point, a manufacturer of guns and gunpowder and a medical center.

A fire in 1916 destroyed 26 blocks, 138 businesses and 526 homes.

A flood 13 years later led to the erection of a levee separating the river from downtown.

Several years later, golfer Bobby Jones came over from Atlanta, built his dream course on the old Fruitlands Plantation and formed the Augusta National Golf Club.

It was impossible to envision the new tournament he began in 1934 becoming the dominant image of Augusta. But it surely is.

The irony is that many Augustans rent out their homes and leave town during Masters week; the schools use the week for spring vacation no matter when the tournament is held.

Once the tournament ends Sunday and golf's millionaires take their glittery show elsewhere, the locals will return along with the pace of routine life in Augusta.

People will complain about the reduction of jobs at the Savannah River

Site, brought on by cuts in the federal defense budget.

They will argue about the effectiveness of the new, consolidated government.

They will point proudly to the nearly-completed National Science Center's Fort Discovery and the planned Georgia Golf Hall of Fame, new attractions for the river walk.

And they will breathe a sigh of relief that the Masters won't be back for another 51 weeks.

What's It Like to Be a Member?

A Rare Glimpse Behind the Green Velvet Curtain of the Most Exclusive Club in Golf

by Ron Sirak, *Golf Digest*, April 2003

Washington Road could be just about anywhere in small-town America. It is a bustling eyesore-lined thoroughfare with cheap chain restaurants and bargain retail stores. And while this gaudy strip shouts with a working-class accent, whispering in more genteel tones, behind the sign off Washington Road chat reads "Augusta National Golf Club Members Only," is a peaceful enclave for powerful men. And behind the mystique spawned by the secrecy that surrounds the club is a place of surprising simplicity. It is a haven where important men go to be regular guys and escape in the joys of golf and companionship.

"We don't have anything in here you can't put your feet up on," says an Augusta National member, skirting the club's no-talk policy by speaking under the condition of anonymity. That accurately describes the comfortable atmosphere of the clubhouse, the original part of which was built in 1854 as the home of Dennis Redmond, who ran the land as an indigo plantation. The floorboards creak with age and seem to speak of a bygone era. While time hasn't stopped at Augusta National, it certainly moves at its own casual pace. And casual is the operative word. The clubhouse and the 10 cabins on the grounds have an easy décor that suggests a summer getaway place rather than a stuffy citified club.

"We are not a museum," William W. (Hootie) Johnson told Golf Digest in a recent exclusive interview (as chairman he is the one Augusta National member allowed to speak publicly about club policy). "I don't say that to be cute. The golf course has constantly been improved by Bobby Jones and Mr. [cofounder Clifford] Roberts and on up through the years."

BEHIND THE GATES

At the guardhouse on Washington Road, security personnel know the members by sight, and guests are held until a member comes to collect them. Members are allowed as many as four guests at a time, depending on the time of the year, and guests can play without a member, as long as the member is on the property while his guests are playing. No guests are allowed during the four big member-only events each year.

About 330 yards and 61 magnolia trees off Washington Road and down Magnolia Lane is the front door to the clubhouse, a building that was saved from destruction 70 years ago by the club's early financial problems during the Great Depression (if they'd had the money, they'd have built a new clubhouse). Inside the door, stored beneath the counter at the switchboard, is a humidor with an excellent cigar collection known only to the members. The best go for less than $10. Unlike at many clubs, things are not overpriced at Augusta.

In the downstairs Trophy Room dinner is eaten under portraits of Jones, Roberts and U.S. President Eisenhower, a club member. A set of clubs used by Jones and the ball Gene Sarazen struck when he made his double eagle in the 1935 Masters are on display.

There is some lodging for members just off the Trophy Room. Upstairs, the Library is where card games are played and stories told and re-told. The room is not loud with money but rather quiet with charm. The Champions Locker Room, where Tiger Woods shares a locker with Jackie Burke Jr., is just off the library, as is the recently renovated Grill Room and the Members' Locker Room, complete with masseuse. Among the art in the Library is the first watercolor sketch of the course by architect Alister MacKenzie and a portrait of Roberts painted by Eisenhower.

Up a near-vertical flight of stairs, in a room with windows on all four sides that would be called a widow's walk if only there were an ocean nearby, is the Crow's Nest, the first on-site housing at the club. Originally a dormitory that slept six, it now has a sitting room, a bathroom and four enclosed rooms sleeping a total of five. This is where amateur contestants in the Masters stay, and it is still used by visiting members and guests.

Although Augusta National boasts a world-class wine cellar and high-quality food, the dining-room menu speaks to the relaxed atmosphere of the place. Only the soups vary daily. Otherwise, the choices include steak, broiled fish ("with no fancy sauces on it," a regular diner says), fried chicken, macaroni and cheese, green beans, squash and corn bread. There is shrimp cocktail for an appetizer and ice cream or a delicious peach cobbler for dessert. French fries are not served, because Roberts thought they were unhealthy.

"I think it is very comfortable, but understated," Johnson says of the clubhouse. "We try to make everyone who comes to Augusta National feel at home, whether they are members or guests."

Part of the comfort is the staff. Although the paternalistic manner in which Roberts viewed the almost exclusively black workforce can be regarded as condescending, it produced a loyalty that not only resulted in very little turnover but created multi-generation employees. The son of Eisenhower's regular caddie, Cemetery, is a caddie at Augusta today. Frank Carpenter, who recently retired, worked at Augusta for more than 50 years, starting as a waiter and ending up as the wine steward and reputedly a first-class wine buyer. The longtime chef, the late James Clark, was an active participant in the Closing Party every year. No tipping is allowed, but Roberts was known to intervene if a caddie was underpaid and always told guests to "pay what you think he was worth," which almost always ensured a healthy remuneration.

"We have just unbelievably dedicated people who work here," Johnson says. "And I think that is the first thing that stands out when people come here, and that includes members. Every time we come, I think we are impressed with our service and with our people and with their dedication."

Between the clubhouse and the first tee is the massive live oak under which the most powerful people in golf gather to chat during Masters week. Winding through the tree and around the clubhouse is a gnarled Chinese wisteria vine brought to the grounds when the pre-club owners, the Berckmans family, ran the estate as a nursery. The vine is said to be the parent of all such wisteria in America.

Off to the left as you gaze at the course from the clubhouse is the 10th tee, and to the left of that is the Eisenhower Cabin, one of seven cottages that form a semicircle between the 10th hole and the Par-3 Course. While the term "cabin" is an understatement, the interior is astonishing in its simplicity. Again, the furniture is much like you would gather for a casual summer hideaway, except here the simple wood dressers have had land-scape scenes painted on them by Eisenhower. On the wall is a series of photos taken by Mamie Eisenhower of the various places she and her husband lived: There is Fort Benning in Georgia; Morningside Drive in New York City, from when Ike was president of Columbia University; and, stuck quietly among the other residences, is 1600 Pennsylvania Avenue-the White House.

NO ORDINARY GOLF CLUB

The National is different from most other golf clubs in more than just its membership. First, it is closed all summer, from the third week of May until mid-October, primarily for renovations. Also, you don't apply to join, you are invited (making it known you are interested in being a member is a surefire way not to be invited). A new member finds out he has been asked to join when a letter arrives in the mail. And legend has it that a member who falls out of favor will find out about it when a bill doesn't arrive in late summer, although one Augusta insider says he can't remember the last time that happened.

The club operates under the firm hand of the chairman, a classic benevolent-dictator system created by Roberts. There have been only five chairmen in the club's 70-year history. Advising the chairman is the board of governors. Among the key insiders are Joe Ford, the vice chairman; Will Nicholson, the chairman of the competition committees for the Masters; Billy Payne, the chairman of the media committee; and Charley Yates, the 1938 British Amateur champion, close friend of Bob Jones and the only current member who joined before World War II. Club rules are not so much written as they are hints, and those who don't get the hint get the boot. The code word is "favorably." High-stakes gambling, for example, is not looked upon favorably.

In 1937, Roberts decided members should wear green jackets during Masters week so patrons could easily identify them if they had any questions. Beginning in 1949, the Masters champion, too, received a green jacket. Each member gets one jacket, for which he is billed a small fee. Members are not allowed to take the jacket from the grounds. A Masters winner is an honorary member and may take the coat off the premises the year he is champion. When a member arrives at the club, he finds the jacket hanging in his closet. If it begins to get threadbare or if a button comes loose, a sharp-eyed employee spots the defect and has it fixed.

"Despite the secrecy surrounding the club, there are no mysterious rituals shared by the members," says one insider. "Instead of a secret handshake you're more likely to get a slap on the back."

Augusta National is more about power than it is about money. It is not what you can afford but who you know, and how you act. The initiation fee is in the "low five figures," according to one source, and a member adds, "You could afford it," knowing full well he was speaking to someone making a journalist's salary. The annual dues, two insiders say, amount to "a few thousand dollars," and it costs about $100 a night to stay in one of the 105 beds that are on site.

According to Johnson, a typical weekend might have as few as 20 or 30 people playing golf, or as many as 80. Some members may come to the club only three to five times a year, and others might come 15 or 20 times. It is a close-knit group that resembles in many ways a college fraternity. Members volunteer to chair the 24 committees needed to put on the Masters, and dozens of other members chip in to help on those committees. Former Sen. Sam Nunn is on the media committee.

There is no member-guest tournament, but there are four big member-only social events a year (no guests or wives allowed) that are spirited competitions: the Opening Party in October, the Governors Party in November, the Jamboree in late March and the Closing Party the third week of May. At the last Governors Party, 130 of the 300 members showed up. After the competitive rounds, some members move inside for a drink and cigar and maybe some cards. Others head back out and squeeze in another 18 holes. Except for one day at the Jamboree when two-man teams compete, the competitions are four-man best ball with adjustments for pars and birdies, according to Augusta's unique handicap system. (The course has no Slope Rating—instead, two points are awarded for birdies or better, one for pars, everything else counts for nothing, and a handicap is derived by deducting the total number of points from 18.)

"At the time of the Jamboree our scoreboards [for the Masters] are up," Johnson says, laughing. "It might be Johnson-Chapman, that's my partner

[Hugh Chapman], or it might be Stephens-Johnson—Jack Stephens and I won twice. It's as exciting as heck. You see your name up on the scoreboard with your partner's, then if you start stumbling around your names come off the board and somebody else goes up. You have eight or 10 leaders up there. If you win that, you receive a silver box with every attendee's name engraved on it."

These are some of the most powerful men in America, yet they are thrilled by receiving a silver box they could easily buy—because they won it on the golf course.

"Everybody plays a nassau," says another member, also speaking on the condition of anonymity, in describing the competition at the fall Governors Party. "If you win $75, you had a helluva great day. If you lose $75, you had a horrible day. And if you break even, you're lucky."

WHAT WOULD MR. ROBERTS DO?

When Cliff Roberts ran the place, the Jamboree was not only a time to celebrate the club but was also a time to poke fun at his own autocratic rule. Each year he would show a short movie at the party. One time he depicted himself making a hole-in-one on No. 16 and then walking on water from the tee to the green, a feat pulled off by the construction of a bridge just under the surface of the pond. To add to the effect, his caddie was shown tumbling into the water. Another time, the movie had a bear chasing golfers across the course. Then the camera pulled in for a close-up of the bear—the head was lifted off to reveal Roberts. Several times Roberts showed himself singing to a rubber duck.

"There is still a six- to eight-minute movie shown at the Jamboree with a mix of a little comedy, golf course beauty shots and sentiment," says someone who spends a lot of time inside the gates of Augusta. "There might be a piece on a member who recently passed away." Perhaps this year there will be a tongue-in-cheek reference to the membership confrontation with Martha Burk.

Although the legend of Jones is at the heart of Augusta, the essence of Roberts is its soul. The single-minded efficiency—some would say arrogance—with which Roberts ran the club as chairman from 1934 to 1976 established a road map for other chairmen to follow. Ask an Augusta member about a club policy, and the answer is likely to begin with the words: "Well, Mr. Roberts felt…" Though Jones is listed as president in perpetuity, it is, in fact, Roberts who still rules.

"I'll tell you, he had a great sense of humor," Johnson says. "He'd kind of let you know what he was thinking without being too harsh sometimes. When shorts first came in on the golf course, men wearing shorts, Mr. Roberts was having lunch when Charley Yates bounded up with his shorts on. Mr. Roberts looked at him and said, 'Charley, what are you doing this afternoon?' And he said, 'Well, I'm going to play golf, Cliff, of course.' And Mr. Roberts said, 'Well, I hope the course is nearby.' It didn't take Charley long to change the shorts."

So what would happen if a member showed up now wearing shorts?

"We wouldn't look too favorably on it," Johnson says with a chuckle. "It's all right for ladies to have down-to-the-knee shorts. But men, we don't look too favorably on that."

When Johnson, 72, speaks of Augusta National, it is with a genuine affection. He first set foot on the grounds shortly after World War II, first played there 50 years ago and became a member, at the suggestion of Roberts, in 1968. Time and again as he shares stories about the club his sentences are punctuated with laughter or interrupted by wistful pauses as if a particular fond memory is replaying in his mind.

"The Closing Party is a great party," Johnson says. "We have a barbecue down by the Par-3 [Course], and we hit balls to the first green down there and all walk around with our drinks and our chef, James Clark, he'd get into it with us. He usually ended up winning the money. I only say those things," Johnson says, pausing to collect the words he wanted to use. "It's just a…" Again he stops and laughs a private laugh as if remembering a story or a long-ago incident. "There is a great camaraderie among the membership," he says finally.

"One of the greatest things I see is when two members, who likely haven't seen each other in several months, meet on the practice tee," says one who has been there to witness such reunions. "It's like two old college buddies meeting for alumni weekend. It's just good guys who like golf and each other's company."

Because of the difficulty of getting to Augusta (the town is almost a three-hour drive from Atlanta—many arrive by private jet and fly into Augusta's tiny airport), members begin arriving on a Wednesday night for the big parties. It is those intimate gatherings when people are trickling in that Johnson remembers with the greatest fondness.

"There might be just 25 or 30 people, and we have a great get-together up there [in the Library]," he says. "And it's just an intimate place, a warm place. Most of the time we go to bed at a reasonable hour, but every now and then we might be up a little while."

The club frowns upon lights being on after midnight (the New Year's Eve countdown takes place at 10:30). But there are some nights when the rules are bent just a little. Especially when one of those sharing stories and playing bridge or gin rummy is the chairman, who most likely is beginning a yarn with the words, "I remember the time Mr. Roberts..."

Before the Masters There's the Madness

Monday Through Wednesday, Fans Swarm to the Merchandise Pavilion in a Buying Binge

by Bob Harig, *St. Petersburg Times*, April 4, 2006

There is no tournament in the world like the Masters, and no tournament like the Masters on Monday. For that matter, there is no tournament like the Masters on Tuesday and Wednesday.

A Monday at a regular PGA Tour stop would see last-minute preparations, a smattering of players showing up to register and practice, and perhaps a couple of dozen curious spectators.

Then there is Augusta National on the days preceding the Masters. Quite simply, it is bedlam.

Gates open at 8 a.m. and the masses swarm in. They pour into the merchandise pavilion near the entrance, visit the historical exhibits, wander onto the greenest grass they have seen at one of the most exclusive courses in the world. By noon, you can hear roars for practice shots.

Jon Johnson has viewed this scene time and again. A former assistant golf professional at Augusta National, Johnson, 51, now lives in Lutz and has been coming to the Masters for 25 years to work in merchandise sales and now the merchandise checkpoint and shipping area.

Nearly as stunning as the grounds is what goes on in the 12,000-square-foot building that is used one week a year.

Masters memorabilia simply flies out of the building. Shirts with the famous Augusta logo—flagstick inside an outline of the United States—hats, sweaters, golf balls, markers, head covers, calendars, coffee mugs, rain suits ... just about anything you can put a logo on.

And it can be bought only here.

"I think what amazes me is how they can still have the ability to not go on the Internet," Johnson said of Augusta National. "There are no mail-order sales and there used to be sales at the front gate. You either buy it through a member or you buy it that week. They've withheld from taking that plunge. I'm sure they could triple their sales. But you don't know. The more people have it, the less they might want it. It's nice quality items. They don't gouge the eyes out of it, but they make it so you have to get it at Augusta."

Johnson is manager of the Tampa Bay Downs Practice Facility in Oldsmar and has recruited others to take the trip with him.

This year, his son, Kyle, has made his second journey. It's the third time for Bill Gilkes, 58, who works for the North Florida Section of the PGA of America. And Tim Greco, 44, general manager at Lansbrook Golf Club in Palm Harbor, is making his first visit.

"For someone in the golf business, it's like a priest going to the Vatican for the first time," Greco said.

They left early Sunday to drive to Augusta in time for an afternoon meeting at the course, where they could go over last-minute instructions while Augusta was still calm.

Members and their guests could still play the course, while competitors could get in practice rounds away from the commotion that followed on Monday.

Of his first trip last year, Kyle Johnson said, "I thought they painted the concrete, it was so clean. And then all you see is just green grass, as far as you can see. Rolling hills and green grass."

"The thing I distinctly remember," said Gilkes of his first visit in 2004, "was when we drove on the property were the butterflies in my stomach. I remember thinking it was like being in Yankee Stadium on home plate with no one in the stadium and you could hear the sound of Babe Ruth hitting the ball over the fence. When I got on the property, I had that same feeling. It's eerie. The serenity was unreal. Unbelievable. It was breathtaking."

Most of those emotions are gone by Monday, when the hard work begins. Johnson and his group will likely work 7 a.m to 8 p.m. shifts every day this week. Augusta National hires several hundred workers to staff the merchandise outlets, which by Saturday often have been cleaned out of most of the popular items.

The reason Monday through Wednesday is so much different than the tournament rounds has to do with the unique way spectators acquire "badges" for the event. The tournament has been a sellout since 1966, and only "patrons" on a mailing list get the opportunity to buy a four-day badge. There is a waiting list, with a few people moving up each year. Unless you are on that list, there is no way to attend the tournament rounds.

But tickets to the practice rounds were always made available to the public at the gate. Then the demand became so great that in the late 1990s, the club decided to sell them through an annual lottery.

Augusta National does not release attendance figures, but veteran observers are convinced there are far more people on the grounds on Monday, Tuesday and Wednesday than during the tournament.

"It's such a different crowd," Johnson said. "The majority have never been to Augusta. They stand around the museum area, they all want to shop. The lines are seemingly a block long. During the tournament, most of them have been there before. They find a place to sit on the course. It's really easier on Thursday through Sunday."

No one who works at Augusta National is allowed to discuss anything in relation to sales. But one can imagine people buying thousands of dollars in merchandise.

It is impossible to know exactly how much money flows through here, but a simple estimate of 40,000 spectators who spend an average of $100 apiece would bring a conservatively low number of $4 million per day. And that's not counting ticket sales, concessions and television and radio rights fees.

No wonder the place looks so good.

The Masters: Toughest Ticket in Sports

Now That's the Ticket—$2,500 for Four Days: Badge for the Masters Now the Most Expensive Blackmarket Ticket for a National Sporting Event

by Mike Fish, *The Atlanta Constitution*, April 7, 1997

In the good old days of the 1950s, Masters tickets were as easy to get as parking tickets. They were hawked from booths along Broad Street in downtown Augusta. You could buy whatever you liked. The Chamber of Commerce pressed local merchants to sell blocks of 100 or more.

Then Arnold Palmer, hitching his trousers, stormed to four Masters titles. Television viewers, many emerging from a long winter, fell for the colorful azaleas and stately cathedral pines.

Now, Augusta National is the place to be in early April. The Masters is no longer simply an annual bash for the locals and golfing purists. In today's celebrity-obsessed global culture, it's evolved into a gathering place for movers, shakers and corporate bigwigs.

So, you want to drive over to Augusta this week to catch a round? Unless your wallet is stuffed with cash or includes a club membership card, forget it.

For the select group of card-carriers and designated patrons who can purchase a tournament ticket (or badge, as it's called) from the club, it's the Best Bargain in Sports. Four days, $100.

For the industrious seeking to pick up a badge on the sly, it's the Toughest Ticket in Sports. Four days, $2,500 or more, according to the going price on the streets and in the classified ads.

Nothing else compares when it comes to the supply-and-demand dynamic of ticket value. Not the Super Bowl, Kentucky Derby or Wimbledon. Not even Opening Ceremonies at the Summer Olympics.

Inflating the ticket demand this week is the pro debut in Augusta by golf's young gun, Tiger Woods.

And that's music to ticket scalpers' ears.

TILL DEATH DO US PART

Short of paying Augusta National dues, the only access to the event is via the Patron List. Those fortunate fans are described by club spokesman Glen Greenspan as "just people who have had tickets for many years—people who in the 1960s bought a badge, enjoyed themselves and said, 'Hey, we like it, let's renew.'"

The club stopped selling badges to the public in 1972. A waiting list was closed in 1978 and, at last guess, stood near 4,000—shrinking by less than a hundred a year.

"You hear of people who've been on the waiting list 20 years and all of a sudden they get a call: 'You're up,'" Greenspan said.

Greenspan, under orders to reveal few specifics, declined to say how many badges are made available. Nor would he disclose the size of the invitation-only membership roll at Augusta National or how many badges each member can purchase.

A badge can be willed to a spouse but not to anyone else. Those on the waiting list must stand by until ticket-holders' funerals.

One Atlanta law firm entertained clients with Masters tickets provided by a partner's aunt, who lived in a small town just west of Augusta. Her death led to a lighthearted conversation among the law partners about whether her checking account should be kept open to maintain the Masters account.

The players, who at most tournaments get virtually unlimited complimentary tickets, are caught in the crunch. Badges are available to wives and children free of charge, and players can buy a limited number at cost ($100).

"You don't have to pay for immediate family but everything else, including mothers and fathers," former Masters champion Tom Watson said. "That's different. But we make enough money. We can afford it."

BANISHMENT THE CRIME FOR SCALPING

Not many people can afford to buy tickets from scalpers, many of whom operate legally from out-of-state offices and prefer to be called ticket brokers. By any name, they can benefit from a seller's market at the Masters.

One advertiser in the *Atlanta Journal-Constitution*'s classifieds quoted a price of $5,000 for a pair of tickets covering all four days. John Pirample, who operates Ideal Tickets Agency, a broker firm in Cleveland, says he also charges $2,500 apiece. Others ask up to $3,000.

Most business takes place with brokers by telephone. According to Pirample, the broker "buys" the badge off the owner and leaves a deposit, which is returned when the owner retrieves the badge after the tournament. The broker finds a customer willing to pay him enough to make a profit.

Because scalping isn't good for the image, Augusta National frowns on anyone who would stoop to selling their badges for more than list price.

Club officials monitor newspaper ads and follow up on tips. It's not uncommon for them to punish someone for selling a badge.

"If they're caught, they can be taken off the Patron List and not allowed to buy a badge again," said Greenspan. "It has happened, sure."

The threat further drives up the black-market price.

Longtime badge owners are leery of parting with them, fearful of embarrassment and banishment. Besides, most are financially comfortable, thus reducing the urge to scalp.

Pirample says he finds some business through "rich kids."

"The dad gives them the badges and often these kids will look to sell them.

"It's tough, though. The people who generally have the badges don't need money, and they don't want to mess around with Augusta National."

BILL MAY DROP PRICE

One veteran scalper from Marietta rents a house near Augusta National, offering food and drinks for clients before they spend the day walking the historic golf course. It's here that they pick up their Masters badges, park their car on the lawn and turn over a $500 deposit—which is returned that afternoon when they bring back the badge for someone else's use the next day.

For the corporate clients who want to make a week out of it, packages of Masters tickets and living accommodations in Augusta are available. The deal can run into the thousands of dollars.

Only at the Masters are practice round tickets scalped. They are sold by the club through a lottery—with Monday and Tuesday going for $16 each, Wednesday for $21. Ticket brokers have a ready supply, quoting prices ranging from $50 to $200 apiece.

Practice round tickets, unlike the tournament badges, are widely bought and sold on the grounds outside the course. (All badges are marked with holograms, checked at the entrance gate, to prevent counterfeiting.)

The state legislature passed a bill this session that legalizes ticket scalping.

It is awaiting Gov. Zell Miller's signature. The law would be in effect for next year's Masters.

Barry Lefkowitz, executive director of the National Association of Ticket Brokers, says that's good news for badge-seekers who must take out a second mortgage to meet the typical asking price.

Lefkowitz predicts that the new legislation would "dry up the black market and consumers will actually benefit. Once you open it up, allowing for competition in a deregulated market, generally ticket prices go down at the secondary level."

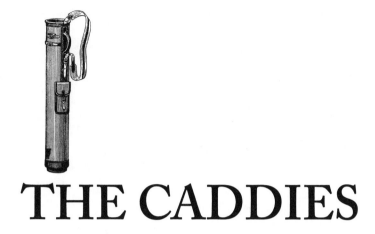

THE CADDIES

Tales From the Caddyshack

With Nicknames Like Stovepipe, Marble Eye, and Fireball, Augusta National Caddies Know the Masters Like No One Else

by David Westin, *The Augusta Chronicle*, April 7, 1996

The Augusta National caddy stories stop, for the most part, the day Craig Stadler won the 1982 Masters.

By the following year, the club had lifted the restriction on using only Augusta National caddies in the Masters. An era was over for the likes of Ironman, Cemetery and Pappy.

That still leaves 48 years of tales from the caddyshack, some of them no doubt embellished by the passage of time.

From the inception of the Masters in 1934 until the lifting of the ban against non-Augusta National caddies 13 years ago, the Augusta National caddy was a constant presence on the course, with his white jump suit with green lettering. Today, they are an invaluable source for insight about the players, pre-1983.

When the Augusta National lifted the ban on outside caddies, some golfers, such as Ben Crenshaw and Bruce Lietzke, continued to use Augusta National caddies. The number of Augusta National caddies, however, has never been more than five or six in a Masters.

What an era is was, though.

"It had a spirit about it; it was a festive-type spirit," said Carl Jackson, a former Augusta National caddy who this week will caddy for two-time Masters champion Crenshaw for the 20th straight year at the tournament.

Jackson, 49, started caddying at the Augusta National when he was 14 years old.

Before hooking up with Crenshaw, Jackson caddied for Davis Love Jr., Gary Player, Tony Jacklin, Bruce Devlin, Steve Melynk, Charlie Coe, R.H. Sikes, Mike Souchak, Billy Burke and Downing Gray.

Gray, a former U.S. Amateur champion, seemed to have a different caddy each year. Though Gray was a low amateur award winner, caddies preferred a pro who had a chance to win the tournament.

"I think we all had to go through Downing Gray," Jackson said, referring to young caddies.

Jackson has a treasure trove of Augusta National memories from the bygone time.

"My first year, in 1961, I caddied for Billy Burke," Jackson said. "He played in a white dress shirt and a necktie."

In 1964, Jackson had the bag of struggling 26-year-old Australian Bruce Devlin, who would go on to win eight times on the PGA Tour and earn nearly $1 million. Devlin currently plays on the Senior PGA Tour, where he has career earnings approaching $2 million.

"That year there was a big story that if he didn't have success in the Masters he was going back home to Australia to be a plumber," Jackson said.

Devlin finished fourth and never had to learn how to unclog a drain.

The great Augusta National caddies from the early years of the tournament are getting up in age. Some are dead, such as Nathaniel "Ironman" Avery, Leon McCladdie and Willie "Cemetery" Poteat.

The legendary Willie "Pappy" Stokes, who caddied for five Masters winners, is 75, frail and has arthritis in one leg. Willie Peterson, Jack Nicklaus' caddy for his first five Masters victories, is retired and living in Florida.

Ironman caddied for all four of Palmer's Masters victories, while McCladdie was Tom Watson's right-hand man in both his victories.

"Ironman was the best caddy up there," said Stokes, his brother-in-law.

Cemetery caddied in the Masters but was best known for being President Dwight David Eisenhower's caddy whenever Ike made one of his visits (the total numbered 29 during his two terms as president) to the Augusta National.

Palmer recalls that Ironman "kind of gave me a little push to play. That was the major thing. His enthusiasm was natural. It wasn't anthing he thought he had to do. Everything he did was out of enthusiasm for me to win."

Cemetery and Ironman were just two of many caddies with colorful nicknames. Most of the caddies were given their monikers by Willie Mason, who was the caddy master at the Augusta Country Club, located adjacent the Augusta National. Almost all the caddies started at "the Club" as youngsters and then moved on to Augusta National.

"He gave everybody nicknames," Jariah Beard said of Mason. "He always called me 'Little Earl,' because that was my dad's name."

Other nicknames were Stovepipe, 8-Ball, Marble Eye, Daybreak, Long Distance, Cigarette, Pokie, Rat, First Baseman, Mutt and Fireball.

Cemetery was also called Dead Man.

In an interview with sports commentator John Derr at the 1953 Masters, Cemetery confirmed a story Derr had heard about how the nickname originated.

Related in Derr's 1996 book Don't Forget to Wind the Clock, Derr told Cemetery that his fellow caddies "said when you were younger, you were quite a ladies' man and that one day you were over at a friend's house, romancing his wife, and he came home and caught you.

"He pulled out a razor and sliced your throat pretty good. You escaped and left Augusta. When your friends asked what had happened to you, the razor man told them, 'You won't be seeing him anymore. He's a dead man.'"

Cemetery told Derr the story was accurate, with one exception.

"No, it wasn't his wife, it was his girlfriend," Cemetery said.

"He stayed in the hospital three or four months," Pappy Stokes said of Cemetery. "They thought he was dead. When he came out of there, they called him Cemetery."

Beard thinks Ironman got his nickname because the tips of a couple of his fingers were missing.

"It might have been something that happened as a kid where a firecracker blew up in his hand," Beard said. "People would say, 'What did you think, you were an iron man or something?'"

Stokes was nicknamed Pappy by the late Augusta National chairman Clifford Roberts. Other highly-respected caddies are Jackson, Ernest Nipper and Matthew Palmer. Nipper caddied for Gary Player until 1970, and Palmer caddied for Billy Casper when he won in 1970.

"If I got out with any of those guys, I was happy just to be walking down the fairway with them," Augusta National caddy Tommy Bennett said. "I tried to learn from those guys."

Pappy, who is living in the Hemingway Services boarding house on Tobacco Road, is the only man to have caddied for four different Masters champions. The victories came in 1938 (Henry Picard), 1948 (Claude Harmon), 1951 (Ben Hogan), 1953 (Hogan again) and 1956 (Jack Burke Jr.).

"Pappy's family had property on the course and he lived there for a long time," Jackson said. "He was 'the man' around there for years."

Indeed, Pappy was born on May 22, 1920 on what had been the Fruitlands Nurseries and would become the Augusta National Golf Club. The Fruitlands closed in 1919 and ground-breaking for the Augusta National started in 1931. Pappy helped clear the course of trees as Bobby Jones and Alister MacKenzie did the routing of the holes.

"I was born and raised there," Pappy said. "It was a farm when I was young. I went out there every morning and I'd plow for cotton and corn. When they started building the course, I remember cutting down trees on No. 10 and 11."

Once the Augusta National was built, Pappy was one of the first caddies out on the course. He didn't have far to walk; his family's house stood near the clubhouse.

"I could always caddy," Pappy said. "I was raised on a golf course. I was the ace caddy at the Augusta National. The members would ask for Pappy. They'd say, 'Where's Pappy at?'"

"Pappy was a great caddy and a good guy," said Otis 'Buck' Moore, a caddy in 24 Masters and the father of University of Massachusetts point guard Ricky Moore. "He took pride in what he was doing. He loved the game. You couldn't help but like him. He was comical (off the golf course). He'd always say something funny if you had a bad day to pep you up."

Bennett said Pappy "would tell you a story, and just the way he'd say it, he was so funny."

"Pappy taught most of us how to caddy," Jackson said. "He knew the golf course like the back of his hand. He could be in the middle of a fairway, look up at the green and say a certain putt was going to break 6 inches to the right."

"When Pappy caddied for Jackie Burke, Mr. Roberts told him whatever Pappy tells you, you do it," said current Augusta National caddy Pee Wee Reid.

Pappy took caddying seriously and expected the other caddies to do the same.

If you were lackidasical, "Pappy would say, 'God's got his eyes on you,'" Reid said.

"I didn't go out there on the golf course to play," Pappy says, "I went out there to try to make a living. Some of them couldn't caddy; they were just bag toters. They never did nothing but tote a bag."

Jackson is 'the man' among Augusta National caddies today in the Masters. This will be his 34th straight Masters, the longest-running current streak among caddies. Of course, he has carried the bag for both of Crenshaw's victories.

"We have been through so much together there," Crenshaw said of Jackson. "He knows me very well. He knows that golf course as well as anyone. It's sort of different the way we approach it. I don't rely on yardage on the golf course that heavily. We know how certain shots play. We're very much a team there."

"Ben has a saying that of all the years I've caddied for him, I've misread one putt," Jackson said.

It happened about 15 years ago, on the par-5 15th hole, Jackson said.

"It was a silly mistake," Jackson said. "It was an eagle putt and I probably went brain dead by the time we decided where he was going to putt the ball. I knew better. My mind just went somewhere else."

These days, Jackson is a full-time caddy on the PGA Tour for Sean Murphy. Jackson and Crenshaw had a run together on the PGA Tour in the early 1990s, but it ended after two seasons.

"I don't know why, but I don't think we work that well as a team in other places," Crenshaw said. "We got to feeling pressure. I was trying too hard for him, and he was trying so hard for me. It just didn't work on a full-time basis. We just have a special relationship. I see him every week (on the PGA Tour). We talk all the time."

There is another former Augusta National caddy who is well-known in golf circles, but not for his caddying. Augusta native Jim Dent, now a star on the Senior PGA Tour, caddied for Bob Rosburg in the Masters in the early 1960s.

***

The caddies have a wealth of stories about Roberts, Augusta National's first chairman. Roberts, who died in 1977, ran the tournament with an iron fist. Roberts didn't just suggest that decorum be followed, he insisted on it.

Reid recalls an incident in the 1970s when Roberts threw the late entertainer Jackie Gleason off the course during a Masters round.

According to Reid, Gleason and some friends were being boisterous behind one of the greens and were disturbing some of the golfers coming through.

"He pulled his tickets," Reid said. "Mr. Roberts told him, 'This is the Augusta National, not Broadway.' Whatever Mr. Roberts said, went."

Roberts looked out for the caddies. According to Reid, if a player didn't pay a caddy at least the standard rate for his services during the tournament, the caddy could go to Roberts and "he'd get everything straight."

To a man, the caddies believe there would still be only Augusta National caddies in the Masters if Roberts were alive.

Leroy Schultz, who has caddied in 22 Masters, said the pros "wouldn't have gone" to Roberts asking for him to lift the ban on non-Augusta National caddies.

Why not?

"Because he was Mr. Roberts," Schultz said.

"Mr. Roberts died and things really changed," said Bennett, who has caddied in 20 Masters and was the man on the bag for Tiger Woods last year.

"We were kicked aside," Schultz said. "When Clifford Roberts died we went downhill and they've continued to go downhill. It's not the old Augusta National and I hope you put that in the paper."

When Jack Nicklaus was a fresh-faced Masters rookie in 1959, there was no infighting to be his caddy, though his talent was obvious.

"Nobody wanted to caddy for him; he'd keep you out there all day hitting balls," said Reid.

"I caddied for Jack Nicklaus the first year and I put him down and Willie Peterson got him," Pappy Stokes said. "Jack was too slow for me. I wanted somebody who would hit the ball and walk. I said 'Pete, I'm going to give him to you.' Jack was paying good money, but he'd go out there at 7 in the morning and come back at night. I said 'Man, you walked my legs off.'"

"Willie would stay with him all day," Beard said. "Basically, nobody else wanted the bag because of that work."

"Willie Peterson was just right for Jack Nicklaus," Jackson said. "Nicklaus can do his own caddying. But Peterson was a good pep man. He was a good 'pat you on the back and let's go' man. He was good for Jack Nicklaus."

"Willie Peterson was a bag toter, but Jack Nicklaus liked him," Pappy said. "He liked Willie Peterson."

Beard said the caddies could "see the potential Nicklaus had, but at the time, the King (four-time Masters champ Arnold Palmer) was on top. Everybody was watching the King. The King was playing super, super golf."

After caddying in the same group with Nicklaus in the early 1960's, Beard had a feeling he was looking at the next King.

"Jack couldn't have been 20 or 21," Beard said. "I was caddying for Don January. On the 13th hole (a 465-yard par-5) we outdrove Jack by 40 yards and we still had 190 yards to the green."

Beard and January assumed Nicklaus would lay up short of the tributary to Rae's Creek that guards the front of the green.

"I heard Willie tell Jack he didn't think he could get there (in two shots)," Beard recalled. "Jack said, 'Gimme my 3-wood, I can hit it as far as I want to,' and he blistered it. It landed on the green. January turned around to me and said, 'He's going to run us all off the tour,' which is basically what Jack did."

Nearly 20 years later, Beard would have a Masters champion's bag of his own. Fuzzy Zoeller credited Beard with leading him around the golf course as he became the second golfer to win the Masters in his first appearance, joining Gene Sarazen, who did it in 1935.

"He told me, 'This is your course, tell me what to hit and I'll hit it,'" Beard said of Zoeller.

Beard never asked to caddy for Zoeller.

"I said, 'Who is Fuzzy Zoeller?' I didn't know anything about him."

Mike Shannon, an Augusta National assistant pro at the time, did. Shannon and Zoeller had been college roommates.

It so happened that Shannon and Beard played golf together every Monday at Augusta's Forest Hills Golf Club.

"At the time I was caddying for Don January and had been since 1967, but Mike said he wanted me to caddy for his buddy," Beard said.

The caddies had their favorite golfers and the ones they tried to avoid at all costs, such as Nicklaus.

At one point in his career, Andy Bean was among the least popular.

"He paid good money, but he'd throw golf clubs," Reid said. "Some caddies just didn't feel like chasing no clubs out there. Then others said, 'You can keep throwing them as long as you want if you keep paying like that.' He'd pay something like $1,300 even if he missed the cut."

"Andy was mean and so was Bob Goalby," Beard said. "Goalby had a heck-uva temper. He'd raise hell if you pulled a bad club or misread a putt."

When the ban restricting outside caddies was lifted for the 1983 Masters, the death knell sounded for the Augusta National caddies. Since the course is open only from mid-October through late May each year, caddies counted on a big-money week during the Masters to get them through the year. Without it, most couldn't make ends meet and were forced to quit and take other employment.

"We lost most of the good ones," Schultz said.

The ban was lifted in part because some caddies showed up late for the completion of a rain-suspended round in the 1982 Masters. Play picked up at 7:30 a.m., the day after the suspension. Some caddies thought the round had been washed out and showed up at the time of previous day's starting time.

"Those guys who were drinking and stuff should have been expelled," Bennett said. "They didn't have any pride and they hurt the caddies at Augusta."

"All the caddies were weeded out because of four or five guys," Moore said. "They should have gotten rid of them instead of punishing the whole group." Jackson said he never thought the day would come when anyone but Augusta National caddies would be putting on that white jump suit and lacing up those white sneakers with green trim.

"I didn't see it ending until it ended," Jackson said. "There was a lot of talk about guys showing up unprepared and staying out late. The caddies did enough things they shouldn't have done to help make what happened happen. They're not blameless. Some guys weren't doing right. That (what happened after the suspended round in 1982) just put fuel on the fire."

What could the caddies do without the big Masters week check? There were bills to pay and mouths to feed. So what happened to that 48-year tradition of knowledgable Augusta National caddies?

"All they could do," recalled Jackson, "was say to heck with it."

Those New
Masters Caddies

by Dave Anderson, *The New York Times*, April 10, 1983

In the rain yesterday, they still wore the green caps and the white coveralls with the names of their golfers on the backs in green lettering. But the caddies at the Masters have a different look. For the first time in the 47 tournaments, some Masters caddies are white. For the first time, the Masters golfers have been allowed to use caddies of their choice rather than being required to hire one of the black Augusta National caddies.

Black caddies were a tradition here, part of the Masters lore. Willie Peterson jumping up and down on the 18th green after Jack Nicklaus holed a long putt there in 1975. Ironman Avery striding along behind Arnold Palmer.

All those black caddies also were part of the image that Augusta National projected, knowingly or not, as America's last plantation with the caddie yard over there in the pine trees beyond the delivery driveway.

In the sprawling white clubhouse, the wealthy Augusta National members in their green jackets still are served by black waiters, black bartenders and black locker-room attendants.

But during the Masters now, some of the caddies are white, following the dictum by Hord Hardin, the Masters chairman, that competing golfers no longer had to use an Augusta National caddie. Understandably, the black club caddies who were replaced by touring caddies, whether white or black, don't appreciate the new system. But they appreciate the significance. During a practice round last weekend, Jim Ballet, the New England amateur champion, walked onto the first tee with his caddie and close friend, Jack Tosone, a 22-year-old Bryant College student.

"You just made history," a club caddie called to Jim Hallet's caddie. "You're the first white man ever to caddie here."

Not all the touring pros chose to bring their tour caddies. Jack Nicklaus was using Willie Peterson again until the five-time Masters champion withdrew yesterday because of back spasms. Craig Stadler, the defending champion, retained Ben Bussey, another club caddie. But many touring pros preferred the caddies they regularly employ in the weekly PGA Tour events, and a former Masters champion, George Archer, brought his 19-year-old daughter Jill, the first woman caddie in Masters history. Tom Watson has Bruce Edwards, his tour caddie for a decade, rather than Leon McClattie, his club caddie during two Masters triumphs.

"After playing in the Masters for 10 years, I know the yardage and I know the club," Tom Watson says. "Bruce doesn't know the course that well yet. but he knows me."

That knowledge of the golfer is often a caddie's most important contribution. During the opening round Tom Watson was grousing about rain having interrupted play but Bruce Edwards didn't sympathize.

"I told him to stop complaining," Bruce Edwards says, "and let's get going."

Tom Watson finished with a two-under par 70 that day and added a 71 yesterday.

"Anytime I'm uncertain about which club to use, I know Bruce is a good sounding board for me," Tom Watson says. "Most of the time I'll ask him which club just to be reassured, but sometimes I'm not that sure myself. I'd say 75 percent of the time I want that reassurance; the other 25 percent I want him to suggest which club he thinks I should use."

In the months following last years Masters, several leading touring pros suggested that the Masters, like every other important tournament, permit a caddie of the golfer's choice. Hord Hardin agreed.

"We have some excellent caddies here at the club," Hord Hardin says, "but we're not" naive enough to think that we have 80 caddies who can be classified at the same level of competence as the tour caddies. If I were a player under today's conditions, and I think Bobby Jones would agree, I would want to bring my own caddie."

The mystique of Bobby Jones remains as much a part of the Masters as the azaleas and the dogwood. Bobby Jones founded the Masters in 1934 as the "Augusta Invitational" after having retired at age 28 following his 1930 grand slam of the United States Open, the British Open, the United States Amateur and the British Amateur.

"I like to think our tradition is change," Hord Hardin says.

"From the beginning Cliff Roberts and Bobby Jones," he adds, speaking of his predecessors, "were innovators. They did not stick to things because they did 'em that way before."

In addition to the caddie ruling, the Masters has provided the golfers for the first time with pin-placement diagrams of each green as well as booklets that show yardage-diagrams of each hole. The club also improved the two practice ranges that extend down the vast lawns on each side of Magnolia Drive leading to and from the clubhouse from the Washington Road guard house.

The influx of different caddies, of course, is the Masters' most visible change this year.

Several touring pros had felt the overall quality of Augusta National caddies had slowly deteriorated in recent years. On the undulating Masters greens, a club caddie might read a break that his golfer wouldn't see. But the golfer still has to stroke the putts, as Arnold Palmer did in winning four Masters titles.

After one of those victories, Arnold Palmer tipped Ironman Avery $1,500. In the excitement of the moment, Palmer's wife Winnie wrote a check for $15,000, which Ironman immediately returned.

"But no matter how I did in the Masters in those years, I never depended on Ironman for advice," Arnold Palmer says. "He was just there to carry the bag and to offer encouragement—which he did very well."

Years ago, Sam Snead had a caddie named O'Brien, but the three-time champion, who Thursday shot 79 in his last of a record 146 rounds in the Masters, made his own decisions as to which club to use and how a putt would break.

"I once told O'Brien," Sam Snead says, "if I asked him which club to use, don't tell me."

But for a new caddie, Augusta National presents at least one problem that might not be that apparent. John White, a Florida caddie imported by Arnold Palmer for this year's tournament was puffing hard as he trudged off the 18th green after the opening round.

"The hills here," he said, "don't come across on TV."

The Masters: Get Your Mouth Off My Ball!

from *Who's Your Caddy?* by Rick Reilly

Having never caddied in my life, I needed a smallish place to start out, away from the spotlight, a podunk kind of tournament.

Naturally, I chose The Masters.

In front of thousands of people, in the greatest tournament in golf, I made my professional caddying debut, looping for 64-year-old Tommy Aaron, the 1973 champion. I think he'd tell you it went quite well, unless you count tiny, little nitpickings, such as my dropping the towel eleven times, the headcover four, the puttercover six, standing in the wrong place at the wrong time, standing in the right place at the wrong time, forgetting to give him his putter, his ball, his driver, being too close to him, being too far from him, letting the clubs clink too much as I walked, letting myself clink too much as I walked, the infamous "mouth" incident, and the awful, shameful thing that happened on No. 5 that none involved shall ever forget.

This was Friday. We were paired with "Sponge," who caddies for New Zealander Michael Campbell, and "Fanny" Sunneson, who won six majors with Nick Faldo and now is the bagwoman for Notah Begay, who hates me very much, despite the fact that I've never caddied for him.

Sponge and Fanny. Sounds like a British sex club.

I say, Nigel, didn't I see you last night at The Sponge and Fanny?

What happened was, Aaron hit a 3-iron at No. 5 into the left greenside bunker, then splashed out. I handed him his putter and then nervously set about my raking duties. The crowd was huge around that green, as they are around most Augusta greens, and nobody was ready to putt yet, so I could feel all the eyes on me. I had dropped my towel once already that day and had 500 people yell, "Caddy! Caddy! Towel!" as though I were President Bush's Secret Service agent and had dropped my gun. *Caddy! Caddy! Uzi!* So I knew they were watching. I raked as I have raked my own bunkers far too many times, climbed out, then placed the rake on the grass behind.

That's when I noticed Aaron staring at my rake job, then glancing at Fanny. Aaron nodded at her. She nodded back. Begay nodded. Sponge nodded back. For all I know, the huge crowd nodded. Only one of us had no idea what all the nodding was about. Suddenly, Fanny dashed over to the rake, picked it up, got back in the bunker, and did it again. Completely.

I was to suffer the ultimate caddy humiliation: Reraked.

I was left with nothing to do but stand there and watch, humiliated. It was like a coach calling time-out in the middle of the Super Bowl and showing a quarterback how to put his hands under the center's butt.

And that's when I realized the horrible flaw in this book idea: Just because somebody "lets" you do something, doesn't mean you necessarily should go out and "do" it.

The fact that I, an absolute novice know-nothing, could get a bag and traipse my size 12s across the hallowed ground of Augusta National tells you how dangerously easy this whole idea was.

At the 2000 Masters, every past champion got a lifetime invitation, even if they were 111 years old. The rule has changed now, but then, it meant if Byron Nelson, then 89, felt like playing in next year's Masters, he could play. Naturally, since 1966, he has had the good sense not to.

Luckily, guys like 1957 champion Doug Ford (then 78) did not have good sense. He played every year until they made him stop in 2002. In the 2000 Masters, he went out there, threw a little 94 at them, and then withdrew. Meanwhile, a very good player sat home and bit his putter.

Naturally, figuring Ford was not exactly "counting" on winning and therefore might suffer an insufferable caddy and get in a book, I called him first.

"Mr. Ford," I began, "I'm doing a book on caddying and—"

"Already got a caddy," Ford snapped. "Had him for 25 years."

"Sure," I said, "but I was thinking, just this once, you might allow—"

Click.

May his bunions burst.

Finally, the agent for Aaron called back and said Aaron would let me caddy Wednesday only, as a tryout for the next year. Said we'd play nine holes and then the par-3 contest and that would give him an idea of exactly how horrible I was.

Yes!

I started researching Aaron, who, it turns out, is famous for three things: 1) Saving the Masters from having to put up with J. C. Snead every year by beating him by one shot in 1973; 2) Writing down an incorrect par "4" instead of a birdie "3" on the 17th hole for Sunday playing partner Roberto De Vicenzo in 1968. De Vicenzo signed the card anyway, causing him to keep that one-stroke higher score, causing him to miss his rightful spot in what would've been a two-man playoff with Bob Goalby, who was then declared the winner. When told of it, De Vicenzo did not blame Aaron. Instead he said, "What a 'stupid' I am." 3) Not being Hank Aaron's brother, though people ask him all the time anyway, despite the fact that the baseball Aarons are black and this golfing Aaron is white. ("No," Tommy tells them, "I'm taller.")

He'd played in 37 Masters, won the par-3 tournament one year with a five-under 22, and had missed more cuts than a drunk surgeon. However, in 2000, Aaron became the oldest player ever to make the cut—63 years, one month—when he shot 72-74-146, three under the cut, the first two days. Of course, he wound up dead last by five shots at 25-over, but still, on that Friday night, he was three shots better than Ollie, seven than Daly, and nine than Ben Crenshaw.

My man!

I reached him on his cellphone. "Meet me at the bag room at 7:30 sharp tomorrow morning," he said. "We'll play a practice round and then we'll play the par 3."

Having slept not at all, I was at the holy place by 7 a.m., and by this I mean the Augusta caddyshack. It was a white brick building, with lockers, tables, a TV playing ESPN, and a little caddyshack grill where a huge black man cooks delicacies for the caddies, such as hamburger ($2), cheeseburger (also $2), soup (50 cents), and fries (50 cents). Of course, business was a little slow this week on account of—for Masters week only—a giant cake-display case being brought in and filled with pimento-cheese sandwiches, fruit, Gatorade, pop, and candy. Now who is going to pay a whole 50 cents for soup when you can get free pimento-cheese sandwiches?

I saw Pete Bender, who carried Ian Baker-Finch at the 1993 British Open—which tells you how good Bender is—and he said that Augusta is good, but the best caddy room in the free world is the Players Championship. "Oh, man, hot breakfasts, hot lunch, big-screen TV, couches," Bender said wistfully. Here's a guy carrying Rocco Mediate and probably making $100,000 a year, and he's thrilled at the idea of being able to actually eat a meal during his 10-hour workday. The worst, he said, was Arnold Palmer's tournament, Bay Hill. "They got nothin'. Zero. Not even a room to change in."

Shame, Arnie, shame.

I put on the classic all-white painter overalls with the green Masters hat they give you (free!). It's the classiest uniform in golf, with the player's number Velcroed on the left breast (I got No. 411—the defending champ's caddy always gets "1"), the Augusta logo on the right breast pocket, and the player's name on the back. Beautiful. Like a fool, I forgot to steal it when I was done.

I tried to ignore the sign that read, "Caddies are required to wear white flat-soled sneakers." All I had were black Softspiked golf shoes. This made me stand out like a bridesmaid in construction boots. Also, I found out later, on hot days, guys wear nothing but boxers underneath. There have been rumors of guys going "commando" under them, and I can only pray that: a) it isn't true and b) if it is true, I didn't get Fluff's old overalls.

They handed me a yardage book, which looked like Sanskrit. It made no sense, just numbers and swirls and acronyms. It must be how *The New Yorker* looks to an illiterate. I was standing there, looking like Rubik's twit brother, when Cubby, Davis Love's caddy, said, "Don't even bother, Rook, you'll never understand it."

Cubby is one of the great lads. When not caddying, he's always got the sports section in one hand and an unlit cigar in the mouth. His breakup with Brad Faxon was one of the most tragic in tour history—13 years together. But that's how it is. No alimony, no keeping the China. Just like that, everybody notices you're not lugging the old bag with you everywhere you go.

Cubby and Faxon used to be quite a pair. They had a language all their own. For yardages, for instance, Cubby would say, "OK, you got 123 plus Elway, and a little Reagan." Which meant, "You have 123 yards to the front of the green, plus another seven yards (Elway's jersey number) to the flagstick, with the wind throwing your ball a little to the right (Reagan's politics)." Or Cubby would say, "You got 214 (yards to the front) plus Michael (Jordan, which is 23 yards), and a little Clinton (wind going left)." What, you don't speak fluent Cubby?

Cubby has a jersey number for every conceivable yardage, but I always thought there were more they didn't use. For instance, what about: "You got

134 plus Hal (four, for the number of Hal Sutton's wives)," or "You got 189 plus O. J. (Simpson's two murders)," or "It's 201 plus Anna (Kournikova, a perfect 10)."

The yardages in the book were from every conceivable place you could think of—sprinkler heads, bushes, benches. You half expected to see distances marked to Martha Burk's offices written in. But there were also strange numbers way to the sides of the hole drawings accompanied by strange letters—like ICYFU: 219. And ICYRFU: 174. Cubby explained it to me. "ICYFU means 'In Case You Fuck Up.' And ICYRFU means 'In Case You Really Fuck Up.'"

Then somebody came up to him and said, "Cubby, did you get those bad numbers on 11?"

"What bad numbers?" Cubby said.

And the guy said, "Where it says 64 and 56, it's really 60 and 51." I made a secretive note of it in my book, which Cubby slyly noticed. Then Cubby said to the guy, "And did you get the one on 16? It's 144 from the front tee there, not 164." And his buddy goes, "Yeah, I got it. But did you get the one on 18? That first bush isn't there anymore, so that 128 is really 182." And I'm flipping frantically through the pages, trying to find the stupid 16th hole when I hear them both suddenly break up into hysterics. Great fun to con The Rook.

As God is my witness, I will get them someday.

I jammed the yardage book in the overall pockets, plus some sandwiches and apples, plus I had my wallet in there, my notepad, four pens, and a cell-phone, which I forgot to leave in the car and is strictly forbidden at Augusta. I walked out of there looking like a man shoplifting porcupines.

I checked my watch. It was 7:29. I started sprinting for the bag room. Then I was reminded of one of Augusta's big rules: No running. I sprint-walked. People suddenly started parting seas for me. People jabbed each other. I was wondering what was going on when I heard: "There's Aaron's caddy." The overalls were, it turns out, a big deal. I was Augusta royalty. I was wearing the white, the green, the logo. I was the real deal. You know, if a guy were single ...

I made it by 7:30. Luckily, Aaron wasn't there yet.

And he wasn't there by 7:45 either. Or 8. Or 8:30, 9, or 9:30.

"Welcome to the Pro Gap," Joe LaCava, caddy for Fred Couples, told me.

"What's the Pro Gap?" I asked.

"The difference between when the pro says he'll meet you and when he actually shows up."

Of course, caddies accept the Pro Gap as part of caddy life. But, as they pointed out, let "you" be late and you're as fired as Anna Nicole Smith's dietician.

Still, it was sort of caddy *Star Wars* outside that bag room. Fluff was there (for Jim Furyk). LaCava was there. Jim Mackay, the world-renowned "Bones," my personal caddy hero who had hauled Phil Mickelson for 10 years by then. And, of course, the Joe Namath of caddies, Bruce Edwards, Tom Watson's longtime Sancho Panza.

Edwards happened to be the person Tom Watson told, "I'm going to chip this in," on the 17th hole at Pebble Beach at the 1982 U.S. Open, which he did, to beat J. W. Nicklaus himself.

Finally, at 11:30, four hours late, Aaron showed up. He was much taller than I thought he'd be. Maybe 6-1, still slender, elegantly dressed, curly gray hair, glasses, and a visor.

"I'm just going to go into the Champion's Room (the locker room at Augusta reserved for past champions) and then we'll go. Meet me on the range in, what, 45 minutes?"

"Sure," I said, cheerfully. *Sure! What's another 45 minutes!?! No problem! Perhaps I'll knit another sweater!*

The bag was simple and blue, with no sponsor on it, and heavier than Meatloaf. What's this guy got in there, anvils? I remembered the time British golf writer Bill Elliott spent a day caddying for Faldo for a story. Elliott struggled under its weight all day, until he discovered, afterward, that Faldo had snuck a brick and three dozen extra balls into the bottom of the bag for a laugh. There is nobody that will crack you up like that madcap Nick Faldo.

I made my way past the ropes, into forbidden territory—the range—the place where no writer is allowed to go at the Masters, nor fan, nor photographer. Self-conscious and thrilled, I tried to think of what to do so as not to appear self-conscious and thrilled. So, naturally, I decided to eat.

I sat on the bench and pulled a pimento-cheese sandwich out, and an apple and a Gatorade. I was about to take my first bite when I noticed, for the first time, approximately 1,000 people watching me. The bleachers behind the range were full of fans and, at that moment, nobody was actually hitting balls, so they were watching me. I tried not to spill.

Just then, Bruce Edwards sat down next to me. Sitting on that bench, him waiting for the great Watson and me waiting for Aaron, I, naturally, ruined the moment by hounding him desperately for advice.

"Just remember the three ups," he said.

"Three ups?" I asked.

"Show up, keep up, and shut up."

I asked Edwards if he ever wished he'd have done something else for a living.

"Never," he said. "In fact, in 1976, Tom wanted me to quit caddying for him and go to school. He even offered to pay for it. He wasn't winning much then and he said, 'Look, go get your degree and have a real life.' So I thought about it and I came back to him and said, 'No. I like *this* life.' And I'm sure as hell glad I did. Because that next year he won four times and the next year five." And went on to a career that has so far paid like a winning Lotto ticket and kept Edwards in cold beer and nice boats ever since. Finally, Watson himself showed up, about an hour late.

"I'm sorry," Edwards chided. "Did you mean 12 o'clock, Kansas City time?"

Caddies 1, Pro Gap 0.

They walked off and Edwards grinned at me. I thought maybe I should say that to my man. "I'm sorry, did you mean 7:30 a.m., sharp THURSDAY?"

but then I thought, perhaps this is a wisecrack one might try after caddying 30 years, not 30 seconds.

Aaron came striding onto the range and I came striding after him, holding a bag of balls which I—ever the sharp caddy—had secured and made ready. Except when we got to our stall on the range and I plopped them down, they turned out to be the wrong balls. "I play Callaway," he said, staring at me. I jog-walked (no running!) back to the ball boys and said, "I need Callaway, fast!" and they said, "Red or blue?" And I said, "Bloody hell? You have red or blue?" I took a bag of each.

Aaron was accompanied by his coach, 79-year-old Manuel de la Torre, the head pro at Milwaukee Country Club, one of the foremost teachers of the "swing the club" school of golf. And already, he was tutoring Aaron on how to swing the club.

"What happened there?" Manuel said.

"I felt like I swung it a little right of the target."

"And where did it go?" said Manuel.

"Right of the target."

"Correct," said Manuel.

Whoa, this is the magic that they're discussing? This is the inside conversation that we're all dying to get up close and hear?

We went through two bags of BLUE Callaways, went through another bag in the bunker—where I learned upon receiving a dirty look that you want to flip the practice ball to him so that he doesn't have to move his feet—putted for a while, and then, suddenly, miraculously, we were on the first tee at Augusta National during the 65th playing of the Masters Tournament. It was wonderful... until Aaron uttered five awful words: "Do you know Scott Hoch?"

"Uh..."

"He's got nobody going with him, either, so we're going with him."

Suddenly, I was turning around to shake the hand of a man I'd mocked to 21 million readers more than once in print for: a) skipping the British Open every year because it's too "expensive"; b) missing a 2-foot putt that would've won him the 1989 Masters; and, c) being voted Least Liked Player on Tour in a poll of his peers.

Hoch looked at me. I looked at him. He knew.

"Scott, Rick Reilly," I said, holding my hand out.

He looked at me, looked at the hand, said, "I know who you are," and began to tee up his ball.

Oops.

Aaron gave me a look. I stared at my shoes. Not a shot hit yet and I was already causing him problems.

Still, I was thinking that Scott Hoch has had to play with people he dislikes and who dislike him quite often in his career. Like, say, on the order of every Thursday through Sunday. So, off we went.

Of all the signs in the world, the most ignored has to be the little white-and-green sign on the first tee at the Masters that reads, "Play Only One Ball Please." In fact, about the only place only one ball is played during practice rounds is at that first tee. Otherwise, players play about eight balls. Players hit all kinds of second shots, third shots, dozens of chips, putts, bunker shots, pitches, and lags from every possible angle on every green.

This makes practice days very difficult for your average everyday caddy and absolute, pure Dante's *Inferno* for your basic Rook. It was "throw those back to me" and "rake those spots" and "let me hit those again, Rick." If I'd had a methamphetamine habit, I couldn't have done it all: clubs to be cleaned, clubs to be exchanged for different clubs, balls to be cleaned, balls to be retrieved, bunkers to be raked. And that was just the stuff I knew I should be doing. God knows what I wasn't doing. I almost quit. If it hadn't been the first hole, I might have.

At one point on No. 1, I got so confused I put our 8-iron in Hoch's bag—they were both white—until Hoch's caddy cleared his throat. Caddy etiquette. If it were one day later and Hoch played the hole with the club in there, it would've been a two-shot penalty—on Hoch. And then he really wouldn't like me.

Exhausted and dehydrated by the time we reached the No. 2 tee box, I stood the bag up and went for a cup of water. When I came back, Tommy was pissed. "You *never* take your hand off the bag when it's standing up," he growled. "It can—and will—tip over at the worst possible time and place, like on my golf ball." Good point.

That would be another two-stroke penalty, wouldn't it? Played one hole, nearly caused four shots in penalties. Nice start.

Tommy Aaron is just slightly more finicky than the Sultan of Brunei. For instance, he informed me on the second hole not to hand him his putter until he reached the green. I always thought there's nothing better than a long walk with your putter, meaning you've hit the green, life is good, but, no.

One time, on No. 5, he hit a chip that looked like it was going to be short. "Get up!" I said to it.

He turned to me. "Keep your mouth off my ball."

I was confused.

"I don't use my mouth," I said, earnestly. "I'm using this wet towel here." I held it up for him as proof that I wasn't popping his ball in my mouth to wash it.

"No, no. Keep your mouth off my ball. Don't talk to it. I want it to get up as much as you do. It doesn't help me to know that you're over there, telling it to get up or get down or whatever. It just adds to the pressure."

I said OK, and I thought about it. It "adds to the pressure"? You'd think he'd want to know that somebody is cheering him on, rooting for him "and" his stupid ball! How is that "more" pressure? It seems to me it's dividing the pressure in half, you and me, pal, a team! But the more I thought about it, the more I understood what he was trying to say. What he was saying is, "If I hear you urging my shots to do a certain thing—Sit! Bite! Run! Cut!—and they *don't*, I'm going to feel like I've let *you* down, too. I've got a family to support, and friends here, and fans, and press. The last thing I need is a caddy piling on, OK?"

It's like me. I write a weekly sports column. The "last" thing I want is my wife to call at the office and say, "Hey, how are you doing this week? Is the lead going to be good? The kids and I are really hoping it's going to be funny!"

Still, there were other things. He'd hit a drive and people would applaud and we'd walk down the fairway and he'd say to me, "I can't understand that."

"I'm sorry?" I said, fingering my wet towel, in case I needed it as evidence again.

"The gallery applauding. Can't they see I hit that one in the heel? I mean, don't they know anything about golf?"

I wanted to say, "Well, you're 64 years old. You've already told me you're playing with a painful hammertoe, an arthritic hip, a bone spur in your neck, a little vertigo, and insomnia. I suppose they're just glad you got it airborne."

One time, somebody in the crowd hollered, "Hey, Tommy!" and Tommy gave them the tiniest of waves.

"That's funny, isn't it?" he said.

"I'm sorry?" I said, for the 116th time.

"If I were at a tournament, I don't think I'd speak unless I was spoken to. I'm trying to work here, you know? How would they like it if I hung around the insurance office all day while they were working and said, 'Hey, Fred, way to go!'"

I agreed, of course. They should all be hung from the old tree on the clubhouse veranda.

On the third hole, Aaron said, "Seemed like there was some tension between you and Scott on the first tee." Uh-oh. Here it comes. I've got no chance now. I'll get the rest of this day and see ya later.

"Yeah, well, I noticed that, too," I said. "Not sure what that was about."

He stared at me for a second and then walked on.

Uh-oh.

At the end of nine, Aaron had played well. I had us at one-over-par 37. But he suddenly decided to quit for the day. He also said he wasn't going to play the par-3 tournament. "And I'm afraid I'm going to stay with the caddy

I was given," he said. "You can take the clubs to the bag room. Thanks for your help."

Crushed. Heartbroken. Untipped.

Sacked after nine practice holes at the Masters. If not Aaron, who would ever let me out? My book advance flashed before my eyes. I was doomed.

Desperate, I said, "You sure? Because I'll be here all week. Maybe if your caddy comes up hurt or something?"

He just smiled and said, "I doubt it."

I hung around in my beloved caddy overalls as long as I could. A few Japanese people took my picture. I finally had to take them off. I didn't see how a caddy could ask Tiger Woods a question in the press conference.

"Uh, Tiger, how do you feel about people's mouths on your balls?"

The next day, Thursday, I followed Aaron and his caddy, a local, a few holes. I felt like a jilted lover.

But then I noticed something wonderful. I couldn't hear, but Aaron was jawing at him animatedly. I thought maybe it was the dreaded Mouth-on-Ball Syndrome, but it seemed worse. Aaron was walking away, shaking his head. And the caddy was shrugging his shoulders.

Could he have accidentally said, "Good shot?"

Aaron shot 81. I found him in the clubhouse after lunch and said it looked like he'd played fairly well, but something seemed to be bothering him.

"That caddy," he said, shaking his head, "has the *worst* damn attitude of any caddy I've ever had. Just a *piss-poor* attitude. He was pouting the *whole* time. He gave me a read that was just flat wrong on 16 and I told him so and he pouted. He had his head down all the time. The most miserable, worst goddamn *horrible* attitude I've ever seen."

Hope springs anew.

I cleared my throat. "Well, if he's that bad, how about this? I'll 'pay' him to stay off your bag the rest of the week and I'll work for you for free!"

Aaron thought about it and thought about it some more and finally said, "OK."

Pinocchio, you're a real boy.

On the way to the pressroom, higher than Tokyo rent, I saw Carl Jackson, Ben Crenshaw's Masters-only caddy, the one who gave Crenshaw the little ball-positioning tip before the 1995 Masters that Crenshaw credited for helping him win. I imagined me doing that for Aaron.

Aaron to Press: I know it's incredible, a 64-year-old man winning, but it never would've happened without my caddy, Rick. He noticed my left pinky knuckle was pronating slightly and it made all the difference in the world. Rick, I want you to have the jacket.

Me: No, I couldn't.

Aaron: Oh, nonsense. Try it on!

Me: Well...

I paid the old caddy $150 for the day he missed on Wednesday and another $150 for the day he was going to miss Friday, and I said I'd pay him $150 for any day after that, although, after the 81, Masters chairman Hootie Johnson was going to vogue across the 18th green naked before that happened. Still, the guy made $300 for sitting on his couch watching on television while I humped the bag up Augusta's hills for bupkus. OK, I undermined him, but I ain't holding any telethons for him.

Friday morning came and as Aaron met me, he warned, "Now, don't get too excited out there."

"I'm sorry?" I said.

"If the caddy gets all nervous and excited, it seeps into me. So just be quiet and calm."

Got it.

When we got to the first tee, Aaron said, "Rick, do you know Notah Begay?" Uh-oh.

I did know Begay and he knew me and I could tell that from the glare I was getting. Begay had spent a week in an Albuquerque prison after his second DUI, only it wasn't exactly the gulag. He was part of a "work-release" program, so he was allowed to get up in the morning, go hit balls at his club, have lunch at the club, then play 18 holes in the afternoon, then dinner at the club, then back to the prison to sleep. I said they ought to call the jail Swing-Swing. I said that for most guys, that wasn't prison, that was a week at the Myrtle Beach Red Roof Inn. I'd heard Begay was ticked off about it. Still, unlike Hoch, he begrudgingly shook my hand. I made a note to stay very clear of his tee shots.

Aaron might have said something to me like, "I noticed some tension between you and Notah there," except for the fact that he found something that annoyed him about Begay and Campbell right off. He canned a 40-footer on No. 1 to save par, walked over to me, and whispered, "Did you see that?"

"I'm sorry?" I said, nervously fingering my wet towel and trying to figure out what I'd done now.

"Neither of those guys said, 'Nice putt.' That's the way it is with these younger players. They don't see any shot but their own."

"Selfish," I said, shaking my head. For once, he was mad at somebody other than me. It didn't last long.

On No. 2, Aaron had a little chip back from above the green. I gave him the wedge and stood there a second and then realized I better get the bag to the side of the hole that would lead to the next tee box, as all good caddies do. He was still eyeing the chip from behind the shot and he gave me a dirty little look. I froze. Then he chipped.

Going down the third fairway, he said, "The clubs are making too much noise."

"I'm sorry?"

"They're making too much noise. Listen to the noise they're making. Quiet them down."

He walked ahead of me in a kind of huff. I wandered over to Fanny. "I can't *believe* this guy!" I complained to her, struggling up the hill at No. 3. "He says my clubs make too much noise when I walk. I mean, Christ, what am I supposed to do, buy fourteen mufflers and—"

"Yes," she said. "Yours do make too much noise."

I stared at her. She stared at me. "Take your towel and wrap it through the middle of the irons, like this. Then walk with your hand over them."

I tried it. They quieted right down. Fanny Sunneson is a goddess.

On No. 4, the par 3, he was standing in the middle of the tee box, about eight feet from where I was standing with the bag, just to the left of the tee markers. "Rick, come over here," he said.

I had a flutter of excitement. He was finally trusting me enough to ask me advice. Maybe he wanted to talk wind. Maybe yardage. Maybe club selection. So I stood the bag up where it was and walked over to him. He looked at me like he'd just swallowed a cockroach. "*With* the bag," he said, irritated.

I didn't understand why he wanted me to drag the bag the eight feet out to the middle of the tee markers when it was much easier for him to simply take the club himself. Fanny and Sponge weren't doing that. Their guys would stand by their bag, pick the stick, and walk the eight feet. But so be it. I got the bag and brought it to him. He took his club. I went back to where I was and he hit it.

But on the sixth hole, another par 3, I forgot and the same thing happened. "Rick, bring the bag," he said sharply, and I schlepped it out there again. He took a 6-iron and made the most gorgeous swing, nearly making a hole-in-one, missing by inches left. As the huge crowd roared, he came over to me and looked me right in the eye. I figured he was going to say something clever or snappy, something like, "Pulled it." Or, "Take a suck of that!" But instead he yelled—YELLED—"Now, goddammit, I'm not gonna tell you again! I don't wanna have to walk clear over there to get a goddamn club!" There was a hush around the crowd at the tee box. Caddy whipping. All I could do was clean my little 6-iron and stare at the bottom of the bag.

I would ask Couples' caddy, Joe LaCava, about this later. I said, "Why would a guy want me to pick up the bag and take it to the middle of the tee box when he could just take it with him when he steps out there?" And Joe LaCava said, simply, "Because he is a professional golfer."

I didn't know what that answer meant then. But I'd learn. I'd learn.

On No. 8, I watched Sponge and Fanny give their guys 3-woods so they didn't have to walk clear back to the tee, so I did the same. I was kneeling there, trying to catch my wind, when I felt a tap on my shoulder. It was Begay. "Here is where he lets me have it," I thought. Here is where he spikes my kidneys. Or gets me with a homemade prison shiv. Instead, he said, "You should go wait with the others." I looked around and Sponge and Fanny were 150 yards up the 8th fairway, resting happily in the shade.

Left the Rook behind.

After that, it all fell apart for us. Aaron bogeyed the par-5 8th despite being right in front in two and then doubled 10, where he chunked a chip into a bunker, then three-putted.

Then we headed into Amen Corner and it was a thrill to be inside the ropes at the most famous section of holes in golf. "Nobody" gets inside the ropes at Augusta except players and caddies and the scorer. Not coaches. Not photographers. Not press. Not rules officials. Nobody. It's virginal land, pristine. If Ansel Adams were around, he'd shoot it. Walking down 11 fairway, I was struck by the hugeness of the place, the vast "space." I'd covered thirteen Masters and yet I'd never noticed how deep the woods went to the left of 11 and 12. It looked like *Blair Witch 3* in there.

Another odd thing. Since the crowds are so huge at Amen Corner, I was aware that every time I moved a step, I was blocking the views of maybe 100 people or more. It was an odd feeling. Move one yard this way and those 100 can't see. One yard that way and those 100 can't see. Great, great fun. I was the God of Views, free to give and take away as I saw fit. "Oh, you drove the Dodge Dart clear from Manitoba for your first Masters? Sorry. I choose to stand . . . *here.*"

All my life I'd wanted to stand on the 12 green during The Masters. I'd always wondered what it's like out there, viewed by thousands of fans, but all from 160 yards away—every movement watched through binoculars but not a sound heard. For fans, it's like watching a silent movie. But on the green, so far away from the thousands watching, you find out. "Fuck me," Begay said when his par putt missed. Aaron missed a four-footer for par, but, to his credit, did not say, "Fuck me." The thousands back in the gallery probably assume they're saying, "Well played there, Tommy," and "Oh, a spot of bad luck there, chum," and instead they're going, "Fuck me."

There is nothing in golf like the 13th tee box, either. Set back into the azaleas and dogwoods, it must be the most beautiful inland tee in the world. And yet, to the players, it is more famously known as the home of the "pee bush." Players and caddies go back behind a huge bush and pee. There are not many Porta Potties at Augusta and the ones they have are packed, so 13 has become the traditional whizzing ground. Not wanting to piss on history, I also loosed the lizard back there, and as I was doing so it hit me that some of the great names in golf history—Jones, Snead, Hogan, Nicklaus—had all squirted on this very bush. It made me proud. It also made me want to throw out my shoes first chance I got.

We made an awful double bogey at 13, but it wasn't our fault. We wound up in a divot after our second shot, had to blade it out of there and over, putted way, way by in 4, half-lagged it up in 5, and missed a three-footer for 6. I still feel if I could've spoken to his ball, it would've helped. Now we were 10 over par with five holes to go. We were headed for 90. Doug Ford, here we come.

But at 14, 15, and 16, we made great pars—nearly made three birdies—and it was a privilege to carry the bag of a man who can play that well at 64 years old with more ailments than the Mayo Clinic. The pars made him so chipper, in fact, that I offered a small bit of chitchat. "This place has great memories for you, huh?"

He said it did. He said he hated to come and play so badly as he did this week. "Shooting in the 80s is not my idea of fun," he said. He said he loved

Augusta and loved the memories of his win here, when he made birdie at 18 and had no idea he'd won until later, since he wasn't in the last group.

I offered up a potential grenade, seeing as how we were coming to the 18th tee box. "How did the whole De Vicenzo snafu happen?" I said, walking just out of swinging-putter range.

He was quite happy to talk about it. "It was really so ridiculous," he said. "In those days, you'd check your scorecard at a little card table they set up, right out in the open, under the sun. Roberto was a little mad that he'd made bogey on the last hole and so he just signed the card without even looking at it. He threw it on the table and left. Whoosh. Now, I'm very meticulous about my scores. I double and triple-check them. My card checked out and I was about to leave when I looked up at the scoreboard and saw that it said 'De Vicenzo, 11-under.' And it hit me that something was wrong. I had him at one 'higher' than that, 10-under. I checked it against the scoreboard and realized what had happened. I said to one of the officials, 'Better get Roberto back here. This isn't right.' I felt bad, but people make mistakes on your scorecard. Happens all the time. You *have* to check it."

At 18, Aaron made an unbelievable chip shot, a purposely bladed chip from against the collar that he aimed 180 degrees away from the hole, ran over the green, down the hump, over the fringe on the other side, and back to within six inches of the hole. It was the kind of shot only a man who'd played 37 Masters could've made, and even Begay and Campbell put their putters down to applaud.

Tommy checked his card, meticulously, then gave me a tour of the Champions's Locker Room, which is the tiniest locker room you've ever been in, yet with the greatest collection of nameplates ever in one room. His was under Jimmy Demaret's. Then he had a lunch and a couple vodkas and I had a beer, and suddenly he was the nicest man you'd ever want to meet, chatty, funny, cordial.

He gave me his critique of my maiden loop. "For a first-time caddy, you weren't *that* bad" he said. "It seemed like you wanted to get rid of the bag at all costs. Most caddies walk right up on the green with the bag on their shoulder, wash the ball, make sure everything's right, and *then* get rid of the bag. You just wanted to get rid of the bag right away, no matter what, get rid of the bag, then come and check on me."

That was true, of course, for two reasons. One, I was taught you don't walk on the green with your bag on your shoulder as it makes deep footprints in the green. Guess not. And two, that stupid bag was heavier than a lead piano.

I asked him if there were any scorecard problems this time, 33 years later. "As a matter of fact," he said, "Michael Campbell had two incorrect scores for me—on 2 and on 8. I had sixes on both and he had me for fives. I'm telling you, it happens all the time!"

What a stupid Campbell is.

We could've used those fives, by the way. We finished fourth worst in the tournament at 163, just 27 shots behind Tiger's two-day 136, which would lead to his four-day 16-under 272, which would merely win him the Consecutive Grand Slam is all. Only Billy Casper had a higher two-day score at 167. Gay Brewer had an 84 the first day and withdrew. We were 90th out of 96 in driving distance at 241 yards (66 yards behind Tiger), and 90th in greens in regulation (13 total), but we were 30th in putts. Then again, we did a whole helluva lot better than the charming Doug Ford, who made a six on the first hole, withdrew immediately, took his $5,000 participant's honorarium, and went home. Class guy. I'll bet he voted against Lincoln, too.

Actually, $5,000 to play one hole is about what third-place finisher Phil Mickelson ($380,000) made per hole after playing 72.

Maybe he's not so dumb after all.

THE MOMENTS

War Comes to Augusta

Curtain Calls for the Masters and PGA Championship

from *When War Played Through: Golf During World War II* by John Strege

Uncertainty permeated the Augusta National Golf Club and the Masters in April of 1942, inviting nostalgia to overwhelm a man. When he arrived, Grantland Rice, the poet laureate of American sportswriting, gazed pensively at the flora that ushered in the spring there—the flowering dogwood, pink and white, the azaleas and camellias and purple wisteria—and was inspired to craft an ode to old friends and better days:

> *Back to the red clay hills again,*
> *back to a trail I know,*
> *Where the ghostly tramp of the years returns*
> *to a spring in the long ago.*
> *When a mockingbird and a bluebird call,*

"Don't you remember the day
When Bobby Jones was the Grand Slam
kid and Ty had the right of way?"
Back to the red clay hills again,
back where the years were young,
When Uncle Remus was still
around and Stanton's songs were sung.
And a mockingbird calls from a dogwood flame,
"Here's to an ancient toast—
When Bobby Jones was the king of golf
and Ty was the Georgia Ghost!"

Jones vying for first, Cobb breaking for second—these were memories that for Rice provided a measure of warmth against the chilling reality that encompassed the Augusta landscape. They couldn't smell the war in Augusta, but they could feel it. Augusta was a military town, ninety miles due east of Atlanta, the home to the United States Army's Camp Gordon, and already it was on its war footing. Military planes passed overhead every couple of minutes. In town, uniformed personnel seemingly outnumbered civilians.

Augusta was also home to the Augusta National Golf Club, a private sanctuary created by the renowned Atlanta lawyer and Rice's dear friend, the inestimable Bobby Jones. Jones's involvement in founding the club, as well as the annual exercise that had come to be known as the Masters, had restored Augusta's prominence, which had largely been moribund since it had relinquished its role as the capital of Georgia nearly one hundred fifty years earlier.

The war had caused Camp Gordon to eclipse the Masters on the scale of importance there. The tenor and the time were wrong for a rite of spring, as the Masters had become. Now, as the ninth playing of the Masters approached, there was a foreboding sense that it would be the last for a while. The U.S. Open had already been canceled. Gasoline rationing and Augusta's isolation challenged the logic of keeping the course open over the duration of the war. Each week, the ranks of professional golf were thinned by the call to serve. The Masters this time around seemed not so much an opportunity to say hello to old friends as it was as an occasion to say good-bye to them.

The press sensed it too. It was determined to elevate the stature of the 1942 Masters to a degree that it would be regarded an appropriate send-off, if indeed this was its farewell pending the return of peace in the world. Writers were selling it as the de facto national championship. "This year, with the U.S. Open tournament canceled by war, the Masters' title will be regarded by many as equivalent to a national championship," *The Atlanta Constitution* wrote.

The membership at Augusta National did not summarily reject the media's hyperbole. Indeed, it helped reinforce what Clifford Roberts, the cofounder of the club and the tournament chairman, had come to believe about the tournament. Roberts wrote, "While we may not have expected it originally, we have created a tournament of such importance that we are bound to see that it continues."

Another reason for the welcome injection of hype was that it introduced the possibility of an attendance spike. To its credit, the club had earmarked the Masters gate receipts for a worthy cause that demonstrated on behalf of the membership a greater concern for the plight of its country than its country club: Augusta National had offered to bankroll and build a practice facility at Camp Gordon, to stock it with equipment, and to periodically supply renowned tour pros to conduct clinics for the soldiers.

Jones and Roberts had considered a variety of suggestions of ways in which the club and its members might assist in the war effort, including one culled from the radio program *Information, Please*. A tobacco company that sponsored the show donated twenty-five dollars to charity for every question that was answered incorrectly. Roberts and Jones concocted the idea of soliciting pledges from the members, who would donate to the Red Cross each time a Masters contestant made a birdie.

That idea gave way to Jones and Roberts deciding that proceeds from the Masters would go for a golf facility at Camp Gordon. The club's news release announcing the project began: "A man in an Army training camp can't come to a golf course—at least, not often. So golf is coming to him."

Officers at Camp Gordon were thrilled with Augusta National's benevolence and pledged their support. Jones was enlisted as the club's emissary, and he met with Camp Gordon officers and an architect whom the camp was employing and drew up a design, which began with a putting green large enough to accommodate seventy-five players. Adjacent to the green was a large, gradual slope that overlooked the practice range and was capable of holding as many as two thousand spectators for those occasions when Augusta National would send over marquee professionals to conduct clinics.

The range itself would have room enough for fifty golfers, most of whom would never be able to reach the far end of the range, two hundred fifty yards off. Four greens (made from sand, actually) would be situated at intervals from one hundred to one hundred seventy-five yards away, providing a series of targets. Augusta National also intended to supply the camp with seventy-five woods and irons and fifty putters, as well as upwards of a thousand golf balls. It even intended to install floodlighting, for night practice, at a cost of about a thousand dollars.

Roberts concluded that it would be money well spent on soldiers otherwise unable to entertain themselves during downtime. "To my mind," Roberts wrote in a letter to the United States Golf Association, "the one controlling thought to keep in mind about this whole thing is the fact that a great deal of money is being raised to entertain soldiers and sailors in the cities and in the towns, but for every soldier boy seen on the streets of our cities, there are probably ten out at some camp who cannot get a pass to leave the camp or who haven't the money to go outside."

The Bobby Jones Driving Range at Camp Gordon was finished in time for players from the Masters field to participate in its inauguration. The bill came to $2,669, while the equipment was donated by club members and the Augusta National pro shop. The facility was dedicated on the eve of the Masters, a five o'clock ceremony that allowed the players to complete practice rounds and still make their way over to the camp.

Practice rounds were not trivial affairs. Newspapers covered them as though information might be gleaned that could help them with their tournament form charts, disregarding the fact that what a player scores on Tuesday has no bearing on what he'll shoot on Thursday. Still, their diligence in reporting on practice rounds often turned up, if not useful intelligence, at least amusing asides. Two days before the Masters was to begin, Sam Snead was at the first tee, ready to play a practice round. Also there were Fred Corcoran, the PGA tournament manager, and a couple of sportswriters. Corcoran had a keen eye for promotion, and he began boasting about Snead's talent, even suggesting that he could win the Masters playing barefoot.

"You should kick off those shoes," Corcoran said. "Remember, you played five holes in practice in your socks before the Canadian Open last year and won it."

The writers similarly urged him to remove his shoes and socks. Snead pondered whether it might be bad form to do so at an upscale club, but eventually he succumbed to the challenge.

He rolled up his pants and removed his shoes and socks, then playfully wiggled his toes in the grass.

"You know," he said, "it sure feels good to get your feet on the ground. I used to play barefoot all the time back home on the goat course at Hot Springs, Virginia."

He stepped up to the tee and hit a perfect drive, long and straight. He followed with a perfect second, the ball stopping three feet from the hole. He made the birdie putt.

"Honestly, I'm telling you the truth," he said. "I feel better when I stand up to the ball in my bare feet. Those thick-soled shoes keep you too far off the ground."

Snead went around Augusta National in 68 strokes and even hinted that he might play the tournament sans shoes. Word of Snead's escapade, meanwhile, had traveled all the way back to the clubhouse, where Gene Sarazen was waiting for him. Sarazen was spitting angry at Snead, whom he accused of acting like a "barefoot hillbilly" on this hallowed course. "Can you imagine Walter Hagen or Henry Cotton playing barefoot on this course?" Sarazen asked.

Corcoran predictably sided with Snead; he told Sarazen that he'd bet on Snead barefoot in a match with Sarazen, who went off again, reciting his record and contrasting it with that of Snead, who had won nothing of substance to that point in his career.

To Sarazen's chagrin, the media generally sided with Snead as well. "Wild man Walter Hagen not play barefoot?" Bill Corum wrote in the *New York Journal*. "Hagen would play in a bathing suit if the mood struck him. Sarazen would, too, if he thought it'd help win. Gene should be the last to squawk—all golfers remember his weird proposal to enlarge the cups to eight inches." The California Golf Writers Association, coming down on the side of "barefoot hillbillies" over the game's elitism, made Snead an honorary member "for putting the game back on its feet."

Another practice round produced some of the finest, most spirited golf of the week. Bobby Jones had been retired from competitive golf for nearly twelve years, though once a year he pulled his rusty skills out of storage and allowed himself to play in the Masters. In the practice round, he paired with Byron Nelson in a match with Gene Sarazen and Henry Picard, and he showed that on a given day he could still provide a reasonable impersonation of Bobby Jones. Even with a ball in the water at the thirteenth hole, Jones shot a five-under-par 31 on the back nine for a round of 68 that enabled him and his partner to halve their match.

"What do you think of that?" Sarazen said. "Picard and I scored seven birdies in the last nine holes and didn't win a hole."

After their practice rounds, Jones and another thirty players from the field of forty-two made their way to Camp Gordon for the dedication ceremony. Craig Wood was there, as were Ed Dudley, the host pro and the PGA president, Nelson, Sam Snead, and Ben Hogan. The master of ceremonies was Grantland Rice, who opened his remarks with a lighthearted apology:

"We're sorry we can't offer you soldier boys a better bunch of golfers for this show, but there aren't any better golfers in this world today."

An assortment of military dignitaries was there, including the camp's commanding officer, which ensured that the hundreds of enlisted men in the crowd behaved in an orderly manner. Eventually, Jones was introduced to a standing ovation.

"I hope you boys find sport, relaxation, and a lot of fun in the range and putting green," he said.'

The microphone worked its way to Horton Smith, a successful tour pro who could talk as good a game as he played. Smith emceed the clinic and brought on Jones to strike the ceremonial first shots. "Bobby Jones led off with three dedicatory wallops, all beautifully struck," his friend and biographer, O. B. Keeler, wrote in *The Atlanta Journal* the next day.

For the next four days, golf moved to the fore, a brief respite from the real world represented by the uniformed spectators lining the fairways, as well as the military cadets, more than a hundred of them, recruited from a dozen academies to control and direct the galleries. If the uniforms provided a visible reminder of the challenges ahead, the golfers delivered an oral reminder that they were going about their business as usual. It manifested itself in the obligatory whining about the difficulty of the course, specifically the speed of the greens, unduly fast, an Augusta tradition.

The year before, a couple of pros complained about the speed of the greens within earshot of Ed Dudley, Augusta National's head professional. "If you don't like them that way," Dudley replied, "I'll put the blades down on those mowers in the morning and you'll think you're on a billiard table."

Al Sharp wrote in his column "Sharp Shootin" in *The Atlanta Constitution*, "It isn't true that men with razor blades manicure the greens to make them so perfect ... but it does look as if that's what happens."

Golfer Henry Picard noted, "We aren't used to tapping six-foot putts, and that's what you have to do here. Stroke a short one and it'll end up in the fairway."

One particular habitual whiner, who built his reputation complaint by complaint, entered the clubhouse and headed for the bar, grumbling all the way about how unfair the layout was. Tommy Armour, the Silver Scot and the preeminent raconteur in the field, listened to the diatribe, accompanied by the tinkling of ice in his own cocktail. Armour took a drink, while considering the man's complaint and weighing it against the difficulty quotient experienced by Americans and Brits required to carry weapons more lethal than irons. Finally, he felt compelled to issue a rejoinder.

"There weren't any bombs out there, were there?" Armour said.

The quality of the competition was high, as the war had not yet appreciably thinned the talent—Hogan and Nelson were entered, as was Snead, and defending champion Craig Wood. The Navy was generously allowing Ensign Charles Yates, a former British Amateur champion and an Augusta National member, to participate. The Army gave a pass to Corporal Bud Ward, the reigning U.S. Amateur champion, to participate.

Players polled in the run-up to the Masters established Nelson, Hogan, and Snead as the favorites. It was a demonstration of sound judgment; they were the three best players in the world. Still, the year before the players had established Wood as the favorite, and he delivered on their behalf.

The tournament actually delivered on behalf of those in the press who were determined that it should be special. Jones was in contention briefly—he was tied for fifth after the first round. Sam Byrd, the former

New York Yankees outfielder, was the first-round leader. Nelson opened with rounds of 68 and 67 to take the lead after thirty-six holes, while Ben Hogan, the pretournament betting favorite at five to one, was eight shots in arrears at the halfway mark. "The impossible impediment," Grantland Rice called the deficit, for once choosing the wrong words.

Hogan erased five shots of Nelson's advantage in the third round, and whittled away two more shots on the first seventeen holes of the final round. On the difficult par-four eighteenth hole, Hogan hit his second to three feet of the hole and made the birdie putt to pull even with Nelson, forcing an eighteen-hole play-off the following day.

"When the showdown came on the final green," Rice wrote, "with Army men helping to check the human surge, Ben Hogan and Byron Nelson, the two star Texans, were all snarled up at 280 in a tie for first place .... Hogan cleared away the killing margin with one of the greatest finishes I've ever seen in golf."

The play-off was not anticlimactic either. The crowd was two thousand— "many of them in the khaki and blue of the armed forces," the *Constitution* wrote—forming a horde crowding around the only hole on which there were players. Among them was virtually every player who had competed in the Masters, each of them staying in town one more day to bear witness to a duel between the two best players in the game. Tommy Armour, Jimmy Demaret, Henry Picard, Jug McSpaden, Ralph Guldahl—they were there as well to pay tribute to the men who were selling their sport better than anyone else.

Hogan opened a three-stroke lead through four holes. By the eighth hole, Nelson had erased the deficit and had taken a one-stroke lead that he never relinquished. Nelson shot 69 to Hogan's 70, to win the tournament for the second time in six years.

The show that Nelson and Hogan put on over five days elevated the stature of the Masters, stamping it distinctive, a cut above the endless succession of *opens* that more or less followed a road map from town to town. Clifford Roberts considered that the 1942 Masters had two winners—two champions, certainly—and he expressed his thanks in a letter to each of them, enclosing as well checks for two hundred dollars, extra prize money, he told them. The four hundred dollars erased the net profit the club realized from the additional day of revenues, but the sum was less important than the gesture, one of profound gratitude.

O. B. Keeler saw Nelson's victory as possibly preordained. At the beginning of the week, a package had arrived at the club at about the same time that Nelson did. The package contained plaques, individually wrapped, each with a name and a year etched onto it. The plaques were to be awarded to each of the past Masters champions.

"Open it up," Clifford Roberts said to Nelson. Nelson obliged.

"Draw one," Roberts said.

Nelson selected one, unwrapped it, and saw that it had been emblazoned with the name *Byron Nelson* and the year *1937*, representing his Masters victory five years earlier.

"It's an omen," Roberts said elatedly. "If there's anything in hunches, you're going to win this tournament."

Roberts noted that were Nelson to win, the club would only have to add *1942* to the plaque, absolving it from having to spend money on another one.

"I'll show you," Roberts said. "Draw another one."

Nelson unwrapped a second plaque. The name on it was Horton Smith, under which the years *1934* and *1936* were etched.

"See?" Roberts said. "You can't miss. It's your tournament." Keeler considered the evidence. "Golf," he wrote, "is a Scottish game, and Scots run largely to Presbyterians, and Presbyterians have always stuck more or less to the plan of predestination; it's all in the Book, they say, before ever a ball is struck off the first tee, in the game of golf, or in that other game we call Life."

The diversion known as the Masters was over and "that other game" reappeared, in all its myriad forms. For some of those who played in the Masters, it appeared as a draft notice. In the back rooms of the Augusta

National Golf Club, it appeared as a challenge: Which way to turn? Jones and Roberts began the year with the idea that they would keep the club and the tournament operating until circumstances erected an obstacle that was simply too considerable to overcome. In the aftermath of the Masters, Jones and Roberts each concluded that moving forward was going to be problematic, though they at least had time to contemplate alternatives—the club would soon close for the summer and was not scheduled to reopen until October.

The outlook was bleak at any rate. The war raged on, hinting at an epic struggle rather than an abbreviated one. Indeed, there was nothing to look forward to in the near term at Augusta National. Grantland Rice, of course, had already recognized the dearth of options and chosen a convenient one. He took comfort in his nostalgia, destined as it was to return him to Georgia's red clay hills and the bygone era that he cherished most . . .

> *When Bobby Jones was the king of golf*
> *and Ty was the Georgia Ghost!*

The Day When Burke Roared

50 Years Ago, the 'Pro From Boys Town' Snuck Off With The Masters

by Steve Campbell, *Houston Chronicle*, April 2, 2006

The Technicolor splashes—the azaleas, the magnolias, the dogwoods, the deep blue waters, the greenest shades of green in creation—are only part of the sensory overload that is the Masters.

The sounds of Sunday at the Masters "toon-uh-ment", as the green coats are wont to call it, are unlike anywhere else in golf.

Distinctive birdie roars and eagle roars and even hole-in-one roars reverberate though the pine trees and hollows at Augusta National Golf Club. There are Tiger Woods roars and Phil Mickelson roars, just as there used to be Sam Snead roars and Ben Hogan roars and Arnold Palmer roars and Jack Nicklaus roars.

On the Sunday that Houston's Jackie Burke Jr., won the Masters, the soundtrack at Augusta National was unlike any heard before. Or the 50 years since.

"That day, nobody was doing anything," Burke said. "I never heard anything."

As quietly as a tree falling in a forest with nobody there to hear it, Burke rallied from eight strokes off the lead to win the 1956 Masters by one stroke over Ken Venturi. Playing in what Augusta National co-founder Bobby Jones called "the hardest playing conditions we have had in this tournament," Burke pulled off the largest final-round comeback in Masters history.

Burke made his move up the leader board by shooting a 1-under-par 71. On a damp, dreary day on which wind blew through Augusta, Ga., at a guesstimated 40-50 mph, the huddled masses watched and shivered as player after player faltered. Burke remembers telling Doug Ford on the putting green before the final round, "I'll take 76 and go take these shoes off.

"I didn't see any way on earth you could break 80," Burke said.

Twenty-nine players—including Byron Nelson, Jimmy Demaret and Julius Boros—found themselves on the wrong end of 79. The 1956 Sunday scoring average of 78.261 remains the highest for the last round in tournament history. The 1-over-par winning score of 289 matched the highest since the Masters began in 1934.

FIRST MASTERS ON TV

The 1956 Masters was the first shown on television. Burke made such a stealthy move into the lead, the only air time he received was when he finished his round. Three birdies, two bogeys, one green jacket.

"Jackie just kept making putt after putt," said Mike Souchak, who was Burke's final-round playing partner. "He was the only one who could handle that weather and the greens."

Jackie Burke Jr., son of the 1920 U.S. Open runner-up, turned pro before his 20th birthday. He was so conspicuously fresh-faced, Bob Hope nicknamed Burke "the pro from Boys Town." Burke proved he was ready to sit at the PGA Tour grown-ups' table in 1952, winning four tournaments—including the Texas and Houston Opens—in a four-week stretch.

When Burke teed it up at the 1956 Masters, he was 33 years old. His most recent victory had come in 1953. His closest brush with winning a major came at the 1952 Masters, where he finished second, three behind Snead.

Now at 83, with 17 tour victories and a World Golf Hall of Fame induction in the rearview mirror, Burke has a book ("It's Only a Game: Words of Wisdom from a Lifetime in Golf") out.

"I was never preoccupied with winning majors," Burke said. "When we were out there, you were trying to play as good as you could because you might get a better club job. It wasn't like there was a tour going on in the summer. There were hardly any summer tournaments in the summer for pros."

Burke tied Snead for the victory lead with five in 1952, when the entire tour played for $498,016 spread over 32 events. The leading money-winner that year, Boros, pocketed $37,032.97. By 1956, the tour's purses rose to $847,070.

"I remember when 20th place was $100," Burke said. "I was betting more every day than that."

At the '56 Masters, the professionals found themselves playing catch-up with an amateur long shot. Venturi, a 24-year-old car salesman from San Francisco, opened with a 66 that put him one stroke ahead of defending champion Cary Middlecoff. A second-round 69 left Venturi 9 under and four strokes ahead of the field. Burke attracted little notice with a 72-71 that left him in seventh place. Eight strokes out of the lead when the weekend began, Burke shot a 75 that proved to be much better than the score indicated. Burke actually moved up to fourth with his 3-over round that Saturday.

"They had little grass on the greens" Souchak said. "Every day they cut 'em lower and lower, 'til they were down into the roots."

HIGHEST AVERAGE SCORE

The more the wind blew, the more the greens hardened. The average score that Saturday was 78.565, still the highest in Masters history. Nobody broke par; only three players (Snead, Boros, and Lloyd Mangrum) matched it. Especially down in Amen Corner, players found themselves baffled by the wind.

"You're in a valley, and it goes in a circle," Burke said. "You think the wind is behind you and by the time you swing, it went the other way."

At the par-3 No. 12, Bob Rosburg felt the wind blowing into his face in the third round. Rosburg nailed a 4-iron, only to get caught by the switching wind. His ball sailed over the green, all the way to the adjacent Augusta Country Club, on the way to an 81. Playing into the wind at the par-3 No. 4 in the final round, Burke hit driver-wedge to the back of the green. He rolled in a 30-foot putt to save par.

"It's a downhill putt that I would lay you odds that you couldn't two-putt," Burke said. "It's 1,000-to-1 you're not going to make it. I could have putted it in the front bunker."

Still, Burke found himself trailing by nine strokes early in the final round. With 10 holes to play, Venturi still clung to a six-stroke lead. Though Venturi hit 15 greens in regulation the final round, he started making one bogey after another.

"The greens were like rocks," Souchak said. "When you putted the ball, you could hear the ball rolling on the green. That's how hard it was."

Burke had inched to within one stroke of the lead when he got to the par-4 No. 17. With the gale at his back, Burke became the only player all day to hold the green on his approach—a high, sliced 8-iron. Original press reports had Burke leaving himself with a 15-foot birdie attempt. Burke remembers it as a 30-footer. Whatever, Burke rolled in the putt.

"I saw how sandy the green was, and I had played on sand greens in East Texas and knew how slick they could be," Burke said. "When I hit my putt, I thought, 'Oh, God, I hit it halfway.' Had I hit it the way I wanted to hit it, I would have run it by 15 feet. And the wind just blew the damn thing in."

For the first time of the tournament, Burke was in the lead.

"I didn't know Venturi and those guys were falling out of the chair," Burke said. "Actually, there was no pressure on me. The pressure was on Middlecoff and Venturi. Souchak and I were just out there trying to make sure we didn't shoot 100."

AN IMPRESSIVE SAVE

Burke proceeded to put his approach into No. 18 in a greenside bunker. He blasted to just inside 5 feet, leaving him a dreaded downhill putt for par.

"I see it in my sleep, that putt," Burke said. "You don't ever want it. I don't."

Burke nudged the ball into the hole with the toe of his putter. It was his seventh one-putt of the final round. Middlecoff, for his part, three-putted No. 17 for a double bogey and finished two strokes behind Burke. Venturi could have gotten into a playoff by parring the final two holes. Like Middlecoff, Venturi couldn't get up and down at No. 17. Until Paul Lawrie rallied from 10 back to win the 1999 British Open at Carnoustie, the biggest final-round comeback in major-champion- ship history belonged to Burke.

"I don't see how anybody can go out and plan on winning major events," Burke said. "There's so much luck involved. There's a lot of luck in golf."

Venturi's good fortune and good play expired before he could become the first amateur to win a major since Johnny Goodman at the 1933 U.S. Open. Instead, Venturi went down in Masters lore by shooting 80. Venturi suggested afterward that Burke's victory bore the taint of Souchak helping out with club selection and reading greens. Though Souchak said he was happy to see "a close friend" win the Masters, he wonders what he could have had to do with Burke's $6,000 payday.

"I know I got accused of helping Jackie the last day," Souchak said. "But I shot 80 and took 42 putts. How could I help Jackie?"

Barely three months later at Blue Hill Country Club in Boston, Burke won the PGA Championship, then contested at match play. Burke won seven matches in five days, twice going into extra holes. The payoff for becoming the seventh player in history to win two majors in the same year: $5,000.

"It wasn't like you were on top of the mountain," Burke said.

Reality really set in when Burke tried to collect his PGA winnings.

"The check was hot," Burke said. "The PGA had to guarantee my check."

CHAMPIONS BECKONS

Burke and Demaret opened the doors to Champions Golf Club on Nov. 1, 1958. At age 35, Jackie Burke Jr. gave up playing the tour full time so he could try to make a real living.

"I remember driving down the highway after leaving a tournament early in those days," Burke said. "A guy would roll down his window and tell you, 'You finished eighth. You got $380. Meet me at the next barbecue place.'"

Strokes of Genius

Overpowering a Storied Course and a Stellar Field, Tiger Woods Heralded a New Era in Golf with an Awesome 12-Shot Victory in the Masters

by Rick Reilly, *Sports Illustrated,* April 21, 1997

Short and pudgy, he pushed through the crowd, elbowing and worming his way, not stopping for any of the cries of "heyyy, watchit!" as he went. At last he popped through to the front and craned his neck down the line, wide-eyed, hoping to see what he had come for. As Tiger Woods strode past, Jack Nicholson slapped him on the back and grinned, same as everybody else.

It didn't matter who you were; if you were there the week everything changed in golf, you just had to reach out and touch a piece of history. Almost 50 years to the day after Jackie Robinson broke major league baseball's color barrier, at Augusta National, a club that no black man was allowed to join until six years ago, at the tournament whose founder, Clifford Roberts, once said, "As long as I'm alive, golfers will be white, and caddies will be black," a 21-year-old black man delivered the greatest performance ever seen in a golf major.

Someday Eldrick (Tiger) Woods, a mixed-race kid with a middle-class background who grew up on a municipal course in the sprawl of Los Angeles, may be hailed as the greatest golfer who ever lived, but it is likely that his finest day will always be the overcast Sunday in Augusta when he humiliated the world's best golfers, shot 18-under-par 70-66-65-69-270 (the lowest score in tournament history) and won the Masters by a preposterous 12 shots. It was the soundest whipping in a major this century and second only to Old Tom Morris's 13-shot triumph in the 1862 British Open.

When Tiger finally slipped into his green champion's jacket, his 64-year-old father, Earl, drank in a long look and said, "Green and black go well together, don't they?"

So golf is trying to get used to the fact that the man who will rule the game for the next 20 years shaves twice a week and has been drinking legally for almost three months now. "He's more dominant over the guys he's playing against than I ever was over the ones I played against," marveled no less an authority than Jack Nicklaus, whose 17-under Masters record of 271 had held up for 32 years. "He's so long, he reduces the course to nothing. Absolutely nothing."

It was something to see the way a 6´2´´, 155-pounder with a 30-inch waist crumbled one of golf's masterpieces into bite-sized pieces. The longest club he hit into a par-4 all week was a seven-iron. On each of the first two days he hit a wedge into the 500-yard par-5 15th hole—for his second shot. Honey, he shrunk the course. Last Saturday his seven birdies were set up by his nine-iron, pitching wedge, sand wedge, putter, nine-iron, putter and sand wedge. Meanwhile, the rest of the field was trying to catch him with five-irons and three-woods and rosary beads. When Nicklaus said last year that Woods would win 10 green jackets, everybody figured he was way off. We just never thought his number was low.

Said Jesper Parnevik, who finished 19 shots back, "Unless they build Tiger tees about 50 yards back, he's going to win the next 20 of these." (Memo to former Masters winners: Get ready for a whole lot of Tuesday-night champions' dinners you can supersize.)

Woods's performance was the most outstanding in Augusta National history, and that figured, because he stood out all week. He stood out because of the color of his skin against the mostly white crowds. He stood out because of his youth in a field that averaged 38 years. He stood out because of the flabbergasting length of his drives—323 yards on average, 25 yards longer than the next player on the chart. He stood out for the steeliness in his eyes and for the unshakable purpose in his step. "He may be 21," said Mike (Fluff) Cowan, his woolly caddie, "but he ain't no 21 inside those ropes." Said Paul Azinger, who played with Woods last Friday and got poleaxed by seven shots, "I just got outconcentrated today. He never had a mental lapse."

It was a week like nobody had ever seen at Augusta National. Never before had scalpers' prices for a weekly badge been so high. Some were asking $10,000. Even after it was all done, a seemingly useless badge was fetching up to $50 outside the club's gates. Never before had one player attracted such a large following. Folks might have come out with the intention of watching another golfer, but each day the course seemed to tilt toward wherever Woods was playing. Everybody else was Omar Uresti. Never before had so many people stayed at the course so long, filling the stands behind the practice range, 1,500 strong, to watch a lone player hit thrilling wedge shots under the darkening Georgia sky. It was the highest-rated golf telecast in history, yet guys all over the country had to tell their wives that the reason they couldn't help plant the rhododendrons was that they needed to find out whether the champion would win by 11 or 12.

Away from the golf course, Woods didn't look much like a god. He ate burgers and fries, played Ping-Pong and P-I-G with his buddies, screamed at videogames and drove his parents to the far end of their rented house.

Michael Jordan called, and Nike czar Phil Knight came by, and the FedExes and telegrams from across the world piled up on the coffee table, but none of it seemed to matter much. What did matter was the Mortal Kombat video game and the fact that he was Motaro and his Stanford buddy Jerry Chang was Kintaro and he had just ripped Kintaro's mutant head off and now there was green slime spewing out and Tiger could roar in his best creature voice, "Mmmmmwaaaaannnnnggh!"

By day Woods went back to changing the world, one mammoth drive at a time, on a course that Nicklaus called "much harder than the one I played" when he delivered his 271.

What's weird is that this was the only Masters in history that began on the back nine on Thursday and ended on Saturday night. For the first nine holes of the tournament the three-time reigning U.S. Amateur champion looked very amateurish. He kept flinching with his driver, visiting many of Augusta's manicured forests, bogeying 1, 4, 8 and 9 and generally being much more about Woods than about Tigers. His 40 was by two shots the worst starting nine ever for a Masters winner.

But something happened to him as he walked to the 10th tee, something that separates him from other humans. He fixed his swing, right there, in his mind. He is nothing if not a quick study. In the six Augusta rounds he played as an amateur, he never broke par, mostly because he flew more greens than Delta with his irons and charged for birdie with his putter, often making bogey instead. This year, though, he realized he had to keep his approach shots below the hole and keep the leash on his putter. "We learned how to hit feeders," Cowan said. Woods figured out how to relax and appreciate the six-inch tap-in. (For the week he had zero three-putts.) And now, at the turn on Thursday, he realized he was bringing the club almost parallel to the ground on his backswing—"way too long for me"—so he shortened his swing right then and there.

He immediately grooved a two-iron down the 10th fairway and birdied the hole from 18 feet. Then he birdied the par-3 12th with a deft chip-in from behind the green and the 13th with two putts. He eagled the 15th with a wedge to four feet. When he finished birdie-par, he had himself a back-nine 30 for a two-under 70—your basic CPR nine. Woods was only three shots behind the first-day leader, John Huston, who moved in front at 18 by holing a five-iron from 180 yards for eagle and then dropped from sight the next day with a double-par beagle 10 on the 13th. Playing in the twosome ahead of Huston, Woods had eagled the same hole after hitting an eight-iron to 20 feet, vaulting into the outright lead, one he would never relinquish.

By Friday night you could feel the sea change coming. Woods's 66 was the finest round of the day, and his lead was three over Colin Montgomerie. Last year's two Goliaths in the Masters drama—Nick Faldo and Greg Norman—had blown the cut, Faldo 20 shots behind Woods and Norman 15. For Norman, even a pretournament session with motivational speaker Tony Robbins didn't help. Next year: Stuart Smalley. I'm good enough, I'm shark enough and, doggone it, people fear me! "I guess I should start hating this bloody place," Norman said as he left, "but I can't."

Saturday was nearly mystical. As the rest of the field slumped, Woods just kept ringing up birdies. He tripled his lead from three to nine with a bogey-less 65. You half expected him to walk across Rae's Creek. Even when Masters officials warned him for slow play on the 14th, he kept his head.

That night there was this loopiness, this giddy sense, even among the players, of needing to laugh in the face of something you never thought you'd see. A 21-year-old in his first major as a pro was about to obliterate every record, and it was almost too big a thought to be thunk. "I might have a chance," said Paul Stankowski, who trailed by 10, "if I make five or six birdies in the first two or three holes." After playing with Woods on Saturday, Montgomerie staggered in looking like a man who had seen a UFO. He plopped his weary meatiness into the interview chair and announced, blankly, "There is no chance. We're all human beings here. There's no chance humanly possible."

What about last year? he was asked, a reference to Norman's blowing a six-shot lead and losing the Masters to Faldo by five. "This is very different. Faldo's not lying second, for a start. And Greg Norman's not Tiger Woods."

Ouch.

Only 47-year-old Tom Kite, who would finish second in the same sense that Germany finished second in World War II, refused to give up. He was a schnauzer with his teeth locked on the tailpipe of a Greyhound bus as it was pulling into beltway traffic. How can you be so optimistic when Woods is leading by nine shots? "Well," said Kite, "we've got it down to single digits, don't we?"

But Kite did not leave Augusta empty-handed. As the captain of a U.S. Ryder Cup team that will try to reclaim the trophy from Europe this September in Spain, he suddenly has a one-man Ryder Wrecking Crew on his hands, for Woods wiped out his playing partners from overseas: England's Faldo by five shots on Thursday, Scotland's Montgomerie by nine on Saturday and Italy's Costantino Rocca by six on Sunday.

The last round was basically a coronation parade with occasional stops to hit a dimpled object. There seemed to be some kind of combat for mortals going on behind Woods for second place, but nothing you needed to notice. Nobody came within a light year. Rocca and Tom Watson each trimmed the lead to eight, but mentioning it at all is like pointing out that the food on the Hindenburg was pretty good. Woods went out on the front nine in even par, then birdied the 11th, the 13th and the 14th and parred the 16th with a curvaceous two-putt. "After that, I knew I could bogey in and win," he said. That's a bit of an understatement, of course. He could've quintuple-bogeyed in and won. He could've used nothing but his putter, his umbrella and a rolled-up *Mad* magazine and won.

He wanted the record, though, and for that there was one last challenge—the 18th. On his tee shot a photographer clicked twice on the backswing, and Woods lurched, hooking his drive way left. On this hole, though, the only trouble comes if you're short or right, and Woods has not been short since grade school. He had a wedge shot to the green—if only he could get his wedge. Fluff was lost. "Fluff!" Woods hollered, jumping as if on a pogo stick to see over the gallery. Fluff finally found him as the crowd chanted, "Fluff! Fluff!" It was not exactly tense.

Still, Woods needed a five-footer for par, and when he sank it, he threw his trademark uppercut. The tournament he had talked about winning since he was five, the tournament he had watched on tape almost every night in his little suburban bedroom all those years, the tournament he had wanted more than all the others, was his, and the dream had only just begun. He was now the youngest man by two years to win the Masters and the first black man to win any major.

He turned and hugged Fluff, and as the two men walked off the green, arms draped over each other's shoulders in joy, you couldn't help but notice that Chairman Roberts's Rule of Golf Order had been turned happily upside down—the golfer was black and the caddie was white. "I've always dreamed of coming up 18 and winning," Woods, still a little shocked, said after slipping on the green jacket. "But I never thought this far through the ceremony."

So golf is all new now. Everything is a fight for place. Win seems to be spoken for. If you are the tournament director of a PGA Tour event, you better do whatever's necessary to get Tiger Woods, because your Wendy's-Shearson Lehman Pensacola Classic is the junior varsity game without him. The Senior tour seems sort of silly next to this. A babe in swaddling pleats with a Slinky for a spine and a computer for a mind had just won a major by more shots than anybody this century. How does he top this? The Grand Slam?

"It can be done," he said, unblinking.

"The bigger the event, the higher he'll raise the bar," Azinger said. "He's Michael Jordan in long pants."

Of course, much more than golf was changed at Augusta National last week. As Woods made his way from Butler Cabin and an interview with

CBS, he brought his phalanx of Pinkerton guards and other escorts to a sudden stop. Out of the corner of his eye Woods spied Lee Elder, the man who at 39 had finally won a PGA Tour event, the Monsanto Open, earning his invitation as the first black man to play the Masters, in 1975, the year Tiger was born. Woods knew Elder's story, knew about Teddy Rhodes, too, the star of the black golf circuit in the 1940s, who might've won here if he'd had the chance; and of Charlie Sifford, who outplayed Masters champions like Doug Ford and Gay Brewer regularly on the Tour but never qualified to play here; and of his own father, who was the first black man to play baseball in the Big Eight and was often forced to stay in separate hotels and eat in separate restaurants, apart from his teammates. Tiger knows all the stories he never had to live, so he stopped and put a giant bear hug on Elder. "Thanks for making this possible," Woods whispered in his ear, and then the parade swept on. Elder had tears in his eyes.

At the very end Woods made it into the elegant Augusta National clubhouse dining room for the traditional winner's dinner. As he entered, the members and their spouses stood and applauded politely, as they have for each champion, applauded as he made his way to his seat at the head table under a somber oil painting of President Eisenhower. But clear in the back, near a service entrance, the black cooks and waiters and busboys ripped off their oven mitts and plastic gloves, put their dishes and trays down for a while, hung their napkins over their arms and clapped the loudest and the hardest and the longest for the kind of winner they never dreamed would come through those doors.

The Tournament Begins on the Back Nine on Sunday

from *The Majors* by John Feinstein

On Saturday night at the Masters, no one goes to bed early.

For those who will be watching on Sunday, it is the last night to party, since almost everyone will head up the road—or in the case of many of the corporate honchos to Daniels Field to fly out in their private jets on Sunday evening.

For those who will be playing, going to bed anytime before midnight is pointless. "You know it isn't going to be easy sleeping to begin with," Mark O'Meara said. "And the last thing you want is to get up really early and then sit around killing time all morning."

So everyone finds different ways to stay up late.

It was closing in on 8 o'clock by the time Couples finished all of his various post-round interviews and left the golf course. He and Thais and his good friend John McLure stopped at an Italian restaurant en route back to the house, and Thais and John went in to pick up take-out to bring back to the house. Couples stretched out in the back seat and closed his eyes. Initially, he decided to lie down to make sure no well-meaning passersby noticed him and stopped to chat, wish him luck, or ask for autographs, but when he put his head back on the seat he realized how tired he was.

"I had played late all three days, and all three days I had to go in and do an hour of media after I was done," he said. "I know that's part of the deal, especially at a major, but it does begin to wear on you."

There may be no feat in golf more difficult than going wire-to-wire with the lead, especially in a major. In the previous sixty-one Masters four winners had led from start to finish: Craig Wood in 1941, Arnold Palmer in 1960, Jack Nicklaus in 1972, and Raymond Floyd in 1976. As dominant as Woods had been in 1997, he had not taken the lead for good until late in the second round. The great players rarely took the lead on Thursday—or wanted to take the lead on Thursday. On his way to winning eighteen major championships, Jack Nicklaus led after all four rounds three times. "I never wanted to go wire-to-wire," he has said. "The best way to play a major is to play good golf on Thursday and Friday and build for the weekend. With luck you peak on Saturday and Sunday."

Of course in golf you can't plan your peak. It isn't like swimming or track where you taper your workouts with an eye toward producing your best performance on one given day. In golf you work and hope your game is where you want it to be when it matters most. This year, more than any year in the past, Couples had tried to bring his game to a peak for the Masters. He had spent four straight days with his teacher, Paul Marchand, working on the practice tee at Bay Hill, the first time he could ever remember practicing that way for four straight days.

The work had paid off for three days. Now, as he waited for Thais and McLure to return to the car, he wondered if he had the emotional energy to get through a Sunday at Augusta. "Physically I knew I'd be fine on Sunday afternoon," he said. "I had really built to the point where I expected to win the golf tournament. I knew that mentally that was the right way to approach it and I felt good about it. But I also knew from experience what a long tough day the last one is at Augusta."

All the players know that. What makes the last day at Augusta different from the last day at other majors is knowing that someone can "go deep," another player term for going low. The golf courses at the other three majors are rarely set up to allow for low scores, especially on Sunday. Yes, Johnny Miller had produced a 63 at Oakmont to win the U.S. Open in 1973; Greg Norman had come up with a 64 to win the British Open at Royal St. George's in 1993; and Steve Elkington had fired a 64 on the last day at the PGA in 1995, on badly beaten-up greens at Riviera Country Club in Los Angeles. But those rounds were aberrations, near miracles. And the USGA liked to point out that rain the night before had softened the greens at Oakmont to the point where they really weren't "U.S. Open" greens.

If you lead a U.S. Open, a British Open, or a PGA on Saturday night and can produce a round near par, you will have an excellent chance of winning. At Augusta, if the weather conditions are good, you have to start out on Sunday assuming that someone is going to shoot in the mid-60s and you are going to have to produce a number of birdies yourself if you hope to hang on and win.

Couples knew that as well as anybody. He was a bit unhappy with himself because he felt he had let an opportunity slip away in the third round. "I played okay," he said later. "But in that weather, under those conditions, 71 was not a great score. If I had made a couple more putts and shot 68 or 69, I could have really put some distance between myself and everyone else. I was a little bit upset that I didn't do it."

Nonetheless, he led by two and felt the same confidence he had felt all week. Once he had been handed his player badge and it was the same num- ber—70—as he had been given in 1992, he had started to buy into all the Jim Nantz notions about omens and karma. Starting the tournament with three straight birdies had confirmed all that and he had gone from there.

He sat around that night watching a baseball game and then "SportsCenter," trying to make it as close to a normal Saturday night as possible. But he knew better. Everyone knew better. Jim Furyk watched his dad fire up the grill, ate his dinner quietly, and then stayed up watching *Forrest Gump* on video after everyone else had gone to bed. David Duval sat up in bed reading because he knew he wasn't going to fall asleep. Mark O'Meara was doing the same thing as Couples—spending a quiet night with his family, trying to keep things as normal as possible—when his phone rang. It was Hank Haney. He was in Atlanta at an airport hotel. He was supposed to fly out in the morning to run a clinic in the afternoon, but he couldn't do it. "I'm driving back in the morning," he said. "I have to be there."

O'Meara had been hearing from his friends about omens too. His car dealer in Orlando, Kevin White, had told him just before he left for Augusta that he had dreamed O'Meara won the Masters. Joe Louis, the owner of Isleworth, always liked to make a couple of bets on players during the major championships. Often, O'Meara would call him after he got on site to tell him who he thought was playing well. He was supposed to call Louis on Tuesday, but he hadn't because he didn't really have a feel for who was hot and he didn't want Louis making a bet based on bad advice. The next day, Louis had called him to wish him luck. O'Meara had told him he was sorry he hadn't called the day before. "Don't worry about it," Louis said. "I bet all my money on you."

O'Meara was stunned. "What are my odds?" he asked. "Thirty-three to one," Louis had answered.

Two shots back with 18 holes to play, his odds were now a lot better than that.

The last day at any major has a special feeling because everyone knows that something dramatic is going to happen by nightfall. At the Masters, the feeling is a little bit different because of the golf course.

"You know where the pins are going to be," Jeff Siuman said as he lingered by the first tee waiting for the leaders to tee off. "You know it's going to be very hard but there are going to be birdies out there to make. And you know someone is going to make a run from back in the pack."

Except of course in 1997, when the pack was so far behind Tiger Woods it wasn't even in Georgia.

All the majors stage a tournament within a tournament on Sunday.

While the leaders sit around the clubhouse killing time before they go out and decide who will be the champion, the second tier of players go out to try and ensure themselves a spot in the field for next year. At the Masters—prior to 1999 when the number dropped to sixteen—the top twenty-four finishers were automatically invited back for the following year. That number was very much on Brad Faxon's mind when he teed off at 1:10. Faxon was in a three-way tie for twenty-third place beginning the day—eight shots behind Couples. Realistically, he knew he wasn't going to win. But he figured he still had a chance to finish in the top ten and, worst-case scenario, he wanted to make certain he held on to his spot in the top twenty-four.

The day was a struggle. Faxon didn't play badly; in fact he drove the ball very well. But, as had been the case all week, his putter failed him. Faxon has built his career around a putter that often acts as a magic wand. No one succeeds on tour if they can't putt. With Faxon that was always the case times two.

"It was aggravating," he said. "Because I might have hit the ball as well as I've ever hit it at Augusta. But nothing went in."

The 18th hole was Faxon's week—his year—in microcosm. He was even par for the day and suspected he was right on the cusp of the top twenty-four. A birdie would probably lock him in, a par would leave him dangling, a bogey would almost certainly knock him out. There was no way to be sure because there are no electronic scoreboards at any of the majors. Week to week on the PGA Tour the electronic boards tell players exactly where they stand. Any time they walk by a scoreboard it will show the names and the position in the field of the players on that hole. At the Masters, unless you are in the top ten and on a leader board, you have no idea where you stand in relation to the field.

Faxon's gut told him he was right on the bubble. He hit two good shots at 18 to a spot 12 feet below the hole. At least now he had taken bogey out of the equation. His playing partner, Stewart Cink, was also on the bubble. Both players were two over par for the week. Cink had a 20-footer for birdie. Calmly, he rolled his putt in. Now, Faxon had to make his putt to tie Cinko He thought he had made it, but at the last possible second the ball veered below the hole. It had been that way for four days.

"Think about this," Faxon said later. "I had one hundred and twenty-five putts for the week. The winner had one hundred and six and I finished eleven shots behind him."

Putting statistics can be deceiving because they don't count putts from the fringe and don't take into account how close a player hits the ball to the hole throughout the week. But Faxon has been near the top of the list in putting statistics almost his entire career. Everyone on tour would rank him among the top five putters out there. For him 125 putts in any week is almost unheard of.

He walked off 18 with a bad feeling in the pit of his stomach. "Something told me that Stewart making and me missing was going to cost me," he said. When he got into the locker room, a check of the computer revealed that Cink had indeed put himself into the top twenty-four by birdieing 18. If Faxon had made his putt, he would have been tied with Cink at one over par, good for a tie for twenty-third. Instead, he finished one shot further back and was tied for twenty-six. Cink making hadn't hurt him, but missing his own putt had.

"There are still plenty of ways to get in next year," Faxon said softly.

"But it would have been nice to get it out of the way right now. I had the chance and didn't get it done."

Another player who had the chance and did get it done was the U.S. Amateur champion, Matt Kuchar. His 68 on Saturday had brought him back to even par for the tournament, and on Sunday he shot a solid, even-par 72 to finish at 288. That left him in a tie for twenty-first place, guaranteeing his return to Augusta in 1999. Not once, it seemed, did he stop smiling.

One person who wasn't smiling at the end of the day was Justin Leonard, who was paired with Kuchar on Sunday. He was happy for Kuchar and admired his ability to stay calm coming down the stretch with the top twenty-four in sight. But Kuchar's caddy almost drove him crazy.

The caddy was Peter Kuchar, Matt's dad. On Thursday, when Peter Kuchar had played cheerleader all the way around the golf course for his son, most people thought it was a nice story. By Sunday the word around the locker room was that the old man never let up and that he was a shameless self-promoter. Since Matt was an amateur, he couldn't pursue any endorsements. According to one clothing company representative, Peter Kuchar had approached him and asked if the company was interested in having *him* wear their clothes. After all, he said, there was nothing illegal about him endorsing a product.

No, there wasn't. But as the rep pointed out, there really wasn't much point in putting someone in their clothing when he would be wearing the Augusta caddy's jump suit over that clothing.

Leonard is a very methodical player. Away from the golf course he likes a good joke as much as anyone. But the last round at the Masters was not a place to be whooping it up as far as he was concerned. He tried to ignore Peter Kuchar's constant cheerleading as best he could. But on the 15th hole, after Matt had hit a fine shot to the green, Peter walked up near the ropes and led cheers for his son.

Leonard, who was about to play his own second shot, waited. Then he got over his ball. The noise continued. He looked up and saw Peter Kuchar still leading cheers. "That was when I just about lost it," he said later. "I mean enough is enough. It's the back nine at Augusta on Sunday. Give me a chance."

Leonard was happy with the way he played, shooting 69 to produce his first top-ten finish (T-8) at Augusta. But he knew that this wasn't going to be the last time he encountered Team Kuchar. At the U.S. Open, the U.S. Amateur champion is paired the first two rounds with the defending

U.S. Open champion and the reigning British Open champion. The reigning British Open champion was Justin Leonard. "Something has to change between now and San Francisco," he said. "I don't want to go through that again."

Generally speaking, anyone who is within five shots of the lead going into the last day of a major is thought to have a chance to win. On this day at this Masters, a lot of people were stretching the five-shot rule to six shots because of the identity of three of the players who were six shots behind Couples.

One was Davis Love, who everyone knew could go as deep as anyone in the field on a given day. Love had loads of confidence going into the last day because he had shot 67 on Saturday, because he had won the most recent major prior to the Masters (the '97 PGA), and because two years earlier he had shot 66 on the last day to come within a shot of winning. CBS's Lance Barrow walked through the clubhouse at lunchtime Sunday telling anyone who would listen that Love was the man to watch.

The other two players worth watching who were tied with Love were Leonard, who had won three tournaments in the last year in which he started the last round five shots back of the leader (including the British Open), and Scott McCarron, who had been very steady—73-71-72—all week but had yet to have a break-out round. The other three players at 216 weren't considered contenders simply because they lacked experience at Augusta and in major championships: Kuchar, Darren Clarke, and Per-Ulrik Johansson. Clarke had started the last round of the British Open in second place in '97 but had never been in serious contention the last day, after hitting his tee shot out of bounds on the second hole.

From 215 on down to Couples at 210, everyone was a contender.

There were five players who had won majors in the past: Couples, Paul Azinger at 212, Jose Maria Olazabal at 214, Ernie Els at 215, and Nicklaus, the Olden Bear trying to turn Golden one last time at 215. One stat on Nicklaus put the field in perspective: if you didn't include Gary Player, who was playing in the first twosome of the day, the other forty-four players in the field had won a combined total of twenty-two professional major titles—only four more than Nicklaus alone. Player had won nine, making him one of the great players ever, but still nowhere close to Nicklaus. Among the under-fifty set playing that Sunday only John Daly (two), Els (two), Bernhard Langer (two), and Fuzzy Zoeller (two) had more than one major on his resume. Els was the only one in that group with a chance to win.

The BPNTHWAM set had several players in contention: Colin Montgomerie at 215, David Duval and Jim Furyk at 213, and Phil Mickelson and Mark O'Meara at 212. Even though he had shot 69 on Saturday, few people expected Montgomerie to be a serious factor. His wife was home in England on the verge of giving birth to their third child. The baby had been due in May but the doctors were now convinced it would be arriving within a week, Montgomerie had already canceled plans to play at the next tour stop at Hilton Head so he could fly directly home from the Masters.

Duval and Furyk were paired together, which pleased both of them.

Both lived in Ponte Vedra, Florida, near PGA Tour headquarters, and they occasionally got together for dinner when they were both at home. They were different in more ways than they were similar. Duval was a southerner who was trying very hard to break his habit of chewing tobacco. He loved to fish, thought hunting wasn't a sport—"What's the challenge of shooting something that can't even see you," he said—and probably read more books than anyone on tour, although he had tired of being portrayed as some kind of intellectual. "Jeez, just because I know who Ayn Rand is people want to make me into a scholar," he said, shaking his head.

Furyk knew who Ayn Rand was too, but his reading interests ran more toward *USA Today* and *Sports Illustrated*. He was a northerner who loved all sports but wasn't likely to be found chewing tobacco or hunting or fishing very often—if ever. He was an only child from a close-knit family; Duval was the second of three children from a family that had scattered when he was a teenager, after his brother's death.

Different as they were, they enjoyed each other's company. They had reached the tour a year apart (Furyk in 1994, Duval in 1995) and both were young rising stars, though Duval's recent victory string had earned him a good deal of unwanted notoriety. They teed off at 2:50, each understanding that this was a day that might represent a great opportunity for a breakthrough.

The 3 o'clock pairing was entirely different. Paul Azinger had lived with the BPNTHWAM label until his emotional victory in the PGA in 1993. Two months later he had been diagnosed with cancer. He had become a symbol of courage during the next year, not only coming back from the cancer but becoming an eloquent spokesman for anyone who had ever fought the disease. He had started a golf tournament to raise money for cancer research and spent a lot of time with children who had cancer. "I just try to tell them that I kicked cancer's butt and they can too," he often said.

But the cancer had interrupted his career right at its peak. In 1993 he had been one of the two or three best players in the world, winning the PGA and two other tour events, anchoring the U.S. Ryder Cup team, and finishing in the top three in tournaments an amazing ten times. In three and a half years back since his illness, he had a total of five top-ten finishes and his best finish in thirteen majors had been a tie for seventeenth at the '95 Masters. He had never really liked the golf course very much—he had finished at least third in the other three majors, never higher than fourteenth at the Masters—and he willingly admitted on Saturday that he was surprised to find himself in the second-to-last group on Sunday.

By contrast, Phil Mickelson wasn't surprised to be in that group.

With the exception of Woods, Mickelson had dealt with more expectations than anyone in the sport. He had first won on tour as a college junior, winning the Tucson Open, and, two months shy of twenty-eight, already had twelve PGA Tour victories. But because he had won so much, because his game was so spectacular at times—especially around the greens—Mickelson had been dealing with the BPNTHWAM label almost since the day he turned pro.

To his credit, he never ducked it, never pretended it didn't matter.

"I should be contending at the majors," he said. "I believe I'm a good enough player to win them and until I do I'm not going to feel satisfied with myself. But I think I will win one soon."

Mickelson made no bones about the fact that seeing Woods win the Masters at twenty-two, Els win his second U.S. Open at twenty-seven, and Leonard win the British Open at twenty-five the previous year had increased the pressure he felt to win his own major. He had put himself into position with his 68 on Saturday and insisted that the bogeys at 17 and 18 hadn't affected his confidence. Still, it probably wasn't a great omen when he pushed his drive off number one into the trees on the left side.

Everyone, it seemed, started out tight. Not surprising under the circumstances. Woods, hoping to get off to a quick start to get the attention of the leaders, opened with a bogey for the second straight day. So did Duval, the third time in four days he had bogeyed number one.

The feeling among the leaders as they started out was best described by Couples in his own unique way: "I'm actually semi-calm," he said, walking out of the locker room. "But I'm also semi-nervous."

Mark O'Meara felt semi-calm when he walked to the driving range with Hank Haney to warm up. But within seconds, he was semi-nervous. Haney was a wreck. He kept talking about what O'Meara needed to do, what this round could mean, what was at stake, how important a good start was. O'Meara finally stopped him. "Hank, I know," he said. "I know everything. It'll be all right. I've been in position to win before. I know how to win golf tournaments."

If O'Meara needed an omen, he might have found one if he had glanced up at the player board next to the first tee. As each group comes onto the tee, one of Phil Harison's nephews slides the names of the players onto a standing board next to the tee. Next to the name of the player, he posts his player number. When Couples and O'Meara walked onto the tee, their numbers had been reversed. Couples had been given O'Meara's 73 and O'Meara had been given Couples's lucky 70. Naturally, neither player noticed. Both were staring down the fairway trying to semi-calm themselves.

Only one person was making a move on the front nine and there wasn't a soul within a hundred miles of the place who didn't know exactly who it was. Augusta crowd roars are different than in other places. They are, as Zoeller had pointed out on Friday, harder to come by. They don't really get loud until Sunday, as if the crowd is saving its energy for the day that really matters. And they are distinctive. The roar for Duval is different from the roar for Couples, the roar for Woods different from the roar for Love.

And then there is the Jack roar. It is like no other because it has been building for forty years. It began as little more than a whimper back in the '60s when he was the black hat to Palmer's white hat. It grew through the '70s as he lost weight and gained titles and stature. And it reached a peak in 1986 when he won at Augusta for the sixth time at the age of forty-six, six years after he had last won a golf tournament. The only other player who could produce a roar that would match a Jack roar was Palmer and he hadn't played the weekend at Augusta since 1983 and hadn't been in the top ten since 1967.

Of course Nicklaus hadn't top-tenned in any major since a sixth place finish at Augusta in 1990. His best finish since then had been a twenty-third at the 1991 PGA. He had gotten into the habit of playing well for 36 holes, then fading on Saturday. That was no doubt a product of age. Which was why everyone had been impressed and surprised when he produced a solid 70 on Saturday. Realistically, he couldn't be expected to play as well on Sunday.

He didn't. Instead, he played better. First, there was a birdie at the second. That was fine, but no big deal since most players birdie the second. But then there was a birdie at the third. That produced the first real Jack roar of the day, echoing off the trees and all the way back to the putting green where the leaders were getting ready to tee off. To a man, they looked up from what they were doing and, to a man, they all looked at their caddy or at each other, smiled, and said, "Jack."

A bogey at the fourth quieted things for a few minutes and, after a par at the fifth, Nicklaus was at two under for the tournament. By now, Couples and O'Meara had teed off and Nicklaus was still four shots behind Couples. Not for long. He rolled in a long birdie putt at the sixth and here came the roar again. Duval and Furyk were standing on the third green when they heard it and both broke into broad grins. "How about that guy?" Duval said to Furyk as they walked to the fourth tee.

"It was one of those things," Furyk said later, "where you're locked into what you're doing but the roars were so loud you couldn't help but notice. "

Nicklaus was now three under and Couples had joined the first-hole bogey parade, dropping to five under. Suddenly, it was Sunday at Augusta and Jack Nicklaus was two shots out of the lead with 12 holes to play. Was he Joe Hardy? Was the devil lurking in the trees somewhere preparing to collect his soul after he holed out on 18? It was too crazy to be true. People came running—yes, running at Augusta—from everywhere to try to get a glimpse of this. All of a sudden, Couples and O'Meara, the last group on the last day of a major championship, found themselves playing almost by themselves.

"We looked up when we got to the third tee," Couples said, "and it was like, where did everybody go?"

They were all over at the seventh, trying to see Nicklaus. And here he came, almost running down the fairway. Els, his playing partner, who was spotting him thirty years, was walking a good 20 yards behind him, a huge grin on his face because, like everyone else, he couldn't believe what he was seeing. "I was completely awed," he said later. "I almost forgot about playing I got so caught up in rooting for him."

Nicklaus floated his second shot to the elevated seventh green, about 15 feet left of the hole. By now they were roaring while he walked, cheering every step he took. Nicklaus couldn't help himself. He was supposed to be concentrating, but he had this big grin on his face, giving the papal wave as often as he could. He stalked his birdie putt like the Bear of old and then drained it. Els was laughing in disbelief. Nicklaus was four under par, two shots behind Couples—who had birdied the second—and O'Meara—who had birdied two and three—and tied with Mickelson and Azinger for third place.

Couples and O'Meara had reached the fourth tee by now and both had silly grins on their faces. "You know what, Joey," Couples said to his caddy, Joe LaCava. "Good for him. If he can pull this thing off, wow, what a thing that would be."

But he couldn't. Mr. Applegate came calling early. A par at the par-five eighth slowed him down a little. But at the ninth, he hit his wedge eight feet from the hole, giving himself another birdie chance. The putt broke hard right, though, stopping on the edge of the hole. The first loud Jack groan of the day went up, and Nicklaus stood looking at the putt in disbelief for several seconds. As he walked through the ropes to the 10th tee, his step had slowed a bit, the waves came a little bit slower. By now, Couples and O'Meara had both birdied the fourth to get to seven under. Three shots on the back nine at Augusta certainly wasn't out of the question, but it seemed apparent now that the leaders weren't going to come sliding backward. Nicklaus felt as if he could have been out in 31; instead it was 33. He hadn't even noticed the pain in his arthritic hip until just now. After he parred the 10th hole, he walked slowly off the green, limping slightly. He had looked about twenty-eight years old going down the seventh and eighth, perhaps thirty-eight coming up the ninth, forty-eight walking off the ninth, and now fifty-eight. A good fifty-eight, but fifty-eight.

He played a solid back nine—one bogey and birdies at the two par-fives, but the miracle wasn't going to happen. When he rolled his birdie attempt to within two inches at the 18th, Els was standing there trying to root the ball into the hole. Els insisted that he mark his ball so that he could tap in after Els holed out and stand on the green and drink in the cheers. He did just that and, as he hugged his son Steve, who was also his caddy, Els stood on the green a few feet away and joined in the applause. "I had chills," he said later.

So did everyone else. Nicklaus had shot 68, which would be good enough to tie for sixth place. It may not have been a miracle, but it was nothing short of remarkable.

When it became apparent that Nicklaus wasn't going to pull off the greatest upset in sports since the United States hockey team had beaten the Soviet Union in the 1980 Olympics, the championship was left to be decided among the mortals.

O'Meara had started with the hot putter, making a 10-footer for birdie at two, a 30-footer for birdie at three, and a 50-foot bomb for birdie at four. "All I wanted to do was get that one close," he said later. "When it was about halfway there, I thought, Oh my God, it's going in."

It was at that moment that O'Meara first thought he might be on to something special. That thought had occurred to Couples too, because he knew how good O'Meara could be when his putter got hot. But he was still completely confident. He had matched O'Meara's birdie at the fourth, and even though the whole world was focused on Nicklaus at that moment, they stood on the fifth tee tied for first, two shots clear of the field.

No one really expects to go low on the front nine at Augusta on Sunday. If it happens, it is almost a lucky break. The only true birdie hole is the second. The eighth is the longest of the par-fives, reachable in two only for the longest hitters in the field and, even for them, it is a lot easier to miss the green than hit it. The fourth and sixth are two of the tougher par-threes in major championship golf, and none of the par-fours are easy. That's why Augusta's oldest cliche is the one about the golf tournament not beginning until the back nine on Sunday.

"You get to that stretch from thirteen to fifteen and you have to make something happen," Couples said. "Because if you play them even par, you can start out with a one-shot lead and finish with a two-shot deficit."

That was why Nicklaus's early run was so amazing. It was also why neither Couples nor O'Meara gave much thought to the two-shot lead they had on the field. A lot of people were lurking: Mickelson, whose game plan had been to get through the first six holes without a big mistake and then attack, had done that. He was five under playing the seventh hole. So was Azinger, who had just birdied the sixth.

Duval and Furyk had both started slowly. Duval bounced back from his opening bogey to birdie the second, then made *four* straight pars. On the seventh tee, he was *four* shots back at three under par. Furyk, who had been playing catch-up all week, was five back at two under. Now though, the Mickelson theory about beginning to attack kicked in. Duval birdied seven. Then Duval birdied eight and Furyk eight and nine. Just like that, Duval was five under, Furyk four. Then they both birdied the 10th, Duval chipping in, and their numbers were six and five.

Couples was aware of what they were doing. He was aware of everything. As casual as he may look walking the golf course, he knows exactly what is going on at every moment. He checks the scoreboards constantly. He never plays the mind game some players employ of not checking the board. He wants to know what the other players are doing. "In a way, it's fun," he said. "If you're going bad, hell, it doesn't matter anyway. And if you're going good, you want to know what everyone's doing. Especially at Augusta, where you can make any score on any hole."

Couples thought he had made a big move at the seventh. He and O'Meara both hit wedge shots close to the hole, but O'Meara's putter finally cooled for a moment when he missed from six feet. Couples rammed home his four-footer to take the lead back at eight under, then birdied the eighth while O'Meara settled for par. At that moment, he was two up on O'Meara and *four* up on everyone else. He was settled into the round now, a solid three under par for the day.

At the ninth, he hit a perfect drive all the way to the bottom of the hill. O'Meara, perhaps feeling the pressure of Couples's back-to-back birdies, pulled his tee shot into the trees. When O'Meara got to his ball, his only play was to punch out in front of the green. As he stood in the trees, trying to figure the best route out, Couples stood in the fairway, waiting. As hard as he was trying not to get ahead of himself, he couldn't help it. "I had 107 yards to the hole, a wedge," he said. "Mark has no chance to get his ball on the green. He's looking at bogey. I have a chance for birdie. If that happens, I'm leading by four going to the back nine. Four!

"You know, you tell yourself a million times to go one shot at a time but dammit we are all human. I'm standing there thinking to myself, wow, this thing could be over right here."

Later, Couples would kick himself for letting that thought creep into his head. Because a moment later, after O'Meara had played his shot from the trees, he got just a little bit loose with his wedge shot. There is no room for looseness on the ninth green at Augusta. The front part of the green slopes back to front, and the hill in front of the green is a lot steeper than it looks on TV. In 1996, Greg Norman had spun a wedge from the front of the green all the way down the hill on Sunday. That had led to a bogey that sent Norman to the back nine with his six-shot lead over Nick Faldo down to two. He never recovered.

Now Couples made a mistake similar to Norman's. He didn't get the ball high enough up on the green. He didn't miss by much, maybe a foot or two, but he missed by enough. The ball spun off the green. O'Meara then hit his pitch shot to four feet. His ball landed perhaps a foot farther up the green than Couples's ball. That turned out to be a monumental difference. Annoyed and wanting to be sure he got the ball safely to the pin this time, Couples knocked his third shot 12 feet past the hole. Then he missed the par putt. O'Meara made his.

Wham! In less than ten minutes, Couples had gone from fantasizing about a four-shot lead to the reality of seeing his lead cut to one. "If I'd had a gun walking to the tenth tee," he said, "I'd have shot myself. I mean if you're a hundred and seven yards from the hole with your drive, you can't make a bogey. You just *can't*. It was ridiculous. Now, I had to dig in all over again."

He did, though, producing a solid par at the 10th. Surprisingly, it was O'Meara who played a poor shot at the 10th, laying the sod over a nine-inch and missing the green left. "Worst shot I played all day, no doubt about it," he said. It was the first bogey he had made since the ninth hole on Friday.

Now, though, he was in third place because Duval was on fire. He had made another birdie at the 11th to get to seven under. O'Meara was aggravated by the bogey, but knew it was too early to panic.

By now, the list of potential winners was thinning. Mickelson, having played the first six holes the way he wanted to, had made a bogey on the seventh. He was still hanging in the hunt at four under when he pulled an eight-iron into the water at the 12th. His hopes drowned with the golf ball. Azinger never went away completely all day—in fact he almost chipped in at the 17th to get to within one shot of the lead—but he never got the break that he needed to make a big move.

By the time Couples and O'Meara got to the 13th tee, it looked like a four-man golf tournament. Couples and Duval were tied for the lead at eight under because Duval had birdied 13. O'Meara was two shots back, as was Jim Furyk, but Furyk had only one par-five left to play.

Couples had spent hours and hours on the range with Marchand working on drawing the ball off the tee, the opposite of his natural fade. Three days in a row, he had hit perfect draws with his three-wood on 13, the last one leading to the eagle on Saturday. He set up to hit the exact same shot, but this time he didn't pull it off. Instead, what he got was an ugly pull hook that went screaming over Rae's Creek into the trees and the azaleas on the left. O'Meara took a deep breath. He knew that his chances to win the golf tournament might very well depend on where Couples's ball was and what kind of second shot he had.

Amazingly, Couples had a couple of options. One was to punch it through a hole in the trees at a 45-degree angle and get it safely to the fairway for a reasonable third shot to the green. The other option was to play the ball straight up the path leading through the woods and try to get it hole high to the left of the green. That would be by far the more dangerous of the two shots, but Couples gave it some serious thought. "If it's Thursday, I play it up the path," he said. "It would not have been that hard a shot and I might have ended up still having a chance to make birdie.

"But it wasn't Thursday, it was Sunday. Extra nerves are involved. I didn't want to go down in history as the biggest mental midget ever to lose the Masters. The safe play was the right play."

And so Couples punched the ball between the trees, one hand coming off the club as he did. The ball made it safely to the fairway and it looked as if Couples had dodged the proverbial bullet. He was now 161 yards from the hole and it appeared certain he would walk off the hole with no worse than a par. He could still make birdie. After all, he had gotten up and down from the fairway on Saturday, hitting a three-iron from 205 yards. Now, he was in between six- and seven-iron.

Which was the problem. Couples's golfing instincts told him the right play was a hard seven-iron. He didn't think the creek would come into play unless he completely mishit the ball and he might be able to get it close. LaCava, having just witnessed a near disaster, didn't want to take any risks. "Let's hit six, make sure we get it past the pin, and get out of here," he argued.

The argument made sense. One of the reasons Couples and LaCava have worked so well together for eight years is that LaCava is not a yes caddy. Couples respects him and his opinions even on those occasions when he disagrees and doesn't listen to what he's being told. Standing in the fairway at 13 he was a little bit shellshocked from the tee shot and the escape. Instead of relying on his gut, he decided to rely on LaCava's counsel to play it safe. "It was good, sensible advice," Couples said. "But it wasn't what I needed to do right there. The blame is with me for not going with my gut."

Couples pulled the six and got over the ball. Another mistake. "I needed time to get my mind back together," he said. "I was going in a thousand directions mentally. I needed to walk up to the green, walk back, calm myself down, make a solid decision, and play the shot. I did none of the above."

What he did was take a half-hearted swing with the six-iron, trying to cut the ball softly into the pin. He got a soft cut—too soft a cut. The ball drifted right and short and splashed into the creek. Couples stared at it as if to say, "This can't be happening."

He had to walk up, drop in front of the creek, and chip on. Two putts later he had made seven and as he walked off the green, the mindset of the Masters had changed. Couples, who had believed for 66 holes that it was his destiny to win this Masters, was no longer so sure. He now trailed by two shots with five to play. O'Meara, who had wondered if Couples was catchable, had now caught him, albeit by Couples slipping rather than by him charging. And, up ahead, Duval, seeing the double bogey go on the board as he walked onto the 15th green, suddenly knew it was his Masters to win or lose. Furyk, even after his bogey on the 15th, stood on the 16th tee thinking if he made three straight birdies he could still have a chance because he at least had the advantage of playing with the man he had to catch.

Truly great players do not roll over and die after a disaster. Couples came back and almost birdied the 14th, just missing a 10-foot putt, and then hit an absolutely brilliant five-iron second shot at the 15th to within three feet. When he made the putt for eagle he had played the critical 13-14-15 stretch in even par by going 7-4-3. Even par through that stretch usually isn't good enough, but Couples was again tied for the lead because Duval had followed his birdie at 15 with a bogey at 16.

In Couples's mind at that moment, the tournament was between him and Duval. "No disrespect to Mark," he said. "But when I walked off thirteen, I was chasing Duval. He became the target. I really almost stopped thinking about Mark, which was probably foolish."

O'Meara had birdied 15, meaning he trailed Couples and Duval by one. He walked onto the 16th tee feeling he was in almost perfect position. The par-fives, where Couples's and Duval's length gave them an advantage, were now behind them and he was just one shot back. He was putting well and, for some reason, he felt calmer than he had thought he might be under the circumstances. "All your life you say, "I'd just like to get into position to win a major and see what happens," he said. "Well, here I was. I was in position to win a major."

O'Meara hit a gorgeous tee shot at 16, a five-iron that stopped just behind the hole. Couples, still pumped up, hit his tee shot just over the green. But he chipped close and saved his par. O'Meara's birdie putt just missed. In the meantime, Furyk was two-thirds of the way to his goal, having birdied 16 and 17 to join O'Meara at seven under. Duval had hit his second shot at 17 to 10 feet and knew he had made the putt. Only it hadn't gone in. "I will never know how those putts at 15 and 17 didn't go in," he said. "I thought I had made them both."

As O'Meara and Couples walked up the slight incline from the 16th green to the 17th tee, O'Meara turned to his caddy, Jerry Higginbotham, and said, "You know what, I can make birdie on these last two holes and win this thing."

Higginbotham wasn't about to argue. He loved hearing his man talk with that kind of confidence. "It was amazing how good I felt coming off of sixteen," O'Meara said. "I hit a great shot in there and a great putt even though it didn't go in."

He and Couples both hit excellent drives at 17 and each hit a nine-iron to about 10 feet. Couples was just outside O'Meara and putted first. He wasn't even close, pushing it two feet past the hole. "Worst putt I hit all week," he said. "I never even put a stroke on it."

O'Meara's stroke was perfect. The ball went dead center. It was at that moment that Duval was being taken to the Jones Cabin, having missed his birdie putt at 18. Furyk had come much closer to making his putt, a curling 25-footer that stopped two inches below the cup. If it had gone in, four players would have been tied for the lead. Drained by the effort he had made trying to catch the leaders and coming up two inches shy, Furyk tapped in.

Three men were tied for the lead at eight under. Duval was finished, O'Meara and Couples were on the 18th tee. O'Meara, pumped up and confident, hit a perfect tee shot to the right of the fairway bunker. Couples, not feeling nearly as good and with Saturday's overcut drive into the woods still on his mind, aimed for the bunker, hoping his natural cut would move the ball safely to the right. This time, though, the ball didn't cut. It went dead straight into the bunker.

In the CBS tower, Nantz, still searching for omens, pointed out that Couples had hit his tee shot into that same bunker in 1992 and gone on to win. Then, though, he had a two-shot lead. Now he had an eight-iron in his hands and 135 yards to the hole. He took too much sand, and the ball popped up right and headed straight for the front bunker, right of the green. Couples didn't even look. "I was mad at myself," he said. "It was a bad shot."

O'Meara and Higginbotham weren't certain if the right shot was a six- or a seven-iron. Understanding that he was pumped up by the magnitude of the moment, O'Meara said he liked seven-iron, preferring to hit something hard.

"Perfect," Higginbotham said. "You've got the right club. Just put a good swing on it."

Watching on TV, Brad Faxon heard Higginbotham's comment and thought, that's the right thing to say. Eliminate any doubt from the player's head.

Sure enough, O'Meara's shot landed hole high, 20 feet to the right of the hole. As they walked to the green, their fellow players crowded around TVs in the locker room. They were virtually silent. Everyone knew what was at stake in the next few minutes for all three players who made up the story line.

While Couples was preparing to hit his shot from the bunker, O'Meara looked around at the setting and couldn't help but think about how beautiful this spot was. It was coming up on 7 o'clock and the sun was starting to descend behind the trees on the now empty back nine.

O'Meara snapped out of his reverie as Couples stood over his shot.

"I had this thought that Freddie could make this shot," he said. "At that point, we were in match play and in match play you learn to always expect your opponent to do something spectacular. I had to prepare myself mentally to make my putt to tie if he made the shot."

Couples hit a good shot, but it wasn't going in. It stopped six feet below the hole. He marked and the stage was clear for O'Meara. One putt to win the Masters. One putt to fulfill every golfing dream he had ever had. One putt to prove to himself once and for all that he had been right all along about his ability to close the deal on Sunday—regardless of the stakes.

He stalked the putt, seeing less break than he thought was there. He just knew there was more break than the green was showing. Higginbotham believed what his eyes saw—maybe a cup and a half of break. O'Meara was convinced it was more. And so, at 7:02 P.M., right on Rob Correa's schedule for CBS, he stood over the putt, drew the putter back, and held his breath as the ball came off the club.

"I knew right away that it had a chance," he said. "But I was afraid to move. When it got near the hole, I saw it dying left and I thought, please, please hang on."

It did. O'Meara's arms were in the air, Duval's stomach was upside down, and Couples was looking at LaCava and saying, "You know what, that's the right way for it to end."

Lance Barrow had picked the perfect camera angle for O'Meara's last putt, using the camera behind O'Meara. It showed the line of the putt perfectly and, as a bonus, the viewers could see the fans behind the hole starting to stand in unison as the ball closed in on the cup. It was a great moment of television.

At that same instant, Barrow made another decision. He had a camera rolling on Tiger Woods, who was sitting in Butler Cabin waiting to present the green jacket to the winner. As soon as the putt dropped, Woods was out of his seat, arms in the air, cheering for his pal. Barrow could have called for that shot, but he decided not to. This was O'Meara's moment and he didn't want anything—even Tiger's reaction—intruding. When O'Meara heard what Barrow had done, he was gratified and touched.

Couples congratulated O'Meara, who was trying to apologize because Higginbotham, in his excitement, had winged his cap onto Couples's line. Couples couldn't have cared less. He made the six-footer—"I honestly believe I would have made it if it had mattered," he said—and at 7:04 the Masters was over. As long as O'Meara signed his scorecard correctly.

Coming off the green, O'Meara looked for his family. They were nowhere to be found. Alicia O'Meara had tried to get inside the ropes with her two children, but they had been stopped by security people. A year earlier, those same security people had cleared the way for Earl Woods and Hughes Norton (an agent, for crying out loud) but now they blocked the O'Mearas. It wasn't until after O'Meara had signed his card and walked behind the scorer's tent that he got to see his family. They cried. He didn't. "I was still in shock," he said.

While O'Meara was whisked to Butler Cabin for the televised green jacket ceremony, Duval was taken to the interview room. His stomach and head were pounding. But he handled himself remarkably well, especially when someone asked him if he felt he had lost the Masters, having a three-shot lead with three to play.

"Pards," Duval said evenly, "I shot sixty-seven on Sunday at the Masters. The guy who won birdied three of the last four holes. I feel I gave it everything I had to give."

That didn't lessen the pain. The same was true for Couples. He knew that only two players before O'Meara—Art Wall in 1959 and Arnold Palmer in 1960—had birdied the last two holes to win the Masters. He had seen O'Meara make putt after putt down the stretch. But until the moment that O'Meara made his putt on 18, losing had never really occurred to him.

Everyone was drained. Furyk walked into the men's grill just outside the locker room, sat down, and asked his dad to get him a beer and four Advil. He sat there, saying nothing for a long time. "You played great," Mike Furyk said. "Everyone is outside waiting for us,"

"Not yet," his son answered. "I'm not ready yet."

He needed time to think about what had happened, how close he had come. "In a way, I would have been more heartbroken if Mark hadn't made his putt," he said. "Because then I would have been that two inches on 18 from being in a playoff. Mark's birdie softened it a little. Even so, I was just exhausted, drained, and a little sad."

His father was concerned. He had never seen Jim this down after a tournament. But he had never seen him come this close to winning a major.

Duval and Couples both went out to dinner with the people who had been down for the week. Sitting in the quaint restaurant at the Partridge Inn, Couples felt a little bit like the widow at a funeral. Everyone was on eggshells. "I finally told them all to quit worrying about me, that I was fine. I mean, I felt awful. I played well but I didn't win. There just wasn't anything more to say about it."

Duval's friends kept trying to cheer him up by reminding him how well he played. He put a hand up. "Guys, I know what you're trying to do and I appreciate it," he said. "But you know what? There's nothing you can say that will make me feel better. Not a single thing."

While the others tried to gather themselves to move on, O'Meara made his way to the putting green for the real awards Ceremony, the one that uses a spectacular sunset as the backdrop with all the green coats and the officials from golfdom around the world inside the ropes. Will Nicholson was the master of ceremonies again and he remembered all the foreign dignitaries without needing a mulligan.

Then he asked Woods to put the green jacket on O'Meara. In the TV ceremony, Woods had struggled, holding the jacket up so high that O'Meara almost pulled a muscle reaching for it. Now he got it just right. The jacket, 44-regular, carried to the putting green as always by Arthur Williams, the club's maitre d', felt absolutely perfect as Woods slipped it over O'Meara's shoulders.

"Mark," Nicholson said, "what a birdie that was on eighteen. What a finish."

Mark O'Meara looked around him at all the people, felt the green jacket on his shoulders, and said the most eloquent thing he could think of at that moment in his life:

"Wow."

Holly, Par 4, 465 Yards, Dogleg Right

from *One Magical Sunday (But Winning Isn't Everything)* by Phil Mickelson with Donald T. Phillips

This final hole at Augusta National is the second most difficult on the course. And there are reasons for that. First, it's almost all uphill. Second, there are two fairway bunkers on the left side about 300 yards out (at the elbow of the dogleg). Third, you have to drive through a very narrow chute of trees. Clearly, the most critical shot on #18 is the tee shot. If you hit it in the trees right or left, you're going to be fighting for par. But if you drive it in the fairway, you'll be thinking birdie. Today, the pin is in the lower left portion of the green—and that is a great placement.

Rather than hit a driver, I pull out my 3-wood to get a little more accuracy and to be certain the ball doesn't reach the fairway bunkers. And I've also been hitting this club well all week long.

Using the 3-wood was a very smart shot. Very smart. Phil is a much better player now than he used to be—not because he hits better shots, but
because he doesn't hit as many bad shots. He's hitting smarter shots. He's
not going to beat himself as much as he used to.

Dave Pelz

I tee the ball up on the left side and just rip it as hard as I can. The ball
goes 303 yards and lands right in the middle of the fairway. Nice.

That tee shot was one of the greatest shots I've ever seen Phil hit. Such a
good shot, such a good swing. That ball went so far, it actually stopped a
couple of yards past the fairway bunkers.

Coach Steve Loy

My approach shot is going to be all uphill to a two-tiered green that slopes
from back to front. It's guarded by two front bunkers, one short left and one
right. When I get up to the ball, I have to wait a few minutes for Bernhard
Langer and Paul Casey to finish putting. I have plenty of time to think
about this shot, so Bones and I discuss it in some detail.

It's 162 yards to the pin. Behind the pin, there's a little catch basin that
will funnel the ball toward the hole. I have a huge margin of error. I want
to hit a shot just to the right of the hole so as to catch that basin and let
the ball funnel back down to the pin. I know it's a quick putt down the hill
from there—but it levels off right near the cup, so there's no real threat of
running it five feet by and three-putting. I've seen a lot of guys make that
putt to win by one or two strokes. Vijay Singh, Mark O'Meara, and Tiger

Woods all did it. Bones and I both agree on club selection. It'll be a full 8-iron.

I'm thinking I'd much rather win the tournament right here and avoid a playoff. So I let "Old Phil" step up to the ball and go for the pin. My swing feels good. The ball fades a little like I want it to. It lands six feet right of the hole, catches the basin, and stops 18 feet away from the pin. Perfect!

The walk up to the 18th green on Sunday at the Masters is a big moment for a golfer. All the spectators have gathered from all over the course. We're in the last group and there's no one else playing golf at Augusta National.

The fairway is long and uphill. People are lined up ten to fifteen deep on both sides. As I start my walk, they're all applauding and cheering. It's an impressive sight and a wonderful moment.

When I saw my son walking up the 18th fairway, I thought back to when he was nine years old and had called me out of the kitchen on Masters Sunday. "You see, Mom," he said, "one day that's going to be me—and they're going to be clapping and yelling for me! I'm going to win the Masters and be walking up to the 18th green just like that!"

Mary Mickelson

I look into the crowd and see the faces of many people who are at Augusta year in and year out. It just makes me feel great—and all I can think of is to just enjoy the moment. Just enjoy it. So as I head up the hill, I smile and nod, thank you. I smile and nod.

While I was replacing the divot, Phil got about 30 yards in front of me. Standing there watching him walk up to the 18th green, I noticed that it's much more uphill than you think. The green sits way up on top of a hill.

Jim (Bones) Mackay

During that walk, I recalled the first time I took Philip to the big golf course. He was only three years old and didn't want to play the 18th hole because it would be the end of our round. I told him we had to play it—and he ran right up Cardiac Hill just as fast as he could.
I remember thinking at that moment: "This kid is just destined to play golf."

Phil Mickelson, Sr.

When I get up to the green, I mark my ball and step back out of the way so that Chris DiMarco can hit out of the left front bunker. Unfortunately, just as I had done back on #5, Chris leaves his ball in the bunker. Boy, is that sand tough! Chris doesn't waste any time with his next shot. I'm sure he wants neither to disrupt my concentration nor to leave his ball in the bunker again, so he steps right up and takes another swing.

This time his ball pops out, lands on the green, rolls by the pin, and comes to rest about three inches behind my mark. Of course, that means that Chris will hit first—and I will get an absolutely perfect look at how my own putt will break. Talk about luck!

As soon as that ball came of the bunker, Phil went right over and moved his mark so that Chris would be able to putt. It was my responsibility to clean DiMarco's ball because his caddy was raking out the bunker. So I went over, got the ball from Chris, and was cleaning it. All three of us were grinning. Everybody knew what this meant!

Jim (Bones) Mackay

When I came around to mark my ball, Phil tapped me on the back and said: "Show me something!"

"You got it," I said.

To tell you the truth, I didn't think there was any way Phil was going to miss that putt. It just seemed to be his time.

Chris DiMarco

―――――――――――――――――

While Chris is lining up his putt, I stand quietly off the edge of the green to his back right. As soon as he strokes it, I walk behind him to see what the ball will do. It breaks left, but misses the cup, and rolls about a foot by. Chris taps in. Now it's my turn.

―――――――――――――――――

Just as Phil was lining up his putt, I was taking the children from the family room in the clubhouse over to the scorer's hut near the 18th green. I walked by the practice green and saw Ernie Els munching on an apple. "If Phil misses his birdie putt and makes par," I thought, "then he and Ernie will be in a playoff."

Renee McBride

―――――――――――――――――

This is what it all comes down to, doesn't it? One downhill right-to-left putt. The last golfer to win the Masters with a birdie putt on the 18th green was Mark O'Meara in 1998. The first golfer to do it was Arnold Palmer in 1960.

On all my previous putts today, I've walked around the hole and taken a good look from all angles. But because I've seen Chris's putt, I know precisely how it's going to break. So I just stand behind the ball, visualize it rolling down the line at the right speed, and see it going into the hole.

Then I step up and take one practice stroke. It's a fairly quick downhill putt. I'm going to allow six inches of break and stroke the ball firmly.

Everyone and everything is very quiet. I don't even hear the birds chirping at this point.

I hit the putt. It feels good.

People all around the green stand up and start yelling. "Go in the hole!" "Get in the hole!" "C'mon." "C'mon." "In." "In."

I was standing off the side of the green by the scorer's hut. I closed my eyes and clenched hands with my family.

Amy Mickelson

I closed my eyes while that putt was rolling toward the hole. "Dad, help him," I said to Phil's grandfather. "Just help him. C'mon, Dad. C'mon, Dad."

Mary Mickelson

It's a quick putt, but it seems like the ball is taking forever to get there. It starts out right on my intended line. But will it hang in there for those last four feet or so? When it gets a foot from the hole, it starts to tail a bit to the left and looks like it is going to miss. But it hangs on, and hangs on, and hangs on.

My ball catches the left lip of the cup, slides along the edge all the way over to the right side—and falls into the hole. Birdie!

In the first split-second of that moment, I really believe that my grandfather nudged my ball back to the right just in the nick of time.

I was so excited I jumped up from my flat-footed position six feet above the surface of the green! With my arms and legs extended, and my putter still in my hand, I must have hung in the air for seven seconds.

And everybody else was screaming and yelling and wailing and shouting and smiling—and they had their arms over their heads, too.

———————————

We received letters and phone calls from people all over the nation about what they were doing and what happened when Phil made that putt. On airplanes, the pilots announced that Phil had won the Masters and passengers shouted, cheered, and cried. At the San Diego airport, people poured out of the bars into the concourses with their fists pumping, high-fives flying, and screaming in celebration. In restaurants where there were televisions, diners started applauding and yelling. Just outside Phil's childhood home, a neighbor was out in his front yard when he heard roars coming from the inside of four or five houses on his street. One guy from the Midwest wrote us that he jumped so high, when he came down he actually broke his leg! Others said they could now go eat their Easter dinners.

Gary McBride, Amy's Dad

———————————

When I finally float down to the ground from my Olympic-caliber, NBA-worthy leap, the first thing I do is walk over to Bones, give him a great big hug, and say: "I did it! I did it!"

"You did it! You did it!" he shouts back. Chris DiMarco gives me a high-five and a pat on the back. "Way to go, Phil!"

I walk over to the hole, pull out my golf ball, kiss it, and toss it into the crowd. The people are still screaming, shouting, smiling, and crying. I hand my putter to Bones, who takes it and, along with the flagstick, puts it in my golf bag. I walk through the crowd toward the scorer's hut. People are holding out their hands and I give them high fives. One, two, three, four, five . . . ten high fives in all.

When I get up there, I see Amy. She jumps into my arms and I give her the biggest hug and kiss. She can't speak. She's crying. I see my mom, my dad, my sister, Amy's mom, and Amy's dad. I give them each a hug, look them in the eye, and say, "I did it! I did it!"

My dad leans in and says, "I'm proud of you, son."

I see Steve Loy and give him a bear hug. I'm just about to walk up the steps into the scorer's hut when I hear, "Daddy! Daddy!" It's Amanda calling to me.

I turn around and pick her up. "Amanda, I did it!" I say to her. "Can you believe it?"

He was really excited. He wants to win every tournament and he almost does. I told him I was surprised that he won. Then I gave him a great big hug. I was holding on to his neck and he squeezed me so tight.

Amanda Mickelson, Phil's Daughter

Then I see Sophia. I pick her up and hold her in my arms. "Sophia," I say. "Daddy won! Can you believe it?"

Then I go over to Amy. She's holding our son, Evan, who's just turned one year old. At that moment, I feel so blessed to be Amanda, Sophia, and Evan's dad—and to have them with me.

Phil, you're going to be a father and there's nothing greater in the world.

Payne Stewart, 1999 U.S. Open Champion

Okay, now I've hugged and kissed everybody and it's time to walk up into the scorer's hut. But before I go, I take one look back at Amy. She sees me and we make eye contact. It was just for a moment, but it means so much for me to see her standing there holding Evan. After all we had gone through in 2003, after almost losing them both, here they are sharing in this wonderful, almost miraculous moment. And I realize that winning the Masters, as great as it feels, isn't the most important thing in my life.

In the scorer's hut, all I can think about is to make sure the scorecard I sign is correct. I was thinking about Roberto De Vicenzo who, back in 1968, had signed an incorrect card. He finished in a tie but mistakenly marked his birdie at #17 as a par and lost the tournament by one shot. Bob Goalby got the green jacket that year. "What a stupid I am," said de Vicenzo to the press afterwards.

So I look over my card carefully with Bones and Chris DiMarco. Front nine: 4, 4, 5, 3, 5, 4, 4, 5, 4. Two over par 38. Check. Back nine: 4, 4, 2, 4, 3, 5, 2, 4, 3. A scorching 31 with five birdies. Check. Overall a three under par 69. Check. Grand total of 279, nine under par for the tournament. I win the Masters by one shot. It's my twenty-third career victory—and my first major.

After Phil went into the scorer's hut, a reporter came over and wanted to interview me. But I was too emotional to even speak. So he asked if he could interview Amanda. I nodded yes.

"Amanda, is this the greatest day of your life?" he asked.

"Yes, it is," she replied.

"Is it the greatest day of your life because your daddy won the Masters?"

"No, it's the greatest day because we colored Easter eggs this morning."

Amy Mickelson

Just as I finish signing my scorecard, I take a moment to relax. The scorer's hut is right next to the practice green at the clubhouse. So we've come full circle and we're right back where we started. Somebody else walks through the door and Sophia just follows him right in. She likes to cling to me, and I love that. I pick her up, put her in my lap, and she cups my face in her hand. "I love you, Daddy," she says—her big round eyes melting my heart. Then we turn to the right and look out the window. Everybody is smiling and waving at us. I point to Amy and say, "Wave to the people, Sophia."

At first she doesn't wave. So I take the pacifier out of her mouth and say, "Wave." Sophia, who is right-handed, now smiles and waves with her left hand. Then she takes the pacifier away from me and puts it back in her mouth.

I waved because I was happy. I waved because my daddy is my daddy.
                                    Sophia Mickelson, Phil's Daughter

---

I've won the Masters. Sophia is sitting in my lap. She has her magic back. And all is right with the world.

THE
CONTROVERSIES

More Agony at Augusta

from *Getting Up & Down: My 60 Years in Golf* by Ken Venturi
with Michael Arkush

Spring arrived, which means only one thing in the world of professional
golf: The Masters.

I was going back, of course. Any thought of staying away, due to the neg-
ative public reaction in 1957, had been dismissed long ago. I was no choker,
and I was no quitter. I was a grown-up who could handle the boos. Besides,
in the wake of my wonderful play—I finished first or second in five of the
previous seven events—the golf writers had installed me as the favorite to
win the green jacket. I was determined to prove them right.

I didn't waste any time, shooting an opening 68 to assume a one-stroke
lead over a quartet of players that included Jimmy Demaret. Arnold Palmer
and Cary Middlecoff were two back, while Fred Hawkins, Art Wall Jr.,
Claude Harmon, Byron Nelson, and Billy Maxwell were in a group three
behind. I still detected a scattering of boos, but, for the most part, the gallery
seemed more than willing to afford me a second chance. With warm temperatures and almost no wind the course was playing much easier than usual.

In all, 17 players broke par. I knew I had better take advantage. I was especially effective on the greens, requiring only 28 putts.

Friday was another day entirely. The course took advantage of me. I went out with a 4-over-par 40, which included a very untimely double bogey at the par-5 8th. My fourth shot looked perfect but hit the flagstick and, unluckily, caromed back about 40 feet. I 3-putted. I was discouraged enough to be playing that poorly, but what disturbed me even more were some harsh words from a few of the "patrons." I had allowed myself to believe that the worst was over.

"I'm glad you shot 40," someone remarked at the turn. "I hope you shoot another 40. You chokin' again?"

I was reminded of what Snead said to me in Milwaukee. I vowed to respond the same way, with my clubs.

I rallied with a 32 on the back nine. At 18, I lined up a 20-foot birdie putt that broke from right to left. Even before the putt dropped, I threw my hat to the ground.

"You son of a bitch," I said under my breath. "Take that, you crummy bums. I'll show you chokin'."

Despite the up-and-down even-par 72, I was still on top at the halfway mark, by one stroke over Maxwell and Billy Joe Patton, and by two strokes over Bo Wininger and Stan Leonard. Palmer, Wall, Middlecoff, and Snead were among those who trailed by three.

I didn't fare nearly as well on Saturday, firing a pair of 37s to fall three behind Palmer, who rallied with a 68. Tied with Palmer was the incredible, 45-year-old Snead. Sunday promised to be an important day for Palmer, yet to win a major himself—yet to become, well, Arnold Palmer. I believed that it could be an important day for me, as well. I would be paired with Palmer, which gave me plenty of confidence. After all the matches with Wininger and myself against him and Finsterwald, I felt like I could handle the case.

During the night, there was a heavy downpour. No big deal, I thought. After all, everybody would be dealing with the same soggy conditions. It would, however, turn out to be a very big deal. Early on, Palmer and I were notified that Snead double-bogeyed the first hole. He would not be a factor. The tournament, it became increasingly clear to us, would come down to Palmer against me. Which was exactly what I wanted.

On the front nine, I shot a 35, Palmer a 36. The lead was down to two. On the difficult par-4 10, Palmer finished with a bogey. Now the margin was only one. The momentum was all mine.

After we each paired the 11th, I hit first on the always treacherous par-3 12th, sending the ball to the back edge of the green, about 20 feet from the cup. That was the smart play, especially with the traditional Sunday pin placement far right, and only a few yards behind the water. You don't ever want to mess with the 12th pin in the final round.

Palmer followed by sailing his approach over the green, about a foot and a half from the bunker. Though his ball was embedded in the bank, it seemed he would, under the rules, be entitled to a free drop.

But Arthur Lacey, the rules official, saw the situation differently. "It's not embedded," he told Palmer. "It's only half embedded."

"Half embedded?" I said. "That's like being half pregnant. You're either pregnant or you're not."

Palmer and Lacey continued to argue. Concerned that I would lose my concentration, I told them I would putt out. After barely missing my birdie attempt, I rejoined Palmer and Lacey to catch the rest of their discussion. Nothing was resolved. I sat on my bag with Mutt, my caddie. This matter was obviously going to take longer than I thought. While I sided with Palmer's interpretation, I realized I might capitalize from his misfortune.

Finally, an angry Palmer played the shot. Not surprisingly, he flubbed the chip and the ball did not even reach the putting surface. He hit the next one five feet past the hole but then missed the putt, making a five. The two-shot swing put me in the lead for the first time since early in the third round. Two years after my memorable collapse, I was on my way toward a memorable comeback.

Only Palmer wasn't ready to give up on the 12th hole just yet.

"I didn't like your ruling," he said, glaring at Lacey. "I'm going to play a provisional ball." (He was really playing what is called a "second ball.") "You can't do that," I told him. "You have to declare a second *before* you hit your first one. Suppose you had chipped in with the other ball? Would you still be playing a second?"

But Palmer had his mind made up. I turned to Mutt.

"Mutt, we got 'em now," I said, knowing Palmer was in violation of the rules. "It doesn't make any difference what he does with this ball."

Palmer didn't say another word. He took the drop. The ball rolled toward the hole two times in a row, allowing him to place it. This time, with a better sense of the speed of the green, he almost chipped it in, tapping in for par.

We proceeded to the 13th tee. By the time we arrived, I was no longer angry. If anything, I was amused. I was certain the officials, once they checked the rule book, wouldn't give Palmer the second ball. The five, not three, would stand, and so, too, would my one-stroke advantage.

At 13, Palmer outdrove me by a yard or two. Hitting first, I made the smart play again, laying up with a 4 iron. With the lead, I wasn't going to do anything stupid... or so I thought. But then I committed a big mental blunder, and I didn't even have a club in my hands. Even now, the mere memory makes me ill.

Palmer, preparing to hit an iron to lay up, had stopped and turned to me.

"You know, they're going to give me a five back there at 12, aren't they?" he asked.

"You bet your ass they're going to give you a five," I responded.

That was the worst possible thing I could have said. There were so many better answers, such as: "I don't know, Arnold, we'll have to see when we get in," or "You never really know with rules officials," or "Oh, I'm sure they'll give you a three." At the very least, I should have said nothing. For many years, because of my stammering, I was the man to give short answers. I could have really used one in this situation.

Why was my response so stupid? Because, by telling him that he was sure to get a double bogey at 12, I believe I helped convince him to put the iron back in his bag and go for the green in two. He might have played it more conservatively if he thought he was still in the lead. In any case, I know I shouldn't have tortured myself for all these years. Knowing the aggressive way Palmer played the game, he probably would have gone for it anyway.

Lo and behold, the gamble paid off. His approach bounced on the small neck in front of the green just over the water. A few yards to the left or a few yards to the right and his ball would have gone in the creek. Instead, it came to a rest about 20 feet from the cup. Palmer, of course, would make the putt for an eagle. After a wonderful wedge, I tapped in for a birdie, convinced I was still tied for the lead. I was still pretty confident I could win.

But, walking up the fairway at 14, I saw Bill Kerr, a member of Augusta National and one of Cliff Roberts' assistants. Kerr, wearing his green coat, was running down the middle of the fairway. I soon found out the cause of his exuberance.

"They gave Arnold a 3 at 12," Kerr shouted. "They gave Arnold a 3 at 12."

The gallery went crazy. So did I, for a different reason. This simply was not happening, I kept reassuring myself. Kerr must have received the wrong information.

"Get the hell off the fairway," I told him. "You don't belong in the fairway."

Palmer turned to me, asking, "What do you think?" I didn't answer. Not this time.

I tried not to worry about it, figuring I would deal with the situation when we finished the round. But it was no use. My concentration was shattered for good.

I proceeded to 3-putt 14, 3-putt the par-5 15th after getting on the green in two, and 3-putt 16. Palmer hung on to win by one stroke over Doug Ford and Fred Hawkins. I tied for fourth, two shots back.

In the scoring tent, I gave Palmer another chance.

"You're signing an incorrect card," I told him.

"No, I'm not," he said. "The ruling was made."

Nonetheless, the way I figured it, the matter was still far from over. After signing my scorecard, I went to see Mr. Roberts. All I was trying to do at this point was protect the field. I no longer had a chance to win, but I strongly believed that Ford and Hawkins should, at the very least, be given an opportunity to fight it out between themselves.

I started to lay out the whole sequence of events for Mr. Roberts, that Palmer, under the rules, was required to declare that he was going to play a second ball before hitting the first one.

I was wasting my breath. Mr. Roberts wasn't interested in fact. In his mind, he already knew the facts.

Becoming more frustrated by the second, I asked that Mr. Roberts bring in Arthur Lacey. Lacey would make things right.

Only one problem: Lacey, I was told, had already left the golf course, and there was no way to track him down. There were no cell phones in 1958. A pretty quick exit from the premises, don't you think? I certainly don't have any evidence that Mr. Roberts, anxious to avoid controversy, made sure Lacey got off the grounds in a hurry, but it sure looked fishy. The one person who could clear up the whole mess was nowhere to be found. (I wrote a letter to Lacey, saying, "I'm sorry we didn't get together before the tournament was over, and I'm sure you'll agree that it was not the right ruling, and hopefully we'll see each other some time." I did not receive a response.)

Then I said, to Mr. Roberts: "Bring in Arnold. Rules are rules."

By now, Roberts had listened long enough. He wasn't going to bring in anyone.

"I don't need to know the rules," he said. "I make the rules." There was no doubt. Even the great Bobby Jones, on matters pertaining to the actual running of the golf tournament, deferred to Cliff Roberts.

"I told Cliff the ruling was wrong," Jones told me a few years later. "But I was overruled. I always believed you were right. I'm so sorry."

I thought, briefly, about finding the press to make my case, but I quickly reasoned that such a plea would also get nowhere. If anything, going public would damage my fragile image even further. "Look at that Venturi," they would write. "He's always complaining about something."

What took place at the 12th hole, to be sure, would never happen on today's PGA Tour. There are too many observers—writers, announcers, spotters, rules officials, and cameras—at every tournament to let any infraction go unnoticed. And in the rare case in which they were to miss a violation, believe me, a viewer lounging on his couch in Flint, Michigan, would call the networks in no time to make sure the error was rectified.

The viewer in Flint didn't see Palmer and me play the 12th hole in the 1958 Masters. Television coverage in those days wasn't comprehensive like it is today. Too bad for Doug Ford (the 1957 Masters winner) and for Fred Hawkins, who would never win a major. They were robbed.

As the years went on, even some prominent experts in the game got it wrong, such as former commissioner Joe Dey. Dey wrote an article about the matter for *Golf Digest* magazine in 1983, not knowing the exact chronology of events. When I provided him with the whole explanation, he felt horrible and apologized profusely. Other publications have indicated that Palmer acted properly, citing the rule that allowed a free lift from an embedded ball. I don't disagree. All I'm saying is that Palmer made improper use of the second ball.

I've never gotten over what happened at the 12th hole. Why didn't I come forward sooner? I couldn't, not with my responsibilities and loyalties to CBS. The network needed to maintain a good relationship with Augusta National. If I had spoken out, that relationship might have been irrevocably harmed, and CBS might have lost coverage of The Masters. I couldn't take that risk. But I've retired now from CBS.

I'll start with Palmer. First, like so many others, I am extremely grateful for the contribution he's made to the game. I can't imagine where golf would be without him. Also, regardless of what I believe took place at the

12th hole at Augusta National 46 long years ago, it should not take anything away from that contribution. The game has never known a more deserving ambassador.

At the same time, nobody, not even Palmer, is bigger than the game. I firmly believe that he did wrong, and that he knows that I know he did wrong. That is why, to this day, it has left me with an uncomfortable feeling.

Arnold has never brought up 1958, and neither have I. I understand. The past is the past. What I don't understand is his still believing that he was right, as he said in his 2002 book, *Playing by the Rules*.

If people don't know which interpretation to accept, his or mine, all I ask is that they look up the rule about hitting a second ball and decide for themselves. I have nothing against him personally. But we all know the rules.

My feelings about this matter, at least among close friends, have been no secret. Which is why, in the 2002 Masters, CBS producer Lance Barrow was worried what I might say when Palmer made what was billed then as his farewell appearance (though he came back a year later). Barrow had nothing to worry about. I was as professional as ever, praising Palmer for what he's meant to the game. "How about that applause?" Jim Nantz said, as Palmer approached the 18th green. "They are honoring a man," I said, "who has won four green jackets."

Only once did I let Palmer know exactly how I felt. The scene was the post-tournament ceremony at the 1960 Masters. Palmer birdied the final two holes to beat me by a shot. He leaned over to me, saying softly: "I wish it could have been you. I wish you had won."

"It's two years too late," I said.

In the spring of 1977, I was playing Augusta National's par-3 course a week after the tournament when I ran into Cliff Roberts. Jack Rodgers, who was my best friend, was with me. Beau was in the hospital for a cancer checkup.

Roberts was going for a walk on the old 9th hole of the par-3 course with Jerry Franklin, an Augusta National member.

"Is that you, Ken?" Roberts said.

"Yes, Cliff," I responded. I always called him Cliff because, after the 1958 ruling, I had lost some respect for the man. I stopped calling him Mr. Roberts.

"Can I see you?" he said, telling Franklin he needed some privacy.

Sure, I told him, asking Jack Rodgers to give me a few minutes.

"Ken," he said, after inquiring into Beau's health, "I want to congratulate you for the way you've handled yourself, the respect you have for this golf course and for this tournament. You are a credit to the game. You never said a single word about the episode at 12."

"Thank you," I said.

He then got to the real point he wanted to make.

"I want to ask for your forgiveness," he continued. "When I made the ruling in 1958, it was wrong. I'm ashamed of myself. I made the ruling because of what you said in 1956. I know now that wasn't Ken Venturi, not the Ken Venturi we all know and love. If you can somehow find it in your heart to forgive me, I would certainly appreciate it. I now wish you could have been a Masters champion."

"Mr. Roberts," I said, now willing to afford him the proper respect, "you've soothed a lot of wounds. I'm glad you know the real story, because I never said those things in 1956."

We said our good-byes. I never saw Cliff Roberts again. About six months later, near the lake on the club's par-3 course, he committed suicide. I felt sad. I truly believe he was very sorry about what transpired in 1958.

In the early eighties, there was one more apology, and from a most surprising source. Again, ironically enough, I was with Jack Rodgers at Augusta, this time walking down the 11th fairway late in the afternoon on the Sunday before The Masters. I was able to play on the weekends before the galleries were allowed in on Monday. Suddenly, it occurred to me that I had seen this caddie before, but I couldn't quite place him.

"Where do I know you from?" I finally asked him.

"Mr. Ken, I'm Ironman," the caddie said.

Why, of course, *Ironman*, Palmer's caddie for years at Augusta. Instantly a flood of memories came back, some good, some not good. We exchanged small talk for a few minutes, but as we approached the 12th green, I could no longer avoid the obvious reference.

"Ironman," I said, "will you ever forget this hole?"

It was a light, friendly remark, or so I thought. Within seconds, I realized that I had touched a painful part of his past.

"No, Mr. Ken, I will never forget this hole," he said. "I felt so bad. I told Mr. Palmer, 'You're doing the wrong thing. You can't do that. It's illegal. You got a five there.' He said, 'I'll get the ruling myself.' I hope you do forgive me, Mr. Ken."

He then provided a piece of the story that had been missing.

"I tried to tell them what happened when I got inside the clubhouse, that I thought what Mr. Palmer did was wrong," Ironman said, adding that he was scared that he would never be able to work again if he discussed the matter further.

I could not believe my ears. Ironman started to cry.

"Please forgive me, Mr. Ken," he said.

We hardly spoke the rest of the round. What else was there to say? But when we finished I told him how I felt. I was very glad that Jack Rodgers, who died a few years later, was there to be my witness. He had always believed me, but having him hear the truth firsthand made a big difference. I didn't care who else knew, as long as my best friend knew.

"Ironman, I am so proud of you," I said. "You did the right thing. You should have no regrets. Your family and you are the most important thing. What counts more to me is that I have you as a friend."

I gave him $100. Ironman walked away, still in tears.

I never saw him again.

A Ridiculous Rule

by Arthur Daley, *The New York Times*, April 16, 1968

After the Masters tournament one year a generous Arnold Palmer decided to give his caddie a $1,000 tip. He asked his wife. Winnie, to write out the check and never gave it another thought. Neither did she apparently. She absent-mindedly wrote out a check for $10,000 and left it at the Augusta National where club officials discovered the obvious error. An embarrassed Mrs. Palmer replaced the inflated check with one for the correct amount.

But there was no recall on Sunday at Augusta when a different kind of mistake in penmanship cost the amiable Roberto De Vicenzo of Argentina a tie with Bob Goalby for one of the most cherished prizes in golf. He signed his name on a scorecard that had incorrectly listed his birdie 3 on the 17th as a par 4. At the time the subtotals had not been added. Otherwise he would have instantly sensed that something was wrong when he was given a 66 instead of the 65 he had actually earned on the last round.

Rules are rules, however, no matter how ridiculous they are. The links code ordains that any divot-digger who attests to a higher score than he made is stuck with the higher score. If he signs to a lower score, he is disqualified.

No matter how honorable his intentions are, intent is not permitted to intrude. Neither is justice.

INNOCENT VICTIM

What made this arithmetical mishap seem so scandalous is that it was exposed on nationwide television to countless millions of witness. They watched the happy fella from Argentina roll in the birdie, thought they were seeing a playoff in the making and were horrified to learn later that Roberto's autograph on an erroneous scorecard had nullified everything. No golfer was Gertrude Stein but she might have phrased it: a rule is a rule is a rule.

But why is there such a rule? Golf is the only sport that obliges each contestant to be his own scorekeeper. It was proper enough in ancient days, and still is proper enough in club matches of little consequence. However, it no longer belongs in major championships where milling thousands of fans charge all over the course and where television magnifies the impact of the event and where huge purses add to the emotional pressure.

Furthermore, no other phase of athletic activity demands more intense concentration on the business at hand than golf. No player should be required to risk distraction by also serving as a bookkeeper. Not only does he know every shot he made but he can remember every one. Gene Sarazen, if asked, can still describe in precise detail every stroke he made in shooting a 66 on his final round to win the United States Open championship in 1932.

Golfers also happen to be the most honest competitors of all. Bobby Jones once lost an Open crown by calling an extra stroke on himself, one that no one else saw. He thought he saw the ball move as he addressed it. Maybe it did. Maybe it didn't. But he bent backwards to call it.

Fred Corcoran runs the World Cup tournament—it originally was known as the Canada Cup—and he has had golfers from 40 nations competing over a 15-year period without a disqualification or rhubarb. Fred's committee checks every bag before play starts so that none can accidently break the rule on a maximum of 14 clubs. Don't forget that Sammy Snead was involved in a rather infamous incident on a TV match when he refused to win after discovering late in the show that he had inadvertently placed an extra club in his bag.

The Corcoran officials check scores, bring contestants to the official repository and make sure each signs his card. It's well to remember that Doug Sanders was disqualified once for forgetting to affix his signature to card.

OFFICIAL STATUS

The United States Golf Association sends out gal scorers with each twosome or threesome in major tournaments. But these female volunteers have no official status and are used mainly to keep spectators, news media and scoreboards up to date. It would be simple enough to give them official status, crosschecking with the contestants at the end of each hole. A final crosscheck at the end of the round would lend far more emphasis to the ritual than having players wearily haul scorecards from back pockets for a much too cursory glance.

If the dolls can't be trusted, the U.S.G.A. can use guys. There always are enough club members who would be delighted by such an opportunity. Joe Dey and the other golfing fathers have one of the finest sports organizations in the world but they are the ones who will be regarded as fall guys in the De Vicenzo goof because of the unnecessary inflexibility in their rules.

Although this one should seem to have left them painted into a corner, there is the easy escape of having official scorers relieve the players of a burden they never should be asked to assume. The post-tournament ceremonies at Augusta became a grotesque mockery of the great piece of Americana that the Masters had become. Archaic rules and archaic presenters swept it into sport's dark ages. Something should be done about both.

Mopping Up

from *The Snake in the Sandtrap (and Other Misadventures on the Golf Tour)* by Lee Trevino and Sam Blair

For years I was remembered at the Masters for all the wrong reasons. Twice, in 1970 and 1971, I refused my invitation to play there after loudly criticizing the layout at Augusta National because it has no rough to penalize guys who hit it crooked, and the hills are in places that favor the long knockers.

Then I came back and immediately got hot about a mix-up over a ticket for my caddy during my first practice round. I was close to packing up and leaving again before Clifford Roberts, the man who founded the Masters with Bobby Jones, explained that the season ticket I had bought for my caddy wasn't good on practice days; he needed a separate ticket for those. It's not that way at any other golf tournament in the world, but that's the Masters for you. They do things their own way.

That's why I felt proud that I finally could be remembered at Augusta for doing something right. On that rainy Saturday in April 1984 I won one from the Masters brass because I stood firm for what I knew was right—standing ankle deep in water at the time.

Part of the Masters tradition is all those names they give to different holes and bridges and ponds and flower beds on the course. I don't know what the 16th green is called, but since that day I've felt it should be known as the Mexican Standoff.

You know the definition of a Mexican standoff: we lost our ass but we got out alive. That's what happened to the Masters brass there.

When George Archer, David Graham and I reached the 16th green, we shouldn't have been putting, because the greens were too wet. My ball was about 20 feet from the cup, and so was Graham's. Archer's was about 30 feet away, and the entire hole was covered with water.

I know what the Masters people were thinking. We were on national television and they were insisting we finish this round so we could finish the tournament on time Sunday. There was an official on the green and I asked him, "What are we going to do about putting?"

"Well, you have to putt," he said.

"What do you mean I have to putt?" I asked.

"We've been given instructions to keep play moving," he told me.

"You can't putt to that cup," I told him. "It's surrounded by water."

"Well, I can't help it," he said. "Everybody else has been putting."

So George Archer went ahead and 3-putted. The official looked at me and I just stood there.

"If you think I'm going to putt, you better call the clubhouse and get your lunch," I said. "We're going to be out here awhile."

He got on the radio with tournament headquarters and said, "Trevino won't putt."

"Yeah," I said, "and tell them why I won't putt."

He listened to their answer and nodded. "They say you're going to have to putt," he said.

"No, I'm not," I said. "The rules state that if you are on the putting surface and cannot move your ball to a dry surface to putt, the green has to be toweled or squeegeed. Play has to be suspended until it is."

"Well, they say you have to putt," he said. The guy sounded like a recording.

"Then you had better call somebody else," I said.

He called Clyde Mangum, the deputy commissioner of the PGA Tour, and told him, "Trevino won't putt on the sixteenth."

"Why not?" Mangum asked.

"The hole is surrounded by water," the official told him.

And Mangum shot right back: "He doesn't have to putt. You are going to have to towel or squeegee that green." And that was that.

When all the squeegees came out, I got a standing ovation from about fifteen thousand people around the 16th green. The officials there knew the rule. It was just that they were told to keep play moving and nobody was going to mess around and delay that golf tournament. Again, they were dictating their own rules.

After they finally did the right thing, I wanted to show the television audience how deep the water was on the course. So when I went to 17 I skipped along and dragged my club behind me. Water churned in my wake as if an outboard motorboat had just come through.

Better yet, I should have tried a jackknife dive before swimming down the middle of the fairway. But I made my point. And I had one more memorable Masters. Maybe if I hadn't decided the wide-open Augusta course wasn't for my game I would have won it by now.

Off Course in Augusta

She Went to the Masters to See Hootie, Martha and a Battle of the Sexes. Instead, She Found a Town Trying to Keep Its Tradition Alive

by Susan Reimer, *The Baltimore Sun*, April 20, 2003

It was after midnight when I arrived in Decatur, Ga., just outside Atlanta. In just a few hours, I was supposed to ride with a couple of busloads of indignant feminists to Augusta to protest the men-only membership policy of Augusta National Golf Club, home of the Masters golf tournament.

There, women's rights advocate Martha Burk planned to lead a rally that would raise the shame index of Augusta's corporate members to an intolerable level. Those men would, in turn, prevail upon intractable club chairman William "Hootie" Johnson to back down and finally invite a woman to join them on the best terrain for deal-making—the golf course.

So at dawn on Saturday morning—long before Tiger Woods would scramble to make the cut—I set out to meet the buses.

I had come to Georgia to witness a showdown that had been brewing for months between corporate America and feminism, but I'd had my doubts from the beginning. Was this really the fight women wanted? A nationally televised battle to get one rich woman into one exclusive club?

Still, what I found when I arrived at the buses made my heart sink. A handful of women protesters—nine by my count—had shown up. They were already outnumbered by reporters, photographers and gadflies along for the ride.

Where was the groundswell of anger at the National's stubborn sexism? Where were the voices against the companies its members run—exploiting a woman's purchasing power but keeping her out of its inner circle? Where was the women's movement in all this?

More important, I wondered, where was my story? Where were the women who would articulate for me the unfairness of their exclusion? I had planned to join a lively band of feminists on a crowded, two-hour ride to Augusta. If this was our Freedom Ride, surely I would understand by the time we reached our destination.

But one of the buses was sent away, empty. As the other got ready to take off, its tiny band of protesters rattling around inside like loose change, I had to decide if I would join them.

When I learned that I was being sent to Augusta to cover the scene at the Masters, I was thrilled. I don't get out much anymore.

In my freewheeling youth, I was a sportswriter, traveling to World Series, Super Bowls and the America's Cup. Then I married another sportswriter, we had kids, and one of us had to stop jumping onto airplanes. I cheerfully traded press-box credentials for a grocery list and a kids' sports schedule, and never looked back.

But then, Hootie Johnson, the iron-fisted chairman of Augusta National Golf Club, turned golf's most elegant and refined championship into a nasty bit of grandstanding. He refused, in a most un-Southern gentlemanly way, to consider a request to admit women (who are able to golf there) as members.

The request was made by feminist Martha Burk, president of the National Council of Women's Organizations, an imposing name for a group run by three people working out of a spare room in her Washington townhouse.

It occurred to me, as I arrived in a rainy, miserable Augusta the day before play began, that I would not be here at all if Johnson had not been so hot-headed last summer when Burk wrote him a private letter. She urged him to admit a woman member so it would not become an issue (read: public embarrassment) during the 2003 Masters.

Insiders report that Hootie thought and thought and then thought some more, but his public response was intemperate to say the least. He used the phrase "not at the point of a bayonet," and blustered like the Wizard of Oz when challenged by Dorothy. Not a few of his supporters have said that if he doesn't regret it, he should.

Soon enough, Burk joined him in hyperbole by saying Augusta's men-only policy was an insult to women soldiers fighting in Iraq. Supporters compared the Augusta leadership to the Taliban and Burk to Rosa Parks. Someone pointed out that Saddam Hussein was eligible for membership at Augusta National, but women's golf champion Nancy Lopez was not. It became clear that neither side was going to back down.

I figured I was the perfect person to watch this little drama unfold. I knew my way around a major sporting event, but more important, I am a ground zero feminist with a daughter. Strictly speaking, I had a horse in this race.

Right off, though, there were problems. Masters officials would not grant me a credential to cover the golf tournament. With my application denied, I would not be allowed inside the club or on the course. I couldn't help thinking back to 1979, when Orioles manager Earl Weaver informed me that, despite a federal court order, I would not be allowed in his clubhouse without a note from my father.

If I couldn't get inside the National's gates, I would work outside them. For feminists, it is familiar territory.

Augusta National Golf Club is located along Washington Road, hidden behind a massive bamboo hedge that shields it from noise and traffic and the unsightly suburban hyper-development that surrounds it. It is an oasis amid fast-food joints, chain restaurants, gas stations, motels and car dealerships, many of them trumpeting the Masters, and the climax of Martha vs. Hootie. A Days Inn sign said "Rooms Available. Women Allowed." A sports-bar sign read, "Hootie 4 President."

When Atlanta attorney Robert T. Jones Jr. bought the ground on which to lay out his dream course in 1931, Washington Road was all orchard land.

Better known as golfer Bobby Jones, the greatest amateur ever (there was no money in being a professional back then), he had just won his historic Grand Slam—the U.S. and British Opens and the U.S. and British Amateurs—then retired from competitive golf. He used his prestige and the business sense of friend Clifford Roberts to create a winter golf course for his business friends, most of whom were from New York.

It was the Depression, though, and the National was a tough sell. There were just 59 charter members (the club has 300 members today) who paid $350 each to join. The club opened in 1933, and Jones and Roberts immediately began planning for an invitational tournament Roberts christened the Masters. Roberts, who was both feared and revered, would run the National and the Masters until he committed suicide on the course grounds in 1977.

It is Roberts' ruthless, autocratic style that Johnson appears to want to emulate. He claims to have the support of the membership in his stand against Burk, but it may be that even the most powerful titans of business fear Johnson's power to expel them from the most prestigious golf club in the country more than they fear the anger of women customers. Local mythology has it that Microsoft billionaire Bill Gates was rejected in his first bid for membership, because he had had the audacity to let it be known that he would like to be a member.

Burk, a woman radicalized into a feminism by the tyranny of housewifery, says she cut her teeth on abortion protests where she feared for her life. But she may have met her match in Johnson.

"If I drop dead right now," he said in his press conference kicking off the tournament, "our position will not change on this issue."

On Thursday of Masters week, the continuing rain forced the cancellation of the opening round of play for the first time in 64 years. Golf patrons (here, they're not "fans") departed the course during the late morning and walked, disconsolate, to their cars.

You can tell Masters patrons anywhere. They dress as if they are just coming off the "second nine," as the National prefers to call it. They were wearing windbreakers, ball caps and golf shirts bearing corporate logos or evidence that they had been at one of golf's other big tournaments. And they all have the unmistakable fresh grooming that comes with prosperity.

Some were smoking cigars, even at this early hour of the morning, and it put me in mind of what someone like Margaret Mead might have said about the National's exclusion of women.

Men like to smoke cigars, but they prefer to do it in the company of other men and outside the company of women. Men not only want to be able to smoke cigars freely, they also like to feel like they are getting away with something. Perhaps this is why the members of the National are so stubborn about allowing women members, I thought: They want to smoke cigars in peace.

With no golf to watch, all that was left to do was shop, and most of those leaving Augusta carried bags of official souvenirs: T-shirts, ball caps and other mementos. There was plenty of unofficial shopping outside along Washington Road as well. Business was brisk at the rain-soaked tents thrown up by opportunistic entrepreneurs trying to make a buck off the Martha and Hootie squabble.

Under a tent in a parking lot across from the National, Clifford Hopkins and his son, Jason, were selling "Hootie" ball caps and bumper stickers, and "I Support Hootie" buttons. Many of their customers were women. I hoped some of them could explain to me how they could support a man who would keep women out of a venue where so much important corporate business is reportedly done.

Most, though, didn't want to talk. But Cliff (who proudly pointed out that he shares the first name of Masters founder Roberts, whom he had once met), and Jason, a 21-year-old finance student at the University of South Carolina, were willing to explain the reasons behind their enterprise.

"We'll lose a lot of money," said the elder Hopkins. He can probably absorb it; he's a developer on Hilton Head Island. But this wasn't about money. For Hopkins, and for several men I came across during the tournament, this fight was not about the National's right to free association.

I had come to Augusta looking for women who could explain to me what gaining access to the National would mean to our sex, and instead I found men who wanted to talk about what golf and the traditions of the National means to them. I was looking for argument, and I found sentiment.

"I went to the Masters with my father for the first time when I was 8 years old," said Hopkins. "And that's when he began to teach me that it was about the game, not about the individual. He passed along to us that there was integrity in the game and there was something special about this place."

His father emphasized the life lessons golf teaches: respect other players and be concerned for their safety, leave the course as you found it, play the ball as it lies and record your score honestly. He was furious that Burk had attacked the National, a club that has safeguarded those traditions, without understanding anything about the game.

"Mrs. Burk has the right to her opinion," he said, "but she isn't about the game of golf. She is about the media. And it is about the game. It is always about the game."

While his Dad preached, Jason Hopkins made change. He could barely keep up with the demand for the $20 hats and $5 pins. When he returned to school, this enterprise would become a finance paper. But Jason was also taking something else away from this week: an appreciation for his father and the values he defended.

"I guess you could say that we are just enough alike to get on each other's nerves," said the son. "But I no longer see him as 'Dad.' I see him as Cliff. He chose me to do this with him, and I am honored."

After his grandfather died two years ago, Jason went to the Masters with his father for the first time. The minute he walked through the gate, he said, tradition infused the air around him as thoroughly as the smell of moist earth and abundant flowers.

"It was quite possibly the most beautiful sight I have ever seen," he said. "You could feel the history around you.

"If I hadn't had that experience, I wouldn't be standing here right now."

The Boll Weevil Cafe is a tiny spot of gentrification in the urban blight of Augusta proper. Located downtown, it sits at the end of block after block of boarded-up buildings, empty warehouses and sad storefronts advertising loans, tattoos and second-hand items for sale.

But the Boll Weevil never wants for customers, and certainly not during Masters week. Especially this Masters week. Tournament patrons made the pilgrimage there to shake the hand of Allison Greene, the cafe manager who made national news by forming Women Against Martha Burk and organizing a counter-protest.

"Little lady, I came all this way to shake your hand," said one man, Charles Crawley of Atlanta, who was attending his 45th consecutive Masters.

Behind the bar, pecking away at a new computer system that had him baffled, was Boll Weevil owner George Harrison. He presides with equanimity over a bustling restaurant that not only employs the outspoken Allison, but three of her four outspoken sisters. But just now, Allison was busy being outspoken with *Sports Illustrated*. So, she pressed George on me as the repository of Augusta and National history.

Harrison's grandfather, George Sancken, a legendary quarterback for the Georgia Bulldogs and a prosperous dairyman, was a charter member of

Augusta. Harrison doesn't remember his grandfather ever playing golf, but he does remember gathering at his home for a pre-Masters Sunday dinner. On the table would be a big bowl of tournament tickets, to be distributed by the old man to his five children and his nine grandchildren.

Until Arnold Palmer put golf on the map, and on television, in the early 1960s, the National could hardly give those tickets away. Harrison remembers vividly when that all changed.

As an ROTC student at a local private high school, he was detailed to Augusta during Masters week to help with crowd control. "My friends and I used to manage the gallery ropes across the fairway," Harrison remembered. "But then Arnie's Army started charging up the fairway. We just couldn't handle the crowds that way any more." That's when gallery ropes were moved permanently to the sides of the course.

As an adult, Harrison would take his daughter, Anna, and his son, William, to the Masters for a few hours early in the morning, before the crowds became large enough to overwhelm the children. He would take each child separately. "You know, it had to be equal. But I liked the time with just one of them."

Today, with tickets still in his family, he goes for one day of the tournament and then gives the badges to his kids—all grown up now.

"I do the same thing every year. I buy my Coke and my ham and cheese on rye ($3.50 for as long as anyone can remember) and I go out on the course."

Harrison grew up waving to Jack Nicklaus as he grilled steaks on the patio of the house that the golf legend rented next door during Masters week. He tried to give a sense of what Augusta and the Masters mean to the community, but "good corporate neighbor" and "grown-up Woodstock" didn't seem quite right.

"I'll tell you what," he said, settling on a description. "Time in Augusta is measured Masters to Masters. If you want carpet installed, you might be told you have to wait until after the Masters. If you want to take a trip, you might tell your friends you will try to come before the Masters.

"I'll tell you what," he concluded. "If Hootie Johnson came out and said 'Tomorrow, half the members of Augusta will be women,' it would be all right with the rest of us."

I left the Boll Weevil still in search of a woman, any woman, who could speak for a community suddenly the object of scorn and anger. Before I got far, though, I found myself hopelessly lost in the neighborhoods of Augusta. When my cell phone rang, it was Bradford Woodhull "Woody" Merry, an agent for the MONY Group, returning my call.

I was hoping to find an Augusta business woman for whom membership in the National might be possible, and word came to me that Woody Merry was the guy to help me find her. "He knows everybody," I was told. He also knew the streets of Augusta like a cab driver, and stayed on the phone with me until I was back in familiar territory. He called me "Suzanne" and promised to convert me. To what—Southern girl or National booster—I was never sure.

"This is a lovin' town," he said.

The next time he called, it was to give me directions to a back gate at the National. Meet me at 6 p.m., he said. I'll get you on the course.

Merry is a volunteer with the Chamber of Commerce, but they could do worse than let him run the whole thing. His family has been in this town since the late 1800s, he is a tireless Augusta booster with infectious energy, and during Masters week, he helps show the place off for business owners who might locate their companies in Georgia. From the headquarters tent of Georgia Red Carpet, he and his fellow volunteers play musical badges with guests. By 6 p.m. on Friday, there would be a precious badge allowing me to tour this storied place.

What Augusta National represents might be in dispute, but there is no argument that the course itself is breathtaking. It is more than a horticultural wonderland; it's what the Garden of Eden must have looked like.

In a hoarse whisper, Merry showed me all the sacred places on the course. Like sports fans who recall Brooks Robinson's diving catches at third base during the 1970 World Series or Alan Ameche's overtime touchdown run to win the 1958 title game for the Colts, golf nuts recall precisely the miracle shots, the ferocious charges and the heartbreaking fades of Masters past.

Like so many men in Augusta, Merry has other kinds of Masters memories, too, and they are all tied up in his childhood, his misspent youth and in thoughts of his own son.

"I lost my daddy when I was 7," he said, "but before he died, I fell asleep in his lap in the gallery at the Masters. And you know what? My son fell asleep in my lap, too."

He recalled the 1987 Masters when, with son Brad on his shoulders calling out the shots, he chased Larry Mize, a neighbor and boyhood friend, around the course. Mize qualified for a playoff with a six-foot birdie putt and then chipped in from 140 feet for a birdie on the second playoff hole to win, and Merry can still hear his boy's excited play-by-play.

"I still have the badge from that tournament and I framed it for his 21st birthday and I wrote on it, 'One day I may die, but memories never will.'"

Merry's feelings about Augusta and the National are as thick and deep as his accent. You can see tears in his eyes when he talks about how wounded his town felt at the attacks on the club.

"You ever have a rich uncle?" he asked. "That's how Augusta feels about the National. It's a rich uncle that comes out of an important meetin' the minute he hears you are in the lobby. And he takes you up on his lap and he says, 'Hey boy, tell me 'bout your day. You need anythin'?'"

No one knows exactly what that uncle does in those board meetings, though. Some think the National is the town's shadow government. The club is notoriously secretive, its members are powerful, its pockets are deep and resistance is rare.

Regardless, Merry said, the National is the first in line to write the checks when the town needs something. The Masters alone is the difference between welfare and work for many of Augusta's poorest citizens, who can make a month's wages in a single day. Schools and businesses close so their employees can be drivers, bus boys or waiters. High school teachers and coaches earn extra money during the tournament. They bring along the kids who might get in trouble during the week off and get them jobs picking up litter or working concessions.

Merry was one of those tough kids once, and he has the broken nose and cheek scar to prove it.

"The National has been there for us our whole lives. Most of us had jobs there when we were kids, or we went with our daddies or we had off school," he said.

"The National is my rich uncle, and he loves me unconditionally."

I didn't get on the bus that morning outside Atlanta. Instead, I returned to Augusta by myself and witnessed from a distance the deterioration of Martha Burk's protest into an embarrassing circus that featured a big pink pig, a guy from a KKK fringe group, and giant puppets. It lasted less time than lunch out with friends, and it accomplished much less.

Burk has plans to shift her pressure from the club to its members, naming the corporate big shots who belong, and demanding that they account to their women customers. But the Masters protest surely set her back. It illustrated to all who watched that there isn't much interest in this cause.

For his part, Johnson had said that a woman would become a member of Augusta at a time of the club's choosing. But, apparently flush with triumph, he dug his heels deeper into the Georgia clay. "There never will be a female member, six months after the Masters, a year, 10 years, or ever," Johnson told the *Atlanta Journal Constitution* a few days after the tournament.

The National can no doubt afford the financial repercussions of its position. It reportedly earns enough from foreign television rights to put on the Masters without sponsors and with reduced corporate support until the end of time. And if it chooses to endure the consequences of its decision not to admit women, then the club is, in my mind, entitled to its decision.

I went to Augusta trying to figure out what membership in the National Golf Club meant for women. I wanted to know, when quality child care is scarce, when the wage gap stubbornly refuses to narrow, when health insurance coverage for women and their children is shrinking, when Title IX and affirmative action are threatened—why was it so important to get one rich woman into one exclusive club?

I was looking for righteousness, and I never found it. I went, with my feminist credentials in my shirt pocket, looking for a reason to get on that bus. If it was there in Augusta, I never found it.

What I found instead was what Augusta National means to men. Not to the rich and powerful men who are members, or to those men lucky enough to be their guests or to the talented golfers who compete on its storied greens and fairways. But to the fathers and sons who spend one memorable week a year inside its gates.

Masters of Their Domain

by Bill Simmons, ESPN.com, November 21, 2002

For everyone's sake, I tried to stay away from this whole "Females joining Augusta National Golf Club" controversy. It's like the old saying goes:
"If you don't agree with something, but it isn't bothering anybody too
much, then just shut up, look the other way and concentrate on the
important things in life—like playing 'Grand Theft Auto: Vice City' so
much that you actually lose feeling in some of your extremities." OK, I
made that up.

But every time the name "Augusta" came up, I looked the other way ...
at least until last week, when I heard a Boston sports radio caller invoke
Jackie Robinson's name. That's right, as in, "The first female joining
Augusta would be like Jackie breaking baseball's color line." Apparently,
we've gone collectively insane. Robinson's case centered on an uncon-
scionable level of bigotry, a despicable collection of baseball players and
owners, and a class system that desperately needed an overhaul. Augusta's
case centers on one simple premise: From time to time, guys enjoy hanging out with other guys.

That's the crux of the issue, isn't it? Augusta's members aren't arguing that women are second-class citizens who shouldn't play golf. We're talking about a group of rich Southerners who enjoy hitting golf balls, telling raunchy jokes, playing poker, ordering people around like Judge Smails, and not answering to anybody. Hey, I don't like them, either. But don't guys have the fundamental right to hang out with other guys? Don't females have the right to purchase their own golf clubs and make them exclusionary to men? Doesn't our constitution condone gender-specific clubs? How does any of this involve discrimination and equal rights?

Of course, some women don't see it this way, something I dealt with last month in my "Ten Tips For Watching Football With the Guys" column. Besides having fun with stereotypes, the column's purpose was to bang home that guys enjoy watching football with other guys, it's a time-worn male bonding ritual, and for the love of God, just leave us alone. I even ended the column with the ski bunny story, just to point out that, yes, there are women out there who know sports and love sports. We accept them, we appreciate them ... we would just rather watch sports with our buddies. I can't emphasize this enough: It's nothing personal.

Well, this drives hard-core female sports fans batty. *But I know sports too! I know just as much as you! I'm totally offended that you wouldn't watch sports with me!* Why take it so personally? It's a comfort thing, just like playing at Augusta is a comfort thing for those stuck-up Southerners. Sometimes, guys just enjoy hanging out with other guys. It's really not that complicated.

But here's the thing...

If you're arguing that Augusta should accept female members because (a) this is the 21st century, and (b) the old standby phrase "This is how we've always done it" doesn't fly anymore, that's fine. I'm on your side. Just realize that, if we're operating under that assumption, then we should overhaul every aspect of our culture.

If women are truly equal, then why do so many expect men to buy dinner on the first date? Why are guys always the ones buying introductory drinks at bars? Why are men forced to purchase engagement rings that sometimes cost more than new SUVs? Why do weddings revolve completely around brides, as grooms become hood ornaments for the entire day? Why do the vast majority of married women take their husband's names? Why are America's military forces dominated mostly by men? Why is chivalry still in vogue?

Because this is how we've always done it.

Oh, well, that solves it. So we're living by one rule, unless that rule isn't convenient anymore, then we're throwing it out the window? That makes a ton of sense.

The same hypocrisy thrives in the sports world. The WNBA and XFL suffered the same woeful ratings and limited audiences ... so why has the WNBA been given six years to succeed when the XFL was cancelled after three months? Female reporters and broadcasters want to be given the same chances as their male counterparts ... isn't it ironic how some capitalize on their looks to get ahead? Why can female reporters walk into NBA locker rooms when players are dressing, yet male reporters can't walk into WNBA locker rooms? If colleges exist to make profits, how is Title IX constitutional when it eliminates money-making programs in favor of programs that don't earn a dime? And if colleges exist to provide education, why would they possibly admit rent-an-athletes like DaJuan Wagner and Eddie Griffin? Which is it? Why the two orders, Colonel Jessup?

Again, I'm just pointing this stuff out. I support Title IX, I would much rather watch Bonnie Bernstein than Armen Keteyian, and the XFL sucked just as much as the WNBA does. But you can't have it both ways. For instance, the most fascinating sport of the past decade has been women's tennis, mainly because they exploit the talents and sex appeal of their players, market the hell out of them, and appeal to men *and* women. And nobody says a peep. Men aren't allowed to say why we're really watching— because the sport has more grunting, bouncing, flapping and sweating than the average Skinemax movie—so we make up lame excuses like "They have more rallies" and "They have more personality than the men." Translation: We like breasts.

For some reason, we aren't allowed to say this. It's sexist. And yet there's Serena Williams dressing like a dominatrix at the U.S. Open, and there's Jelena Dokic wearing a sports bra that's looser than Frank Layden's neck, and there's Anna Kournikova raking in $20 million from endorsements without ever winning a tournament. Yup, we just like watching them hit tennis balls. Never has a sport been more honest and dishonest at the same time.

Of course, women know this—they *know* this—and they conveniently look the other way, even as their tennis sisters are apparently filming the upcoming porn movie "Hookers In Spandex." Yet they won't look the other way with Augusta, because that's an "important" cause. Women's rights are at stake. Somebody needs to become the Jackie Robinson of ... um, female country club members, because this group has apparently been exploited long enough. I know it has been keeping me up at night.

If you want females joining Augusta, and if you rightly insist that women are equal to men, then I'm calling you on it. Let's be equal. Completely, totally equal. Let's throw out any tradition that ever revolved around the phrase, "Because this is how we've always done it." Let's start fresh. We'll even hand over the clicker half the time—with the money we would save on engagement rings, we could afford to buy two plasma-screen TVs (one for us, one for you). But if you're not willing to start fresh, and if you keep clinging to these hypocrisies that complicate every aspect of the male-female relationship, you're shooting yourselves in the collective foot. You're right, it *is* time for a change. But you need to change, too.

Whatever happens, one thing will *never* change: Sometimes, guys just enjoy hanging out with other guys. Unfortunately, we aren't as creative and ingenious as women. The only male bonding vehicles we ever came up with? Sports, beer, golfing, Vegas, fantasy drafts, video games, strip joints, poker, Golden Tee and NFL Sundays. Guys can't interact for extended periods of time unless there's some sort of attention-consuming buffer. We can't just say "let's go to dinner," gab about our lives for two hours, glance through some photos, get bombed on two glasses of Chardonnay and call it a successful night. And we can't interact quite as happily and naturally with a woman in the room, mainly because we're always afraid of what we might say or do.

That's what this whole Augusta thing was about—these old geezers are trying to preserve the only form of male bonding they have left. To all the females reading this, don't hate these guys. Feel sorry for them. Pity them. You are turning their pathetic world upside down. If you can't appreciate that, then maybe—just maybe—you're the ones being shortsighted about this whole thing.

Appendix A

The History

1931
Construction on Augusta National Golf Club commences on the Fruitland Nurseries property, with Dr. Alister MacKenzie of Scotland as course architect.

1932
Augusta National opens for course play.

1934
The inaugural tournament is held on March 22, 1934 as the Augusta National Invitation Tournament. Horton Smith is the first champion, while Bobby Jones finishes thirteenth.

1935
Gene Sarazen hits "the shot heard 'round the world" and scores a double eagle on the par-5 15th hole, forcing a 36-hole playoff with Craig Wood that Sarazen eventually wins.

1939
The tournament is officially renamed the Masters Tournament after Bobby Jones relents in his opposition to the name.

1940
The Masters shifts to the first full week in April. Lloyd Mangrum shoots a course record 64 during the opening round, but Jimmy Demaret prevails in the tournament by four strokes.

1942
Byron Nelson edges Ben Hogan by a stroke in an 18-hole playoff in the last tournament before the club closes for three years during World War II.

1950
Jimmy Demaret wins his third tournament.

1952

The first Champions' Dinner for past champions is held, hosted by defending champion Ben Hogan.

1953

Ben Hogan cards a 72-hole score of 274, breaking the old record by five shots.

1954

Sam Snead wins his third Masters Tournament by defeating Ben Hogan in a playoff.

1958

Arnold Palmer captures the first of his four titles, highlighted by an eagle on Sunday at the 13th hole. The term Amen Corner is coined to describe holes 11 through 13.

1960

The Par-3 Contest is introduced, with Sam Snead taking the first title. To date, no winner of the Par-3 tournament has won the Masters in the same year.

1961

After 24 straight tournaments featur-

ing American winners, Gary Player becomes the first non-American Masters champion. Player famously keeps the green jacket past the permissible one-year period and refuses to return it to Augusta National.

1963

Jack Nicklaus wins his first Masters tournament and, at 23 years old, becomes the youngest champion up to that point.

1965

Jack Nicklaus breaks the record for largest margin of victory while defeating Arnold Palmer by nine strokes.

1966

Jack Nicklaus becomes the first champion to successfully defend his title. After the victory, as he is the defending champion, Nicklaus dons the green jacket himself.

1968

Bob Goalby wins the tournament as a result of a scoring error by Roberto De Vicenzo, who returns a scorecard with a par (4) on the 17th hole instead of the birdie (3) that he actually scored. De Vicenzo is forced to take the less favorable score of 278, which costs him the opportunity for a playoff.

1977

Tom Watson wins his first Masters title, defeating Jack Nicklaus by two strokes.

1978

Gary Player joins Jimmy Demaret, Sam Snead, Arnold Palmer, and Jack Nicklaus as three-time winners.

1979

The first sudden-death playoff is decided, and Fuzzy Zoeller emerges victorious over Ed Sneed and Tom Watson.

1980

Seve Ballesteros becomes only the second non-American champion as well as the youngest winner at the time.

1986

Nick Price breaks the course record with a 63 in the third round, but Jack Nicklaus is the real story by becoming the oldest Masters champion at 46 and the only six-time champion.

1987

Larry Mize hits one of the most famous shots in golf by chipping in from 140 feet out on the 11th hole of a sudden death playoff to win the tournament.

1990

Nick Faldo joins Jack Nicklaus as the second player to successfully defend the championship.

1996

Greg Norman shoots a 63 in the first round, but blows a six-stroke final round lead to Nick Faldo by carding a 78.

1997

Tiger Woods breaks the 72-hole scoring record with a 270, earns the largest margin of victory with a 12-stroke rout, and becomes the youngest champion.

2001

Adding to his British Open, U.S.

Open, and PGA Championships won in 2000, Tiger Woods wins the Masters and holds all four major titles at the same time.

2002

Tiger Woods successfully defends the championship.

2004

Phil Mickelson breaks through at the Masters to win his first major title.

2005

Tiger Woods chips in for birdie on the 16th hole on Sunday and wins in a playoff over Chris DiMarco to tie Arnold Palmer at four Masters wins.

2006

Phil Mickelson captures his second Masters title by two strokes over Tim Clark.

2007

Zach Johnson wins his first major tournament with the highest winning score ever recorded for the tournament.

Appendix B

The Champions

Year	Champion	Score	Margin
1934	Horton Smith	284	+1
1935	Gene Sarazen	282	PO
1936	Horton Smith	285	+1
1937	Byron Nelson	283	+2
1938	Henry Picard	285	+2
1939	Ralph Guldahl	279	+1
1940	Jimmy Demaret	280	+4
1941	Craig Wood	280	+3
1942	Byron Nelson	280	PO
1943	no winner; tournament suspended for World War II		
1944	no winner; tournament suspended for World War II		
1945	no winner; tournament suspended for World War II		
1946	Herman Keiser	282	+1
1947	Jimmy Demaret	281	+2
1948	Claude Harmon	279	+5
1949	Sam Snead	282	+3
1950	Jimmy Demaret	283	+2
1951	Ben Hogan	280	+2
1952	Sam Snead	286	+4
1953	Ben Hogan	274	+5
1954	Sam Snead	289	PO
1955	Cary Middlecoff	279	+7

1956	Jack Burke Jr.	289	+1
1957	Doug Ford	283	+3
1958	Arnold Palmer	284	+1
1959	Art Wall Jr.	284	+1
1960	Arnold Palmer	282	+1
1961	Gary Player	280	+1
1962	Arnold Palmer	280	PO
1963	Jack Nicklaus	286	+1
1964	Arnold Palmer	276	+6
1965	Jack Nicklaus	271	+9
1966	Jack Nicklaus	288	PO
1967	Gay Brewer	280	+1
1968	Bob Goalby	277	+1
1969	George Archer	281	+1
1970	Billy Casper	279	PO
1971	Charles Coody	279	+2
1972	Jack Nicklaus	286	+3
1973	Tommy Aaron	283	+1
1974	Gary Player	278	+2
1975	Jack Nicklaus	276	+1
1976	Raymond Floyd	271	+8
1977	Tom Watson	276	+2
1978	Gary Player	277	+1
1979	Fuzzy Zoeller	280	PO
1980	Seve Ballesteros	275	+4
1981	Tom Watson	280	+2
1982	Craig Stadler	284	PO
1983	Seve Ballesteros	280	+4
1984	Ben Crenshaw	277	+2
1985	Bernhard Langer	282	+2
1986	Jack Nicklaus	279	+1

1987	Larry Mize	285	PO
1988	Sandy Lyle	281	+1
1989	Nick Faldo	283	PO
1990	Nick Faldo	278	PO
1991	Ian Woosnam	277	+1
1992	Fred Couples	275	+2
1993	Bernhard Langer	277	+4
1994	Jose Maria Olazabal	279	+2
1995	Ben Crenshaw	274	+1
1996	Nick Faldo	276	+5
1997	Tiger Woods	270	+12
1998	Mark O'Meara	279	+1
1999	Jose Maria Olazabal	280	+2
2000	Vijay Singh	289	+3
2001	Tiger Woods	272	+2
2002	Tiger Woods	276	+3
2003	Mike Weir	281	PO
2004	Phil Mickelson	279	+1
2005	Tiger Woods	276	PO
2006	Phil Mickelson	281	+2
2007	Zach Johnson	289	+2
2008	Trevor Immelman	280	+3

Appendix C

The Records

Most Victories: Jack Nicklaus, 6 (1963, 1965, 1966, 1972, 1975, 1986)
Widest Margin of Victory: Tiger Woods, 12 strokes (1997)
Lowest Winning Score: Tiger Woods, 270 (1997)
Highest Winning Score: Sam Snead, 289 (1954); Jack Burke, 289 (1956);
    Zach Johnson, 289 (2007)
Youngest Champion: Tiger Woods, 21 years 3 months 14 days (1997)
Oldest Champion: Jack Nicklaus, 46 years 2 months 29 days (1986)
Oldest First-Time Champion: Mark O'Meara, 41 years 3 months
    29 days (1998)
Fewest Attempts Before First Victory: Horton Smith, 1 (1934);
    Gene Sarazen, 1 (1935); Fuzzy Zoeller, 1 (1979)
Most Attempts Before First Victory: Mark O'Meara, 15 (1998)
Most Career Eagles: Jack Nicklaus, 24
Most Career Birdies: Jack Nicklaus, 506
Most Cuts Made: Jack Nicklaus, 37
Most Consecutive Cuts Made: Gary Player, 23 (1959–1982)
Most Consecutive Starts: Arnold Palmer, 50 (1955–2004)
Lowest Career Scoring Average (Minimum of 25 Rounds Played):
    Tiger Woods, 70.85

Credits

Index

Note: Page numbers in *italics* indicate articles written or co-written by referenced authors.

Carpenter, Frank, 208
Casey, Paul, 316
Casper, Billy, 81, 85, 92, 173, 230, 260, 368
Cemetery. *See* Poteat, Willie "Cemetery"
Champions, 367–369. *See also specific champion names* green jacket for. *See* Green jacket
lifetime exemptions to, 13, 85, 243
year-by-year list, 367–369
Champions' Dinner, 10, 11, 51, 72, 283, 364
Champions Golf Club, 280
Champions Locker Room, 207
Chirkinian, Frank, 13–14, 29–30, 79–80, 82–83, 114, 115, 124, 128, 131, 132, 133, 136
Cink, Stewart, 294
Clarke, Darren, 296
Clark, James, 208, 212
Clark, Tim, 366
Closing Party, 208, 210, 212–213
Coe, Charlie, 228
Colbert, Jim, 111
Controversies. *See also* Racial segregation; Women, exclusion of
Palmer/Venturi 12th hole (1958), 78–79, 83, 159–160, 161, 162–163, 176–178, *327–336*
signing incorrect card (1968), 243, 337–339
Trevino's putting standoff (1984), 341–343
Coody, Charles, 11, 41, 173, 368
Corcoran, Fred, 267, 268, 338–339
Couples, Fred, 4, 5, 31, 113, 119–123, 128, 142, 247, 289–292, 296, 299–300, 301, 302, 303–305, 306–312, 313, 369
Course. *See* Augusta National Golf Club; Design, of Augusta National
Cowan, Mike (Fluff), 287
Crenshaw, Ben, 41, 152, 153, 173, 228, 232, 254, 368, 369
Crenshaw, Tommy, 179–180, 183
Cubby, 245–246
Cut, making, 21–23
Daley, Arthur, *337–339*
Daly, John, 17–18, 155, 297
Dead Man, 229–230. *See also* Avery, Nathaniel "Ironman"
Demaret, Jimmy, 68, 154, 271, 276, 280, 327, 363, 365, 367
Dent, Jim, 232
Derr, John, 229–230
Design, of Augusta National
Amen Corner, xvi, 25, 78, 116, 152–153, 157–163, 172, 257–258, 278, 364

back nine excitement, 4–5
changes inciting criticism, 189–195
demanding, with opportunities, 148–149
described, 141–149
designers. *See* Jones, Bobby; Mackenzie, Alister
fairway difficulties, 145
front nine, 151–155
greens, 185–187
holes drifting left, 93
holes named for plants, 182, 183–184
ignoring history, 195
land purchased for course, 182
landscaping, 179–184
Oakmont ideal and, 145–146
Old Course (St. Andrews) and, 146–148
penal design and, 145–146, 192–194
Tigerproofing and, 191
12th hole, 165–178
winter play, 183
De Vicenzo, Roberto, 243, 259, 323, 337, 339, 364–365
Devlin, Bruce, 228–229
Dey, Joe, 333, 339
DiMarco, Chris, 318, 319, 321, 323, 366
Drum, Bob, xvii–xviii, 29–30, 40, 44–46, 81–82, 131
Dudley, Ed, 175, 269–270
Duval, David, 5, 117, 137, 292, 297–298, 299, 300, 301, 304, 306, 308–309, 311, 312, 313
Edwards, Bruce, 238–239, 247, 248–249
Edwards, David, 173
18th-hole reminiscences (Mickelson), 315–324
Eisenberg, John, *199–204*
Eisenhower Cabin, 71, 208
Eisenhower, Dwight D., 59–61, 62–63, 169, 206, 207, 229, 288
Eisenhower Tree, 71, 194
Elder, Lee, 105–112, 288
Elliott, Bill, 247–248
Els, Ernie, 19, 20, 24, 30, 117, 296, 297, 299, 301–303, 319
Faldo, Nick, 5, 17, 20, 21, 41, 51, 72, 123–124, 149, 242, 247–248, 285, 286, 305, 365, 369
Faxon, Brad, *3–6*, 245, 293–294, 310
Fazio, Tom, 190
Feinstein, John, xvii, *9–32, 289–313*
Finsterwald, Dow, 43, 173, 328
Floyd, Raymond, 17, 21, 41, 52, 152, 173, 290, 368
Ford, Doug, 78, 85, 159, 162, 243, 258, 260, 276,